AF540807

METHODS OF TEACHING SCIENCE

METHODS OF TEACHING SCIENCE

By

Dr. Kandi Jaya Sree

M.Sc., M.Ed., Ph.D.

Lecturer in Physical Science

St. Joseph's College of Education for Women

Guntur–522 010, (A.P)

General Editor

Dr. Digumarti Bhaskara Rao

M.Sc., M.A., M.A., M.Ed., Ph.D.

Reader

R.V.R. College of Education

Srinivasa Nagar Colony

Guntur–522 006

Andhra Pradesh

India

DISCOVERY PUBLISHING HOUSE

NEW DELHI-110002

First Published - 2004

Reprinted - 2017

ISBN: 978-81-7141-801-5

Methods of Teaching Science

Published by:

DISCOVERY PUBLISHING HOUSE PVT. LTD.

4383/4B, Ansari Road, Darya Ganj

New Delhi-110 002 (India)

Phone: +91-11-23279245, 43596064-65

Fax: +91-11-23253475

E-mail: discoverypublishinghouse@gmail.com

sales@discoverypublishinggroup.com

web: www.discoverypublishinggroup.com

Printed at:

Infinity Imaging Systems

Delhi

Foreword

Teacher education is quantitatively marching ahead towards quality education. The central and state governments through the NCTE and the Directorates of School/Higher Education are rendering their legitimate service in improving the quality of teacher education by formulating and implementing various academic policies and educational programmes. Along with these policies and programmes, the teacher educators and the prospective teachers teaching and studying in teacher education institutions need good curriculum and quality books.

The methods of teaching each subject play a pivotal role in enhancing the efficiency of their practitioners. Identifying the very importance of the methods of teaching and the quality of books, a series of books on the methods of teaching different subjects have been developed by experienced teacher educators for the benefit of teachers in making in teacher education institutions. Thanks to the authors.

Valuable suggestions for the improvement of these books are welcome from fellow teacher educators, prospective teachers and other academicians involved in the arena of teacher education.

The authors and the editor dedicate this series of books on the methodology of teaching to Mr. Tilak Raj Wasan, Proprietor, Discovery Publishing House, New Delhi, for taking up this commendable task of publication to meet the felt needs of teacher education faculty and clientele.

Dr. Digumarti Bhaskara Rao
Research Director in Education
Nagarjuna University
br_digumarti@rediffmail.com

Preface

The movement of modern education in India is almost two century old. It has come of age now. Over the decades, great educationists have contributed towards the development and evolution of education, as a discipline. Thus, education in India has been enriched a lot.

As a result, the Indian education system can be placed at par with any advanced education system in the modern world. In fact, education is a vast sea and Teachers' Training is a stream in it. So, it makes it essential that the responsibilities of the faculty members are focused on the task of providing better training to the future teachers, for their better learning and proper development. And this responsible exercise can only be undertaken, if the trainers are equipped with all the needed skill and knowledge of the subject, they are supposed to teach. Hence, it becomes essential for making adequate provisions, for each course to the teacher-trainees. Methods of Teaching are very important for the successful training of teachers and for their career in future.

In order to provide all related material in one cover, here is this book, on this important subject. Of course there are several books on the subject in the market, but, every book has its own style and way of presentation. Similarly, the present one, too has its own merits and advantages.

During the course of the preparation of this book, the undersigned has done his best for the accomplishment of the job. He would be pleased and feel contented, if this book is acknowledged, as a textbook and a reference tool for the teachers and students, alike.

Author

Contents

1

Teacher's Role

Teacher! I saw a satellite! "Look! One baby mouse is white!" "Can we attempt the experiment this way?" "I have collected all the data — use of log tables and even slide rule is too time consuming and out of date for calculations. May I use a calculator? Please! Now we have computers."

Everyday, they are different — but everyday greetings like these begin the day for science teachers. One day it is satellite, one day the moon, one day how the seesaw operates, one day the why of earthquakes — or another question everyone is asking. Science teachers as well as students; government as well as commentators — everyone needs the answers to questions in science.

It is a wonderful world when you look at it this way — and science is like a key that opens doors everywhere — on the bottom of the ocean — with the astronauts in space — with the plants, animals, and man here on earth — with thousands of conveniences of our daily lives. Learning about science — as you already know — stretches your mind, but gives you a lot in return. You always have something new to bring to your classes. And you as a science teacher have many satisfactions that come from working with young students.

You have been a practising science teacher and now you are ready to be regular science teacher, teaching a class of physics or chemistry, biology or integrated science, you will surely like to be a good science teacher. This is the right time to ask yourself some questions like these:

- What does it take to be a good science teacher?

- How can I use my teacher's training to be a good science teacher?
- Where can I get some more information about good science teaching?
- What things should I do to begin with to be a good science teacher?
- What should I do to be happy as a science teacher?

Teacher's Job

Everyone needs an education in science in order to understand the world and to be a good citizen and good worker. Scientists, leaders in government, industrialists, and the public in general need to be able to understand scientific problems and to make good judgements about them. We need scientific literate and informed people to make decisions about such things as major government projects in space exploration and medical science; health problems, environmental and population problems, such as air and water pollution; diseases such as cancer or tuberculosis and epidemics; or the possible effects of chemical pesticides upon us and our environment.

More and more people will need science in their work, and they must depend on teachers to help them get the knowledge they will need. Each new "breakthrough" or the expanding frontier of science and technology, and the public's need to be informed, require a never-ending supply of well-trained people to fill the ranks. This is also true in engineering, medicine and other fields related to science. The next generation of youngsters, as it passes through school, must be as well-educated in and about science as its talent will permit if we are to continue to prosper in our democratic society. Moreover, the ever-increasing scientific and technological progress challenges man's ingenuity to improve his methods of processing, storing, retrieving and reporting all sorts of scientific information. In a sense, we need "new breeds" of people who can combine science with other talents, as for example, the scientist, librarian and the science reporter.

Good science teaching is one of the most valuable ways to meet this urgent need for science-educated citizens and workers. Enthusiastic, intelligent, and well-educated science teachers inspire and prepare students to investigate the great questions of science and the questions raised by the scientific discoveries which affect us and our society.

Mainly through the inspiration of devoted science teachers, great number of students develop lifelong scientific interests and learn to appreciate and understand the nature of science and its usefulness to mankind.

The science teacher derives great satisfaction from this special importance of his work. And added to it is the great satisfaction that comes from mastering a field of scientific study and from affording a special kind of service to others.

So, when you ask yourself: "What do science teachers do?" You may answer:

"Everyone today needs to understand what science is about. We need it because discoveries in science affect many aspects of society. To be responsible and useful citizens, we must be able to judge how the discoveries of science may be best used for ourselves and society. Many among us will make a career of science, engineering, or technology. We need a good foundation in science to become competent in our chosen work. Therefore, we can say in general that a science teacher, at whatever level he is teaching, is laying the foundations for an understanding of science."

A science teacher is a teacher first and then a science teacher. As a teacher he should be understanding, sympathetic. Teachable and free of prejudices. Science teaching requires a sound knowledge of the subject and a real interest and ability in sharing this knowledge with others. It also requires keeping up-to-date. The work is not easy, but it is creative, and it can be extremely exciting and satisfying. It takes thought, energy, and enthusiasm. Here is an example of what one good school expects of its science teachers:

1. He plans his work for the whole year before school starts its session.
2. He plans his lessons well in advance before he enters the classroom for teaching science.
3. He knows the various practical skills needed in his particular field.
4. He guides and assists his students in their laboratory experiments, field trips and projects. He is also responsible

for the safety of the students and the condition of the laboratory and its equipment. He decides in what way each aspect of his subject can best be taught. Some of the ideas and problems can be most effectively presented by demonstration, others through student investigation, field trips, or by films or lectures. He also masters the finer art of asking the questions that will stimulate his students to think for themselves and to search for answers.

5. He organises class procedures, plans the use of the laboratory, discusses with the class, and helps his students learn how to find information outside the classroom in school and city libraries, local industries, or by consulting experts in the community.

6. He encourages his students to develop a lasting interest in science, its changes, and its methods. He guides both individual and group projects and help the students participate in various programmes of awards and recognition. He may sponsor a school science club and with the help of other science teachers and students, organises a science fair or plan field trips.

7. He keeps both himself and his students informed on the most recent developments in his field. He draws his students attention to the social, economic, political, and other aspects of the relationship between society, people and modern science. Thus he and his students always see that science study is not limited to the classroom.

8. He attends orientation courses in his field (seminars, workshops, summer institutes), as well as science conventions and science conferences for his academic growth.

9. He participates in science curriculum development programme conducted by various agencies like DIETs, SCERTs, LASEs and NCERT etc.

10. He conducts action research in science education and actively participates in innovative science programmes for better science teaching.

11. He always efforts for quality science education to his students. Now you can figure out yourself what should be

the competencies for a good science teacher (Physics/ Chemistry/Biology).

Being a Good Teacher

After completing your teacher training programme, this is the right time to ask yourself whether you possess the basic intellectual and personal qualities necessary to be a good science teacher. Do you have the attributes, such as integrity, drive, and a high sense of responsibility, which are valued in teaching specially science teaching. Besides these, there are special characteristics of successful and happy science teacher.

Checking the following questions may help you decide, how good a science teacher you are going to be.

		Yes	No
1.	Do you enjoy reading and studying in science as well as in other academic areas?	.....	.....
2.	Have you been a good science teacher?	.....	
3.	Do you like working with students and other science teachers?	.....	.....
4.	Do you like to help your students?	.....	.....
5.	Do your students and other science teachers like to work with you?	.....	.....
6.	Could you enjoy and adopt to a career in which the subject is constantly and rapidly changing because of new discoveries?	.....	.....
7.	Do you/ on your own, sometimes do more work than is required by teachers?	.....	
8.	Have you developed science projects and participated in science fairs?	.....	
9.	Do you like to find answers to problems on your own?	.....	
10.	Do you have a sense of humour?	.....	.....

11. Can you accept criticism and profit from it? ....
12. Do you consider that preparing students for living in the World of the future is a challenging job? ....
13. Are you developing the ability to read quickly and with comprehension and to express yourself clearly and interestingly in speaking and writing? ....
14. Are you in good health, both physically and mentally? ....

If you have checked thoughtfully YES for most of the above questions, you very likely would enjoy teaching science at any level, and you should read on to learn how you prepare for this type of exciting career.

EXERCISE

1. What should be the competencies of a science teacher?
2. Go through the CHECK LIST of a good science teacher and find out how good a science teacher you are going to be?

2

Teaching Techniques

What do we teach in Science? Why should we teach what we teach in Science? How should we teach Science? Why should we teach the way we teach Science? How should we evaluate that students have understood what we taught them. These are some very important points to be considered by those who are concerned with science teaching. They may be science teachers, educators, researchers and curriculum developers. This is what is usually taught in Science Method Courses.

The Way of Teaching

What we teach in science is 'content'. Now the question arises, '*what is science*'? Science is a way of describing and explaining some aspects of the world around us. To the extent that a lot of human effort has already been expended in developing such explanations, our students do not have to 'start from scratch'. A large and ever-increasing body of scientific knowledge already exists, and evidently part of the task as teacher is to pass on some of it to the students. But this is only part of the job, for science is also a package of *processes* by which we can increase our knowledge of external world. Teaching science implies involving our students in investigation, so that they become 'scientists for the day'. There are facts, theories, concepts and also a way of working, which together constitute 'the subject science.' Thus science is not just content. Science is content plus processes. This is dual nature of science.

Content. One of the things you will be doing as a science teacher is familiarising your pupils with theories, helping them to develop concepts and appreciate the structure which connects them. However, so extensive and powerful are these networks of concepts that there is a tendency never to put pupils in the position of scientists. Thus, pupils come to believe that science provides no opportunity for the expression of differences of opinion, for imagination and for creative work. They feel that there is no scope for personal contribution, that knowledge is embodied in the natural world waiting to be discovered and, once discovered, must be accepted without question. But scientist makes his own observations and deduces generalisations from them.

Content to be taught at a particular level should be carefully selected. It is a hard task. Scientific knowledge keeps on increasing. It doubles every decade. Our students are to keep pace with increasing scientific knowledge. We should teach them what they really need at a particular level. If it is more to be completed in a classroom in the allotted time, we should develop some techniques so that students could learn a part of content on their own outside the classroom.

Presentation of Content. 'What we teach' should be compatible with:

1. cognitive level of students,
2. identified objectives, and
3. existing classroom conditions.

The 'content' presented to the student should be such that he could understand it, and not just memorise. Learning is understanding, and not memorising. In every class there is some content in science, which most of the students memorise without understanding. Such content should not be included at that level, but shifted to a level where students can really understand it.

The content in the textbook should be presented in such a way that pupils like it. They take interest in it. Sometimes the content given in the syllabus is compatible to the cognitive level of pupils, but it is presented in the textbook in such a way that the pupils have difficulty to follow it. Therefore they do not like to read such textbooks. According to Professor Jack Carter of University of Colorado, USA and Director of B.S.C.S. Project (AISTA Silver Jubilee Conference, New Delhi, December 1981), "the content presented in our science textbooks is just like a scientific paper which is meant for those who are experts in science, rather than for those who are students in science."

Syllabi given by the education departments or education boards are usually outlines. Therefore different authors go to different depths for the same content when writing the textbooks. If our science syllabi are well defined in the form of 'objectives written in behavioural terms' the authors will know exactly what they are to write, students will know what they are to learn and teachers will know what they are to teach, and paper setters will know what is to be evaluated. All of them will be on the same track, and will not go astray.

Science Processes. The current innovations in schools emphasise the processes of science, the ways in which scientists advance their knowledge and solve problems. Science should be presented to pupils as a way in which they can conduct an inquiry into the nature of things as well as a body of information built by other people. In the past, the processes have been neglected, and school science has been concerned almost exclusively with the 'body of information, the concepts, principles and techniques developed by scientists; too rarely have pupils been made 'scientists for the day,' encouraged to become personally involved in solving problems, in discovering some science for themselves.

The teachers' guides of most recently developed school science programmes in United States and United Kingdom suggest ways in which pupils can become involved in scientific inquiry. They ask to follow the stages: Problem-Hypotheses — Experiment — Result, in solving problems. If you as a science teacher, are to engage your pupils in the processes of science, it is important that you should have thought carefully about what these processes are. The sequence of development of the thirteen science processes is as follows:

1 Observing 2 Classifying
3 Using numbers 4 Measuring
5 Using space-time relationships
6 Communicating 7 Predicting
8 Infering 9 Defining operationally
10 Formulating hypotheses 11 Interpreting data
12 Controlling variables, and 13 Experimenting.

Nature of Science. Science is a broad based human enterprise that can be defined differently from different viewpoints The layman might define science as a body of scientific information, the scientist might view it as a method by which hypotheses are tested, a philosopher might regard science as a way of questioning the truthfulness of what we know, All these views are valid, but each presents only a partial definition of science, only collectively do they begin to define the comprehensive nature of science. Therefore, science should be viewed as a way of thinking in the persuit of understanding nature as a way of investigating claims about phyenomena and as a body of knowledge, that has resulted from inquiry.

Science as a Way of Thinking. Science is a human activity that can be characterized by the thinking that occurs in the minds of people who participate in it. The mental work of scientists illustrates human kind's curiosity and desire to understand phenomena. These individuals possess attitudes, beliefs, and values that motivate them to answer questions and solve problems. Scientists are driven by enormous curiosity imagination and reasoning in their quest to figure out and explain natural phenomena. Their work, as viewed by many philosophers of science and cognitive psychologists, is a creative activity whereby ideas and explanations are constructed.Therefore, the thinking and reasoning of scientists as they go about their work offer important causes regarding the nature of science belief. The tendency for scientists to find out seems to be motivated by their belief that a set of laws of nature can be constructed from observation and explained by thought and reasoning.

Science as a Way of Investigation. Science as a way investigation illustrates many approaches to constructing knowledge. Science has many methods which demonstrate human kind's investigation for seeking solutions to problems. Some of the approaches used by scientists rely heavily on observation and prediction as in astronomy and ecology other approaches rely on laboratory experiments that focus on cause and effect relationships such as those used in microbiology and other sciences. Among the many processes associated with science and inquiry as discussed above are observing, classifying, using numbers, measuring, using space-time relationships, communicating, predicting defining operationally, inferring, denning operationally, interpreting data, controlling variables, and experimenting.

Science as a Body of Knowledge (Product). The body of knowledge produced from the scientific disciplines represents the creative products of human invention that have occurred over the centuries. The enormous collection of ideas pertaining to the natural and physical world is organized into astronomy, biology, chemistry, geology, physics and so on. The result is a compilation of carefully catalogued information containing many types of knowledge, each of which makes its own unique contribution to science. The facts, concepts, principles, laws, hypotheses, theories, and models from the content of science. These ideas poses their own specific meaning, which cannot be understood apart from the processes of inquiry that produced them. The facts of science serve as the foundation for concepts, principles, and theories.

According to *'The Columbia Encyclopaedia'* (1963), "Science is an accumulated and systematized learning, in general uses restricted to natural phenomena. The progress of science is marked not only by an accumulation of facts, but by the emergence of scientific method and of the scientific attitude".

From the above definition three basic principles of the nature of science can be identified (1) an accumulated and systematized body of knowledge, (2) the scientific method of investigation, and (3) the scientific attitudes or ways of thinking. The first point indicates the product of science, while second and the third points indicate the process of science. In other words, Science is both a product and process.

Thus Science has a dual nature.

1. Content of science. 2. Process of science.

Why to Teach ?

It can be discussed into two parts:

(i) Why should we teach science?

(ii) Why should we teach what we teach in science at a particular class level?

Why Should We Teach Science? It is very unfortunate that we as science educators never practically think at 'why.' The principal goal of science education is to create men who are capable of doing new things, not simply of repeating what other generations have done — men who are creative, inventive and discoverers. If that is why we teach science, then how far our science education is compatible to achieve this goal?

The key to national prosperity lies in the effective combination of three factors — technology, raw materials and capital, of which perhaps the first one is the most important. Since the creation and adoption of new scientific techniques, technology can, in fact, make up a deficiency in natural resources and reduce the demands on capital. But technology can only grow out of the study of science and its applications. Technology serves man. It gives individuals and nations roots, a frame of reference, horizons, a world view and inner freedom. Science and technology are used to promote the establishment and furtherance of the community of man to the community of nations. We teach or learn science for a variety of reasons.

1. Science is fundamentally concerned with exploring and interpreting the physical world through the three fundamental areas of Physics, Chemistry and Biology. Physicists are concerned with the exploration of energy and general properties of inanimate materials, chemists with the particular properties of inanimate materials, and biologists explore the behaviour and properties of animate materials. The physical and biological world is of fundamental human interest and man has a basic motivation to understand and control the physical world in which he has his being.

2. We live in a scientific and technological age and no citizen can function effectively in a developed society without a basic scientific literacy and certain elementary skills. Every citizen needs to live a healthy life with proper sanitation and clean surroundings. The knowledge and skills required by a modern householder in dealing with electrical, plumbing, and human first-aid may be cited as some justification for teaching science to all children in school.

3. We depend upon scientific knowledge and understanding for economic and material advancement. Science has provided so many aids for 'the good life' from bicycle to jet aircraft, antibiotics to heart surgery, radar to colour television, and fertilisers to plant growth harmones. Although we are beginning to realise many follies in the large-scale application of science and technology in terms of a net environmental damage, the fact is that we will need science again to rectify these follies (like application of science and

technology in a better way which would not affect the environment adversely) and to enable more people to live on this planet in conditions which do greater justice to the dignity of man. The priority which the developing countries like India are giving to basic science education for public health and agriculture can clearly be seen.

4. Science cannot be used in society without a body of men and women who have been specially trained for science-based vocations in industry, research and teaching. A vocational justification is, therefore, possible for science teaching.

5. Science, if studied properly, develops power of thinking, reasoning, curiosity, open-mindedness, and ultimately develops scientific attitude or scientific temper. Thus science could be aimed as an instrument for social change towards a better society.

6. Professor Yashpal (1992) is of the opinion that, instead of considering science as an extraneous activity or as a tool for providing the means to a good life, usually borrowed from outside, we should treat it as a part of the culture of society, integral to our living and thinking and connected to the deepest questions we ask in regard to who we are and where we come from. Although, the tools that technology provides in the form of increased means of productive goods and services, means of communication and transport are important, but if we make science as a part of our culture, they would all come, much more naturally, more creatively and more in tune with our living.

7. Science is essential for helping us to comprehend and establish connections with the physical and biological world around us. It familiarizes students with the empirical modes of investigation. Understanding its conceptual structures and methodologies are an important part of an educated person. It can help in the development of intellectual skills and motor abilities like comprehension and application of understanding to new contexts and accurate observation of phenomena. Scientific knowledge not only influences our thinking about human, political and social affairs but also affects our thinking about ourselves. Its importance for arousing scientific curiousity and in developing scientific attitudes, as well as educating people for science based vocations in industry, research and training cannot be overemphasized. The scientifically literate person has a knowledge

base of facts, concepts, conceptual networks, and processes, which enable the individual to continue to learn throughout life.

Why Should We Teach What We Teach in Science at a Particular Class Level? Who decides what is to be taught in science at a particular class level *i.e.* science syllabus for various classes (I-V, VI-VIII, IX-X, XI-XII)? Perhaps those who never taught those classes. Science teachers who teach those classes are not empowered to make such decisions. Therefore some topics become too difficult to be understood by the children. It will be advisable that syllabus framers should also involve concerned science teachers when they frame science syllabus for various classes. Syllabus framers should be answerable, why they put this science content in the syllabus. They should objectively say, "We put this science content in the syllabus because children need it, children will understand it and children will enjoy it."

How to Teach ?

"To learn science is to do science, there is no other way of learning science," D.S. Kothari. This is how we should teach science. Do we actually do so?

Several methods of teaching science are taught in B.Ed. classes but what B.Ed. students mostly practise are 'lecture method' or lecture-cum-demonstration method' during their practice teaching. And so they usually use the same two methods when they become regular science teachers. They should practise all the methods which they learn in theory. Then they will be able to use what best fits in the actual classroom conditions.

Our science courses are mostly content-oriented. When content worship is becoming old fashioned in developed countries, our country is still behind it. Whenever the courses are updated more content is added. Courses become heavier and heavier while time allotted in the school time-table remains just about the same. Thus students are to cover much more content in comparatively much lesser time. Moreover classes are crowded and teachers are heavily loaded. Thus inspite of sufficiently available science equipment for experiments and demonstrations, content is covered by asking students to read books, or giving lectures to cover more content in lesser time without demonstrations and experiments.

Under such classroom conditions we are to devise some self-learning techniques in teaching science. Programmed Instruction is one such device. When Self-learning Modules, Programmed Instruction Materials in science or Adjunct Programmes on various science textbooks are used, students will be able to cover a part of the syllabus on their own, and teachers will get some time for individualised instruction. If one were to list expressions that best describe science education for the twenty-first century 'Individualised Instruction' certainly has to be included. The Programmed Instruction and Modular Approach are some of the efficient ways of providing individualised instruction. If our science teachers could have well-sequenced programmed materials and self-learning modules, it would be great help to them since they are heavily loaded. Also if the programmed materials and self-learning modules provided activities of 20-25 minutes duration, students would have more opportunity to do the experiments themselves, even in smaller periods.

Constructivism : A Dominant Perspective about How Children Learn Science. Constructivism is a general name given to the dominant perspective on learning and especially in science education. This approach of teaching learning is quite different from traditional views.

"I hear and I forget, I see and I remember, I do and I understand", must be a familiar phrase for you, but this phrase shows the intent of constructivism. Constructivism is not entirely new. Contemporary researchers from various countries have updated the theories and methods and synthesised several dominant perspectives on learning. This perspective is evolved from the research and theories of Piaget, Vygotsky, Bruner and philosophy of John Dewey. There is a consensus among many philosophers of science, psychologists, science educators, scientists and people concerned with the children's learning that learners must construct and reconstruct their own meaning of ideas about how the world works.

Joseph Novak (1986) defines constructivism as the notion that humans construct or build meaning into their ideas and experiences as a result of an effort to understand or make sense of them. According to Duckworth (1989), all people have their own understanding, one cannot make them believe anything unless they construct it by themselves.

There is no one constructivist theory of learning. Therefore students can be encouraged to learn by reinventing the wheel for themselves, so that the learner does the discovering by forming mental connections. The understanding or conceptual clarity is deeper and retention is greater. The teacher mediates the learning environment and thus plays an important role. The hands on activities in science, manipulative skills, process based learning share some common intentions with costructivism, which is becoming popular in education. The constructivist teacher must fulfill many roles, helping the learner to think critically and use information creatively to construct scientific ideas, concepts and largely function as a facilitator of knowledge construction in order to help the learner how to learn. This conceptual clarity through construction of knowledge is ultimately reflects through their attitudes. This should be the constructivist role of a teacher.

Which Way to Teach ?

There are various methods of teaching science "When a particular method is to be used," is very important

In science there are some concepts and some skills "Temperature" is a concept, and "Measuring temperature or reading a thermometer," is a skill. 'Weight" is a concept and "Weighing by a spring balance, weighing machine, physical balance or chemical balance, ' is a skill. "Photosynthesis" is a concept, and "setting up and performing photosynthesis experiment," is a skill.

By researchers it has been found that concepts are best learned by Child Centred Approach (CCA), and skills are best learned by Teacher Centred Approach (TCA).

If you want to develop "creativity ' and "scientific temper," do not give them readymade answers, use "Scientific Method" or "Problem Solving Method". Similarly you can think of when a particular method of teaching science is to be used.

Evaluation of Learning

During Teaching. When teaching science in a classroom, we ask some questions before we start the lesson. The answers of these questions give us some idea, whether the students have the previous knowledge or entry behaviours for the lesson. We ask some questions during the lesson and also encourage students to ask questions if they do not understand anything. Answers to such questions give us the idea whether the students are understanding what we are teaching them. We also ask some questions after the lesson, just to know whether students understand what we taught them in the lesson.

In Examination. Let us look at our examination system. If we analyse the examination questions very critically, we find mostly knowledge questions are asked and very little emphasis is given to comprehension, application and skill questions. Our examination questions should test all the objectives — cognitive, affective as well as psycho-motor. Clearly defined objectives help us in effective and objective evaluation. Therefore we should identify our objectives before-hand and state them very clearly. If our objective is just knowledge, we should not ask comprehension, application or skill questions; and if our objectives are knowledge, comprehension, application and skill, we should test all the objectives and not just the knowledge as it is usually the case. If our objective is 'to develop the skill of reading a thermometer, our test should be, 'Give a thermometer to the student and ask him to read, instead of how will you read a thermometer? Explain with the help of a diagram. Our education is examination-oriented. Though we identify several objectives but they are just on paper. We try to achieve only those objectives which are usually tested in examination. So our examination system has a big hand of providing quality science education to our children.

Present Situation

Let us examine the present situation of science education in our country. First of all let us have a look at the objectives of science teaching as stated by Prof. B. Sharan of NCERT, which are as follows:

1. To make aware of those aspects of science that are environmental based and life centred.
2. To emphasise the scientific method which has helped in solving problems.
3. To train students in the use and maintenance of science equipment.
4. To make students creative.
5. To develop the mental faculty of open-mindedness.
6. To prepare children for change of life.

Now you can yourself examine, how far our existing science curricula, teaching methods and evaluation techniques are compatible to achieve these objectives.

The curricula have been drawn up and textbooks written by those who perhaps have never taught in schools. They have tried to compress in the textbooks, a variety of topics some of which have little utility or relevance. In spite of the Ishwarbhai Patel Committee on Curricula Reforms for the ten-year school submitted in 1977, the curricula have not been updated. Even the Minister of Education presiding over the annual general meeting of the NCERT on March 11, 1981 regretted that attempts at improving the quality of education in terms of upgrading curricula were not heartening.

One of the recommendations of the Education Commission under the chairmanship of Prof. D.S. Kothari (1964-66) was that science should be made a compulsory subject in school education. The recommendation was accepted and science was made compulsory upto class X in several states and Union Territories. 10+2 Education Scheme started in July 1975. Science courses at 10+2 stage were framed in a hurry and they were implemented without any try-out. When framing the courses, not many teachers who actually teach the students at this level were involved, and editorial boards were made of people from Universities and Institutes of Technology. Ishwarbhai Patel Committee for reviewing Class I-XII courses was asked to submit its report within two months' time. Therefore ad-hoc deletions were made. Sometimes diagrams were deleted while content related-to those diagrams remained.

In the old 3-years Higher Secondary Scheme (IX-XI) about one-third of students who were really interested in science used to take science in class IX. But now science is also a required course like other subjects upto class X. Therefore majority of the students (about two-thirds) who perhaps do not have the interest and aptitude for science have to take it. Now the question arises, must every student be forced to learn a subject for which he has no aptitude or a special science course be developed for such students so that they are also attracted toward learning science.

The former Prime Minister Morarji Desai, while addressing the members of the Review Committee on the curriculum for the ten-year school at New Delhi stated, "The books that I did carry in College are being carried by School students today. The students are burdened by how many books, I do not know." Knowledge of science almost doubles every decade. We are to keep pace with this new development. Then the problem is how much knowledge in science should be given to a child at a particular level, so that he is not burdened.

The goals and expectations of the science education change with time and with them the curriculum. Updating, revising, reorganising, or adopting science curricula are not sufficient to reduce the present state of fragmentation and narrowness, what is necessary is the design of science programmes for the-non-specialist, the common man.

The social imperatives of education and specially science education have recently been attributed new importance and urgency. The long-term social problems of: (1) environmental pollution, (2) food shortages, (3) limitations on available energy, and (4) expanding population demand, change the curriculum emphasis and modes of teaching. Students are not only to be informed about these social problems, they also need practice in making decisions, so that as adults they will be wiser in individual and collective decision-making. Since these social imperatives do not conform to the traditional academic boundaries of the sciences, or even of any subjects commonly taught in schools, new curricular patterns must be generated, developed, tested, and evaluated for evidence of effectiveness. Relevant research is needed not only in the development and testing of these new instructional materials, but more basic studies are required on the ways, means and amounts of various experiences which modify the attitudes and enhance decision making skills.

It is time that the country's intelligentsia, educational planners, educational administrators, educationists, politicians, teachers and parents should give some serious thought to what direction the country's education system should go, and what should be the place of science in the curriculum. They owe it to their children and to the future generations. The time seems to be ripe for a serious national debate on the 'future of science education' taking into a serious view of its past and present.

We always say that we should teach science in such a way that we are able to develop scientific attitude and scientific temper among our students. This remains our objective of teaching science. How far we are able to achieve this objective? What is scientific attitude? What is scientific temper? Is there any relation between these two? Can scientific method help us to develop scientific attitude and Scientific temper among our students?

Scientific Attitude

Before talking about scientific attitude let us discuss what is attitude. Attitudes are mental state or individual outlook towards people, objects, events etc. Attitudes are developed and learned/ they are not inborn. Attitudes can be changed through experiences especially in children. They are the result of experiences.

Scientific attitude refers to an individual's outlook towards life. It means a willingness to adopt scientific approaches and procedures for resolving issues/ assessing ideas or information. Robert Ebel (1997)/ defines attitude as a mental condition/ a stabilized mental set which expresses itself in a tendency to react to any member of a class of stimuli in the same general way. Scientific attitude predisposes a person to engage in responsible action after weighing the possible consequences of alternative options/using rational arguments based on evidence. She distinguishes between scientific evidence and personal opinion and between reliable and unreliable information, remains open to new evidence and the tentativeness of scientific knowledge and recognizes that science and technology are human endeavours. Some other manifestations of the scientific attitude are/ questioning/suspension of judgement, appraisal of different sides of an issue, verification of knowledge, curiousity and appreciation of the natural and human-made world, open mindedness/ intellectual honestly/cooperation and tolerance of the point of view of other people.

The complex interactions of science with society need to be understood by individuals and applied in everday decision making. For improving the quality of life through economic and material development/ we depend on the knowledge of science. Developments in science have prepared the way for a more effective/ practical mastery of the environment and the technological innovations in agriculture, industry and medicine have produced transformations in traditional patterns of social living. In the words of Indira Gandhi (1982). "Science has not only radically altered man's material environment/ but what is of still deeper significance/ if has provided new tools of thought and has extended man's mental horizons. It has thus influenced even the basic values of life/ and has given to civilization a new vitality and dynamism".

Scientific attitude or Scientific temper

1. open-mindedness
2. objective decision making
3. critical thinking
4. not believing what other people say unless convinced what is being said is correct
5. desire for accurate knowledge
6. confidence in procedures in seeking knowledge
7. expectation that the solution of the problem will come through the use of verified knowledge
8. using scientific method (problem, hypotheses, experiment, conclusion) in decision making

Recognising a person having scientific attitude (Scientific Temper) through the following episode in which there are four main characters — principal science consultant physics teacher and science students

An Instance

A Science Consultant went to a school. As soon as he entered the Principal's office, Principal requested him to go to Ms X Physics class as she does not do anything and we have lot of complaints against her. The Science Consultant went to her class and observed her lesson. Here are his remarks "The teacher was teaching waves by lecture-demonstration method. She was demonstrating longitudinal and transverse waves, crests and troughs, rarefaction and condensation, nodes and antinodes, frequency and wave length with the help of a SLINKY. It was a very lively class. Students were really enjoying and participating. There was very healthy teacher learner interaction in the class. Questions between and after the lesson were thought-provoking. Homework copies and practical notebooks were checked up to date. The physics lab was well set for the day practical work. "The Principal was shocked to listen to these comments She spoke to the Science Consultant, "Are you sure, these are your comments." "Yes, these are my comments. She is an outstanding physics teacher. How did you know that she does not do anything. Who was complaining against her, the science consultant asked. Some teachers were telling, the Principal replied "Do not believe what others are saying, unless you are convinced that what they are saying is correct," the Science Consultant advised the Principal.

Answer the following Questions

1. Who has scientific temper — Principal or Science Consultant ? Justify your answer
2. Do all science teachers have scientific temper ?
3. Do you have scientific temper?
4. Do non-science teachers also have scientific temper?
5. Do science or non science principals have scientific temper?
6. Do scientists have scientific temper?
7. Do non scientists have scientific temper?
8. What is scientific temper?
9. How will you recognise whether a certain person has scientific temper?

10.(i) What is the difference between "scientific attitude" and scientific temper ?

(ii) What are the characteristics of a person having

(a) scientific attitude ?
(b) scientific temper?

(iii) A Science teacher has the following characteristics:

(a) She is open-minded
(b) She has a burning desire for the acquisition of correct know'edge and search for truth
(c) She has confidence in her abilities to seek knowledge with her own efforts
(d) She has an adequate ability of problem-solving and believes that the problems can be solved through proper efforts involving scientific observations and experimentation.

(e) She has spirit of curiosity.

(f) She believes in cause and effect relationship.

(g) She believes in the theory of evidence.

(h) She has love for truth.

(i) She adopts scientific method (problem, hypotheses, experiment, conclusion) in her thinking and working.

(j) She teaches science by scientific method, and uses the method in her decision making.

Now answer the following questions.

1. Does she have (a) scientific attitude (b) scientific temper?
2. Which of the above characteristics show that she has: (a) scientific attitude, (b) scientific temper?
3. Do you find any difference between scientific attitude and scientific temper? IV. How to develop scientific attitude or scientific temper?

Try for the following:

(i) satisfaction of curiosity.

(ii) to get rid of superstitions.

(iii) proper way of teaching with no ready-made answers.

(iv) utilising co-curricular activities like working on investigatory science projects

(v) open classroom environment.

(vi) inspiring for the study of scientific literature.

(vii) encouraging day to day problems by scientific method.

(viii) develop in students well defined abilities such as the: (a) spirit of inquiry, (b) creativity, (c) objectivity, (d) courage to question, (e) problem solving and decision making skills.

(ix) self example by the teacher.

Answer the Following Questions

(a) Will these help in developing scientific attitude or scientific temper ?

(b) Which of these are not needed in developing scientific attitude or scientific temper

(c) What more will you like to add for developing scientific attitude or scientific temper

(d) Are the answers of these questions same or different for scientific attitude and scientific temper? Justify your answer.

In Twenty-first Century Children Suicide: Why?

A 15-year old boy Saurav ended his life in East Delhi's Nirman Vihar on Sunday night (February 16, 1997) fearing failure in the forthcoming CBSE Class X Examinations. (*The Times of India*, February 18,1997)

Rahul (Bombay) was punished for not studying regularly. At times, he was made to stand in the bitter cold outside his house. Fed up by his parent's expectations and fearing that he would fail in the Class XII Examinations he committed suicide.

On February 13,1997, 21-year old Chemistry student, Mousumi (Bombay) was found hanging in her hostel room. She was afraid she would not get a first class. Her academic record was very good. She committed suicide due to fear.

"I am tired and frustrated with life as I have to study all the time," were the last words of 16-year old Chandrakant (Bombay). Tired of studying by rote, he immolated himself and died of burn injuries in hospital in February 1997.

Saurav, Rahul, Mousumi and Chandrakant are not alone. A good number of students throughout the country end their lives after not performing well as expected in examinations.

Some educationists feel parental and peer pressure, more than school syllabi, put unfair pressure on students. Air Force Bal Bharti School New Delhi, Principal K.K. Mohindroo blamed it on parental and peer pressures. "Parents want their children to score above 90 per cent in all subjects (Physics, Chemistry, Biology, Maths). This, at times, makes students panicky," said Mr. Mohindroo. Delhi Public School R.K. Puram New Delhi Principal Shyama Chona, too had similar views. "The class X (science and other subjects syllabus) is minimal. It is mainly parental and peer pressure which affects the students," said Ms. Chona.

School authorities blame parents for putting undue pressure on children to excel, and parents hold schools and school education boards for the inability of wards to cope with syllabi.

It is time the school education boards revamp the existing system and base it on the three H's of education - head, heart and hands. We need to tackle this issue seriously so as to bring back the simple joys of going to school and to strengthen the bonds between the teacher and the taught. When the syllabus is prescribed by NCERT and various school education boards, not much consideration is given to how much a student of a particular age-group can comprehend and apply.

Many of our students are first generation learners, hence their parents are not able to give any help at all. Many parents put their children in English-medium schools even though they have no such background, and the subjects taught become too difficult for them to understand. The teacher is weighed down by quantity, not quality. The poor child is the silent sufferer - sometimes he breaks down, sometimes he gives up and sometimes he ends his life.

Delhi University educationist Krishna Kumar felt public school students were more vulnerable to pressures. "Prestige is an obsession with most elite public schools. Students are subjected to inhuman pressure. This sometimes takes its toll," said Mr. Kumar. Mr. Kumar felt syllabi were another culprit. "The Yashpal Committee suggested major changes, particularly in science and mathematics. The overall situation could have been much better if the recommendations were implemented," he added.

Parents and Teachers Associations should be empowered and sit down to discuss those problems and put pressures on School Education Boards, NCERT and SCERTs to do some rethinking.

The Curriculum

Now Science is for all upto Class X. Then what type of science curriculum our children need to be functionally literate, as well as achieve optimally in science. Several children, parents, teachers, principals and administrators were interviewed. Here are some suggestions for restructuring school science curriculum at all levels.

(i) For children to do well in science, we need to identify the basics in science. Once the basics have been chosen and implemented, children will have key facts, concepts, and generalisations to achieve. Teaching science will be more professional once the basics have been identified. A sower (the science teacher) that goes out to sow will then reap not ten nor twenty fold, but hundred fold. Why so? Time spent in teaching science will be spent on the relevant basics, and not upon the irrelevant.

(ii) Basics are to be stated in measurable terms. There is no reason for keeping the children in the dark as to what they are to learn. Measurably stated objectives, announced clearly to children, will assist them to achieve as much as possible. Children achieve poorly in science if the evaluation techniques are not matched with the precise objectives.

(iii) Science instruction should be based on the interests of children. Good science teachers find out what children are interested in, and bring these interests into each lesson. Good training (pre-service and in-service) makes good science teachers. Good science teachers make good science students. If these good science students are permitted to give their input into the science curriculum, they will bring many many items of science to make science interesting.

(iv) Research data indicates how important parents are in helping their children learn. If parents assist their children in learning, achievement continues to rise. Teachers, administrators and parents should learn to work cooperatively to increase children's achievement in science. There would be some parents whose input might be taken into the science curriculum.

(v) We need to stimulate children to identify and solve problems within the science curriculum. Subject matter may become outdated due to new research findings in science, but problem solving is always to stay. We should not focus so much on the content of science, but on processes of science.

(vi) In the past the slow learners received an inferior science education. Science teachers should be trained to identify slow learners and teach them science in such a way that they also enjoy science like normal children.

Courses for Twenty-first Century

Now we entered twenty-first century. What types of Teaching

of Science Courses we are going to have? It all depends upon what type of "Science Education" we will have in Twenty-first century. Let us study the existing Teaching of Science Courses, so that they could accordingly be revised for the Twenty-first Century.

(1) Teaching of Science Courses for Universities. At present there are different Teaching of Science Courses, in various universities of the country. As a sample few of them are given here for study (Appendix F).

I Syllabus Outline for Science Method Course

II Syllabus Outline for Integrated Science Method Course

III Syllabus Outline for Secondary Physics Method Course

IV Syllabus Outline for Senior Secondary Physics Method Course

V Syllabus Outline for Secondary Chemistry Method Course

VI Syllabus Outline for Senior Secondary Chemistry Method Course

VII Syllabus Outline for Secondary Biology Method Course

VIII Syllabus Outline for Senior Secondary Biology Method Course.

IX B. El. Ed. (4 years) Science Course

Syllabus Outline for Science Method Course

Paper — 1. Natural Science

Paper — 2. Pedagogy of Environmental Studies

Paper — 3. Pedagogy of Natural Science

Syllabus Outline for Science Content Course

Paper — 4. Physics I

Paper — 5. Physics II

Paper — 6. Chemistry I

Paper — 7. Chemistry II

Paper — 8. Biology I

Paper — 9. Biology II

2. ***Teaching of Science Course for DIETs.*** In some universities Teaching of EVS (science) course is also introduced. This course is for teaching at primary (I-V) level. The syllabus for this course is given in Appendix - B "How to Use This Book in DIETs?" One District Institute of Education and Training (DIET) is to be started in each district of the country. So far (1997) 425 DIETs have been established. These are coming up since 1988-89. NCERT has developed 2 years Elementary Teacher Education Diploma Course for Pre-service Teacher Education (PSTE) students of the DIETs. In 1st year they are trained to teach primary classes (I-V). NCERT developed DIETs syllabus includes a good Teaching of EVS (science) course (Appendix — B). This may be adopted or adapted by universities if they introduce this course at B.Ed. level.

In 2nd year DIETs' PSTE students are trained to teach upper primary or middle classes (VI-VIII). NCERT syllabus for DIETs also includes a good Teaching of Integrated Science Course (Appendix B). This course may be compared with "Syllabus Outline for Integrated Science Method Course (Appendix - F II)/" and adopted or adapted by universities when they introduce this course at B.Ed. level.

Challenges Ahead

Science Teaching today is not so simple as it was in early fifties. But even in those days use of audio-visual aids was quite common, though students and parents were not as demanding as they are now. In those days there was not so much competition, there was not so much load on students, and therefore there was no need of rote memorisation. Now with the loaded curriculum students cannot escape the drudgery of mugging textbooks and learning without tears and fears. Now in the existing school and classroom conditions SCIENCE TEACHING is a CHALLENGE, which a science teacher alone is to face, but he cannot do much unless he has support from the Principal, Education Officers, SCERTs, IASEs, School Education Boards, DIETs, Parents as well as NCERT, NIEPA and NCTE.

Some Teachers, Students, Parents, Principals, Education Officers, and school Managers were interviewed. What they feel about Today's Science Teaching — A Challenge, is given below.

Role of Teachers

1. We should have 24-30 periods a week with no substitution periods so that we could get enough time for planning, evaluating copies, preparing demonstrations and experiments.
2. Well-equipped Science Labs, with enough audio-visual aids for demonstrations and experiments.
3. Lessons to be observed and necessary guidance be given for better science teaching.
4. Giving some demonstration lessons with up-to-date educational technology.
5. To be trained in the latest techniques of teaching science and in new science content enrichment (pre-service and in-service).
6. To be trained in continuous and comprehensive evaluation.
7. Qualified and well trained Lab. Assistants.

Role of Students

8. Good science teaching, every difficulty to be removed in the class, teachers should not proceed further unless all students understand, to avoid private tutions, so that we could have good marks in X and XII to get admission in higher studies.
9. Less homework, more work in school.
10. Less Course, useless course to be removed.
11. Two Science Courses in X - B-Course for those who will not take science in XI-XII; A-Course for those who will take science in XI-XII; A-Course should cover all Entry Behaviours for XI-XII Science (Physics, Chemistry, Biology).
12. Coordination in Theory and Practical, not as we have now — Theory in IX and Practical in XII.
13. Less Extra Classes, in Extra Classes only Remedial and Enrichment Work, Courses to be completed in regular classes.

14. Maximum and Effective use of Audio-Visual Aids, Hardwares and Softwares in Science Teaching, Science Teaching should be Activity Based — Demonstrations, Experiments, Field Trips, Investigatory Science Projects.

15. Use of computers to teach some portion of Physics, Chemistry and Biology.

16. Use of Self-Learning Multimedia Packages-printed, audio, video, audio-video, computers.

17. Make Science Teaching enjoyable at least less Boring.

Role of Parents

18. Good Teaching - No Need of Private Tutions.

19. Remedial and Enrichment Extra Classes.

20. Excellent Results in X and XII to get admission in higher studies without outside coaching.

Role of Principals

21. Intensive Training in Educational Administration, Planning and Management — Pre-service and In-service.

22. Needed support and guidance from officers of education departments.

23. Science Textbooks should be tried out and revised before implementation — Formative Evaluation Before Summative Evaluation.

24. Officers of education departments should also be given proper training to guide and supervise the work of Teachers and Principals, and give some concrete suggestions for improvement of science teaching.

25. Science supervisors of education departments to be very active for giving proper guidance to Science Teachers for quality science Education and good science results.

Role of School Managers and Education Officers

1. All teachers should teach and all students should study.

2. 100 per cent results with ALL First Divisions and Distinctions.

3. Effective use of Audio-Visual Aids and Educational Technology.
4. Use of computers in Learning Science.
5. B.Ed. Courses should be restructured to enable science teachers to teach science very effectively in existing classroom and school conditions, one science teacher should be able to teach full science upto class X.
6. Timely Need-Based and Effective In-service Training of Science Teachers to enable the teachers to teach science very effectively to give good results.

All these issues are to be very seriously taken up by concerned people and agencies to face the challenge in Science Teaching.

Other Issues

(i) Science Teaching is to be made participatory, joyful and relevant for all type of students.

(ii) Environmental Approach is to be used in science teaching like Science Through Kitchen, Exploring Our Body, Science Experiments using Low Cost Teaching Aids prepared by the Material Available in the Environment.

(iii) Students are to learn science by observing, experimenting and participating.

(iv) Home is to be used as Science Lab.

(v) Scientific Method is to be used in Science Teaching to develop Scientific Temper which is a Basic need for survival Today.

Education Policies come and go, but it looks that our children still are to follow the education system invented by Macaulay, and they are to mug up so many things, without understanding. This has become a painful experience for our children. "There is no joy in mugging. Joy lies in understanding, in finding out things on our own" Professor Yashpal. If we link education of a child with his immediate environment, then education will no more be a burden on the child, and the child will be encouraged to create his own knowledge. There is no dearth of resources, human or material in our country. If we are ready to face the challenge, nothing is impossible. When there is a will there is a way, with the right will we can make education and science education more relevant and enjoyable for our children. This is also a challenge for our science teachers. They can do and make others do. Then our Schools will be joyful places for Learning Science. If Children are taught in a Joyful manner, they will leam faster and retain much more.

"It is our solemn duty to do what the children want us to do. Children are a challenge to policy makers and the challenge has to be recognised and accepted" Arjun Singh, says the former Minister of mhrd. Let's make his dream true.

EXERCISE

1. What is the place of: (a) Science, (b) Physics, (c) Chemistry, and (d) Biology in school curriculum? Discuss.
2. What should we teach in science — content, processes or both? Discuss with due importance and reasoning.
3. "To learn science is to do science, there is no other way of learning science." Discuss taking into consideration the existing classroom conditions.
4. How science is being taught in our schools? Are you satisfied with the way it is being taught? If not, discuss how it should be taught in the prevailing classroom conditions?
5. How should we evaluate whether students have learned what we have taught them in science?
6. Discuss the present situation of science education in our country. How can we have better science education programmes for our schools?
7. Describe nature of science at school level.
8. (a) Why should we teach science?

   (b) Why should we teach what we teach in science at a particular class level?
9. (a) How should we teach science?

   (b) Why should we teach the way we teach science?
10. (a) What is scientific attitude?

    (b) What is scientific temper?

(c) What is the difference between scientific attitude and scientific temper? Discuss.

(d) What are the characteristics of a person having scientific temper?

(e) How will you recognise that a particular person has scientific temper?

(f) How will you develop scientific temper among your students?

(g) What is scientific method? How is it related with scientific temper?

11. "Our students are frustrated with the existing science courses and the examination system." How far do you agree with the statement? Justify your answer.

12. How can we restructure the existing science courses so that learning science may be a joyful experience for our students?

13. Make study of the syllabus outline for the science method course taken by you. Compare it with a similar science course given in Appendix B and F and give the strengths and weaknesses of each. How far do you think it may help you to be a good science teacher?

3

Methods in Vogue

Teacher's main job lies to teach. There is not a method or the methods of teaching science which could suit in all the situations. All teachers are different. No two children are alike. Teachers differ in personality. Children differ from family to family and from locality to locality — even in respect of their mental and physical development. Thus a teaching method is largely governed by these three factors — environment, teacher and pupil. It will be advisable to lay down a series of methods of science teaching, so that the teachers could select from them according to their need.

Teaching Method Selection

There are some guiding principles for determining our teaching methods. They are as follows:

1. Every method we use should be based on an understanding of the pupils in our classroom, and not on an understanding of children we have read about.
2. Every method we use should be one which we thoroughly understand and believe will be successful with the pupils in our classroom and not merely one which we have heard is successful.
3. Every method we use should lead the pupils to a sense of achievement through interest and purpose.
4. Every method we use should stimulate the pupils to think and cooperate actively.
5. Every method we use should be based on the realisation that the word education derives from a Latin word 'educo'

which means "I bring up" or "I nourish." Education is a "drawing out" and not a "putting in."

Mindful of the above points there are certain vital instincts which stimulate the child to learn and through which he acquires knowledge and skills. They are instincts of play, imitation, curiosity and competition. These are the instincts which are principally concerned with the educational development of the child and which we must consider when planning our methods of teaching science.

Beside these vital instincts from which the impulse to learn springs, there are some physical agents which enable a child to acquire skills and knowledge. They are as follows:

1. The hands — Learning by touching and doing.
2. The eyes — Learning by seeing.
3. The ears — Learning by hearing.
4. The mouth — Learning by saying.
5. The nose — Learning by smelling.
6. The tongue — Learning by tasting.

These senses should be utilised as much as possible in our method of science teaching for creating effective teaching learning situations

Methods in Practice

Traditional Methods

1. Lecture Method (8 4)
2. (Improved) Lecture Method (8 5)
3. Demonstration Method (8 6)
4. Concrete to Abstract Approach (8 7)
5. Lecture Demostration Method (8 8)
6. (Improved) Lecture Demonstration Method (8 9)
7. Laboratory Method (8 10)

Discovery Methods

8. Scientific Method (8 11)

9. Project Method (8 12)
10. Investigatory Project Method (8 13)
11. Problem Solving Method (8 14)
12. Heuristic Method (8 15)
13. Inquiry Approach (8 16)

Other Methods

14. Discussion or Interactive Approach (8 17)
15. Programmed Instruction Method (8 18)
16. Multimedia Package Approach (8 19)
17. Individualized Instruction Method (8 20)
18. Modular Approach (8 21)
19. Teacher Centred versus Child Centred Approach (8 22)
20. Activity Approach (8 23)
21. Process Approach (8 24)
22. Environmental Studies (EVS) Approach (8 25)

Lecture Method

This is one of the most popular methods of teaching in our schools. This is a teacher structured method, and the students are just passive listeners most of the time. Very few teachers allow questions during the lecture, though some of them give some time to their students to ask questions after the lecture. Many students forget their questions by the time the lecture is over. So their questions remain unanswered. Teachers talk most of the time without using any teaching aid though some of them use blackboard. For them the lecture method is talk and chalk method. Sometime the back benchers cannot even read what is written on the blackboard. Students take notes of the lecture, and slow writers miss many points.

Research studies have been made on what actually happens in classrooms where teacher is teaching by lecture method. 'Step into a classroom and what do you hear. The chances are better than 60 per cent you will hear someone talking. If someone is talking the chances are that it will be the teacher more than 70 per cent of the time. The teachers talk more than all the students combined.

The teacher is the main actor 85 per cent of the time. Pupils receive recognition, praise and encouragement only 1-2 per cent of the time." According to Flanders, N.A. "We want to encourage our pupils to learn to express themselves fluently, yet on average there are two speeches by each pupil each day in class, and the mean length of these is 8.4 words."

Students dislike lectures. In an adult education class those who had heard only 15 minutes of a radio talk could score 41 per cent on a factual recall test while those who listened to the 30 minutes of the lecture could score only 25 per cent on the same test. In other words, the second period of 15 minutes proved to be for less productive as it reduced the listener's ability to recall the first 15 minutes. It may be due to fatigue set in which students lost the concentration. The span of concentration seems to be less for the child than for the adult. Children switch their attention rapidly from one subject to another.

It implies that the teacher should not lecture continuously for more than a very limited time, say 15 minutes with an average secondary school class. After that a change of activity, to practical work, watching a film, writing or working in small groups, or discussion could be submitted.

Lecture method has some advantages and disadvantages.

Advantages

1. It is quick, and a lot of knowledge can be imparted in quite a lesser time.
2. It is highly efficient if teacher teaches in systematic and logical manner.
3. It is convenient and easy and a teacher is free to develop his own style of teaching.

Disadvantages

1. Students' involvement and participation is nil or quite less.
2. Students' previous knowledge or entry behaviours are usually not taken into consideration.

3. Developing scientific skills are neglected.
4. Teacher needs a lot prior knowledge to prepare a lecture.

It is wise to have notes (in points) available while lecturing for ensuring correct sequencing of ideas and figures, but word by word reading from notes should be avoided. Listening to your tape recorded lecture or comments of your colleagues on your lecture will enable you to find out the limitations of the lecture method as well as to enable you to improve your further lectures.

Lecture Method in Improved Form

Lecture Method is perhaps as old as appointment of the first lecturer in our country, as lecturer is one who lectures, and uses Lecture Method in his class. But old is Gold. It is correct that in Lecture Method, no audio-visual aids are used, and we do not need audio-visual aids all the time. If our students have enough experience of what is to be talked about in we do not need to use audio-visual aids in the lesson, and the lecture can be improved (enriched) by adding Teacher-Learner Interaction (TLI) and Learner-Learner Interaction (LLI), into it. Involve your students into your Lecture with the two interactions — TLI and LLI. Adding these two interactions with the lecture, some of the disadvantage of the lecture (8.4) can be removed, and the lecture can be improved.

Encourage your students to ask questions (NPE 1986). You should also ask questions to all types of students (average, below average and slow learners) and not just the above average during your (improved) lecture. Sometimes ask some open question, for which first students had to have LLI, before answering.

Demonstration Method

Demonstration means 'to show. In lecture method, the teacher just talks but in demonstration method he also shows and illustrates certain phenomenon and applications of abstract principles through demonstration of experiments. Demonstrations provide concrete experiences to students. Demonstrations may also include use of films, slides, overhead projector or the micro-projector.

While using the demonstration method the teacher can:

1. provide significant, rich and worthwhile experiences to students enhancing their power of observation.

2. illustrate abstract ideas in concrete form.
3. co-ordinate laboratory work with theory and highlight safety methods.
4. pose a problem to students and gather their hypotheses based on their experiences.
5. provide concrete experiences for the solution of a problem.
6. add additional demonstrations after its review, if considered necessary.
7. do those demonstrations which are dangerous for students to perform themselves.

Characteristics of a Good Demonstration

1. It should be clearly visible to all students, even to the batk benchers.
2. It should be pre-tested so that it may be convincing, striking and clear-cut.
3. Children should also be involved.
4. Results should not be known to students.
5. If there are more than one demonstration in a lesson they should be well-spread.
6. In a demonstration only one idea should be taken at a time. Too many ideas in one demonstration may confuse the children specially the young ones.

Points to be Noted

1. For large scale demonstration, the teacher must spend a good deal of time in thinking and devising experiments to make principles quite clear, and in showing various types of experiments necessary to clarify the numerous difficult concepts of the science course.
2. The teacher should carry out the experiment in such away that the students should learn how to carry it out by themselves.
3. When carrying out demonstration experiments the teacher should make sure that everything is in order before the lesson begins. He should be certain that the demonstrations

will prove his points. The table should be well illuminated either by day light or by electric lights. The background should preferably be white or black so that the apparatus and other materials are clearly visible.

4. The teacher should see the general order and tidiness of the demonstration table. Nothing looks worst than a demonstration table litered with books and other material not to be used. The demonstration table should have only apparatus and materials relevant to the lesson.

5. In this method students are placed in a passive role which may be frustrating or boring for them unless the teacher involves them in thinking behind the experiment and in the manipulation.

This problem can be minimised if the demonstration is assembled ready for action before the lesson and there is every expectation that it will work. Demonstrations need to be rehearsed. For effective demonstration the following questions should be kept in mind:

(a) Is the apparatus clearly laid out from where the students view?

(b) Do instruments have large enough dials to be read by all the students in the class?

Overhead projector has made it possible to modify some demonstrations so that they are more easily seen and students can take readings and plot graphs while demonstration is proceeding. Under such conditions the teacher can involve their students in making predictions, speculations about causes, and thinking of ways of testing ideas.

Advantages

1. There is a possibility of using more sophisticated apparatus.
2. More difficult experiments can be undertaken.
3. More hazardous experiments may be attempted.
4. Expenses may be minimised compared to laboratory method.
5. There is a possibility to demonstrate manipulative and allied practical skills.

6. There is possibility to draw the attention of all the pupils of the class simultaneously.
7. It takes less time compared to laboratory and other innovative methods.
8. This method is more efficient in a way compared to laboratory method as a teacher is more competent than students to handle apparatus.
9. All students can see the same operation and techniques simultaneously.
10. Teacher is in a position to explain each and every step and to ensure that all students see and interpret all the work in the same manner.

Disadvantages

1. All students do not experiment with their own hands. It is a substitute for laboratory work.
2. When the demonstration is complex or there are too many demonstrations in one lesson, students feel difficulty in understanding the basic concepts, principles and skills.
3. Various details of the apparatus, significant reactions and other essential steps undertaken by the teacher in drawing conclusions are not necessarily visible to all the students of the class equally well.
4. It deprives students of many of the advantages of laboratory method such as handling of the apparatus and other materials as well as making their own interpretations.

Approaches : Concrete and Abstract

Whenever you plan a lesson, ask yourself whether you really need audio-visual aids, as sometimes you do not need audio-visual aids. If your answer is "yes" then ask yourself of what type of audio-visual aids. Edger Dale has arranged the various audio-visual aids, from more concrete in nature to comparatively more abstract (5.4)

1. Direct Purposeful Experiences (5.5)
2. Contrived Experiences (5.6)

3. Dramatic Participation (5.7)
4. Demonstrations (5.8)
5. Field Trips or Excursions (5.9)
6. Exhibits (5.10)
7. Motion Pictures and Television (5.11)
8. Radio Recording and Still Pictures (5.12)
9. Visual Symbols (5.13)
10. Verbal Symbols (5.14)

This will help you to select right type of audio-visual aids for your lessons. This arrangement should not be considered as rigid divisions or watertight compartments.

Lecture-demonstration Method

This is a method generally used by our science teachers. Students cannot learn science either by lecture or by demonstration used in isolation. Even most effective demonstration cannot guarantee learning in science. This may also be true for the lecture-demonstration method. It can succeed when lecture is based upon concrete experiences of the students' environment and a demonstration focuses them into scientific phenomenon, while discussion between teacher and students goes on in a permissive atmosphere. Demonstration method when combined with a well directed discussion is a successful teaching technique. It can be modified by allowing limited students participation and by problem solving at times. It fits well into the regular method of uniform class procedure for all students but does not permit of very wide individualisation. If widely individualised and modified, it approaches to a method usually called the problem solving or project method.

Through contrived situations in this method students themselves form concepts. Therefore lecture-demonstration method should achieve the advantages of both lecture and demonstration methods, and minimise their disadvantages. Lecture-demonstration method though widely used in our science classes has a limited role in the teaching-learning process. This is because all students do not participate actively.

Advantages. Lecture-demonstration method, has all the advantages of a demonstration method plus one more that the teacher can also involve the students in discussion.

Disadvantages. Disadvantages of a lecture-demonstration method are the same as of demonstration method.

Lecture-Demonstration Method in Improved Form

Like lecture, Lecture-Demonstration Method (8.8) can also be improved. Here along with Teacher-Learner Interaction (TLI) and Learner-Learner Interaction (LLI) two more interactions, Teacher Material Interaction (TMI) and Learner-Material Interaction (LMI) are to be added in Lecture-Demonstration (8 8). Addmg all the four mteractions — TLI L1L TML and LMI with the Lecture Demonstration (8 8) some of the disadvantages of the Lecture Demonstration (8 8) can be removed. TLI and LLI will improve the Lecture part, and TMI and LMI will improve the Demonstration part of the Lecture Demonstration. This will be (Improved) Lecture Demonstration Method, much better than the Lecture-Demonstration Method of Teaching.

When demonstrating involve students with you instead just teacher demonstrating (TMI) involve also students individually or in small groups in handling the equipment and doing the activities themselves (LMI). During TMI and LMI involve students in TLI and LLI just like you do in (Improved) Lecture. Thus using (Improved) Lecture-Demonstration method students will understand and enjoy the lesson much better.

Laboratory Method

In this method students perform laboratory experiments or laboratory exercises by their own hands individually or in small groups. So here they are more active and involved unlike demonstration method, where teacher was performing experiments involving few students and most of the students in the class were just passive observers.

Unless students carry out experiments by themselves, they will never get to know what science really is. In this method they get an opportunity to do experiments individually or in small groups. In our schools set up there is a provision of separate science labs but in the West like in USA in most of the schools there are classroom cum labs. There is a provision for 55 to 60 minutes class periods. It is upto the teachers, they can utilise this time for theory or practical or both. They carry the needed equipment and material in the classroom-cum laboratory in trolleys, students pick up the material from trolleys, take it to their work tables, and return it to trolleys after doing the laboratory work.

In our schools at secondary and senior secondary stage students go to science labs to do practical work. Usually in every school there are three science labs — Physics Chemistry and Biology For lab work two continuous periods (of about 30 minutes each) are given. At secondary stage students go to lab work once a week If one week they do Physics, the second week they will do Chemistry and the third week they will do Biology, and the same cycle is repeated. Thus for each subject (Physics, Chemistry and Biology) the turn comes every three weeks. At senior secondary stage students go to lab work twice a week m every subject — Physics, Chemistry and Biology. Usually students work in groups of about 20. If there are 40 students in a class, they are divided into 2 groups (if one group is doing Physics, the other will be doing Chemistry or Biology) so that the teacher may supervise their students work (in a smaller group) more satisfactorily as well as to guide them individually or in still smaller groups.

Generally lab experiments are of five kinds

1. Experiments to illustrate scientific principles
2. Experiments to find numerical results
3. Experiments to produce something as preparation of gases or biological slides.
4. Experiments to verify experiments carried out by other scientists.
5. Original work or investigatory science projects or open-ended experiments.

In our science courses there are usually the first four types of experiments. Now a little importance is also being given to the fifth type, the investigatory experiments, at senior secondary stage. Usually there is no coordination between theory and practical work.

The science courses in USA like PSSC, BSCS and CHEM study have employed a more heuristic approach with the practical work embedded right in the middle of the theory. A cycle of events is envisaged. The pupil is given a laboratory problem and his observations give rise to discussion and hypotheses. These hypotheses are tested by experiment, and so the cycle ends where it started at the laboratory table.

Open-ended experiments, are more difficult to organise and supervise than the traditional ones. The heuristic approach (8.15) demands that the pupils should be allowed to stop and think, discuss and suggest modifications for further experiments.

Objectives. When teaching science by laboratory method, the following objectives should be kept in mind:

1. To develop manipulative skills.
2. To arouse and maintain interest in science.
3. To encourage accurate observations and careful recording.
4. To make biological, chemical and physical phenomenon more real through actual experience.
5. To be integral part of the process of finding facts by investigation and arriving at principles.
6. To train the students in science processes and scientific method.
7. To give training in problem solving. To verify facts and principles already taught in theory.
8. To elucidate the theoretical work so as to aid comprehension.
9. To prepare the students for practical examination.

Advantages

1. Learning by doing.
2. Opportunity to handle materials.
3. Learning to follow directions carefully.
4. Learning skills in performing experiments, recording observations and results, summarising data and drawing conclusions.
5. Opportunity for critical thinking.

Disadvantages

1. More expensive if separate equipment is provided to each student.
2. Difficult to schedule in the school timetable when double periods are provided.
3. More time consuming compared to demonstration method as students are unskilled workers and or not as competent to handle apparatus as their teachers.
4. No guarantee that the students will learn to solve problems or think scientifically.

When there are more students and the equipment is not enough for each student to do experiments, then a large number of experiments should be arranged, and different students could do different experiments at the same time. If possible typed instructions should be given to students for each experiment. This-will facilitate, students to work on their own and teacher will have time to go to students who need him most.

Scientific Method

Scientific method is one of the methods for discovery. Training in scientific method necessitates discouraging traditional demonstrations and laboratory experiments. When teaching by scientific method, the students do not perform the prescribed list of experiments in which emphasis is on the verification of some already known science principles and laws. Instead they are involved in investigatory problems whose solutions are not available either in textbook or lab manuals.

Steps of Scientific Method

1. *Problem.* What does a student want to learn?
2. *Hypothesis.* What does a student think the answer would be?
3. *Experiment*
   (a) Testing of Hypothesis by an Experiment. How could a student tell the answer would be what he predicted?
   (b) Collection of Data
   (c) Interpretation of Data. What happened when a student tested his hypothesis?

4. *Conclusion.* What do the results of the experiment show? Is the hypothesis accepted, rejected or needs modification.

Advantages

1. Students do their own learning under the guidance of their teacher.
2. They learn to propose, formulate and structure problems.
3. They learn to collect varied pieces of information relevant to the problem from different sources.
4. They collect the evidence to prove or disprove the identified hypotheses.
5. They learn to solve everyday problems.
6. They are more closely familiar with various things, their applications and relationships instead of having mere knowledge.
7. They establish a healthy and favourable relationship with their teachers.

Disadvantages

1. This method is very slow, long and time consuming. Therefore the syllabus (knowledge and information) could not be covered in the allotted time. Thus a different syllabus is needed for this method as in some American science programmes like PSSC, BSCS and CHEM Study of which formulation of hypotheses and their testing is the dominant feature.
2. There is too much emphasis on practical work which may give a wrong concept of the nature and philosophy of science in general. Learning science is a joyful process but too much practical work may make it dull and routine type of affair.
3. Most of the teachers are perhaps not able to teach by this method, as they have not practised teaching science by this method.
4. All students are not capable to learn by this method.

Project Method

A project is any purposeful activity. It may or may not involve investigation. If it involves investigation it will be investigatory project. In progressive schools students are allotted some projects during summer holidays. It may be a curricular or enrichment activity. Teacher try to cover a part of syllabus by this method. Parents also help their wards when they work on their projects. Titles of some projects generally given to students are as follows:

1. Indian Scientists
2. Story of Wheel
3. From earth to moon

Here students read some reference material, talk to some professional people and the public, observe what is going on around them and so on. This is how they gather data. Then they analyse their data, and prepare their project reports. The report may be hand-written or typed and it may include pictures, charts, graphs, models and so on. Students learn a lot when these project reports are discussed in the Class. Project Method is an example of Assignment Method.

Investigatory Method

The Investigatory Project Method involves investigation, discovery and finding out something which was not known to the student before. An investigation is much more than the repetition of a standard experiment. Here the student is to decide what experiments are necessary and how he is going to carry them out. He may have to design his own apparatus, if that is not available in the laboratory. He has to search for the appropriate principles, laws, formulae, apparatus and data; and originate solution to a problem. The student will act like a scientist.

This method involves the steps of scientific method:

1. Problem
2. Hypotheses
3. Experiment
    - (i) Testing of hypotheses by experiments
    - (ii) Collection of data
    - (iii) Interpretation of data
4. Conclusion.

This is the least used method of teaching science in our schools. In USA, Canada and UK teachers try to cover a part of syllabus by this method. In this method a group of students select a problem in consultation with their teacher/ and then through discussion develop the plan of action and design the type of equipment needed to carry out the experiments to reach the conclusion. Students thus are trained in science processes and scientific method.

Advantages

1. It creates interest in science.
2. It develops understanding.
3. It develops self-confidence, cooperation, leadership and emotional stability.
4. It promotes curiosity and develops scientific temper, interest and appreciation.
5. It develops abstract and concrete scientific skills.
6. It develops interest in scientific hobbies in the right use of leisure time later on.

Limitations

1. This is the most difficult method for the teacher, requiring more planning and more effort of execution.

   Though it is the most difficult method for the teacher requiring more effort and planning, the lack of this effort is one of the reasons for much of the mediocre teaching that is done. The results of this method, when it is properly executed, are more than compensate for the extra work that is required.

2. If properly operated it calls for somewhat more materials and equipment than in the strictly demonstration method.

   The necessity for more materials and equipment is generally an excuse rather than a reason for not using it. he problems and experiments can be so devised that they will require nothing that cannot be had at little or no expense.

3. The amount of time consumed by the projects may be so great as to make it impossible to cover a wide variety of topics thus resulting in an incomplete course.

Also to the economy of time, there is much doubt as to whether time spent upon less subject matter might not be worthwhile to the student than the same time spent in hurrying over more subject matter.

4. It may result in a task of proper coordination of subject matter when individualised, since students may be working upon different problems or projects.

   The lack of coordination which sometimes is the result of individual work is little more than the result of poor planning and less execution upon the part of the teacher.

5. Difficulties of method increase when there are more students in large classes and more periods per day of the teacher.

   In no other method there is equal provision for the essential factors demanded by our objectives. The solving of problems is essential to the training in scientific thinking and the following of projects is a vital part of the production of those attitudes which should be the outgrowth of science teaching. Proper planning will provide for group or even class participation as a means of diminishing the problem of number of students and number of classes that must be taught and will still make possible a sufficient amount of independent work to provide for the necessary individualisation.

Problem-solving Method

Problem is not a problem if a child can solve it by his previous knowledge. Problem solving takes place only when student's previous knowledge is insufficient to enable him to provide an acceptable solution, and so ution becomes possible only when he acquires new knowledge which he does not have before. A method to solve a problem is called a problem solving method.

Steps in Problem Solving Method

I. *Problem*

(i) Identification of problem after problem survey;
(ii) Statement of the problem — a clear description;

questions in "Yes" or "No." The answer of each question may be a small hypothesis.

Inquiry Approach of teaching science may have the following steps.

1. Encounter with the Problem.
2. Formulation of Hypotheses.
3. Data Gathering — Experimentation and Verification.
4. Conclusion — Solution of the problem.

Interactive Method

When teaching science by lecture method or lecture-demonstration method, if students are involved in discussion (interaction) they are in a much more better situation of learning science. As discussed under lecture method, the teacher should not lecture contmuously for more than a very limited time so that the teacher should not lose the concentration of their students. For this he can do a change of activity, and discussion (interaction) is one of the several activities in which students can be involved very actively. So by using lecture-cum-discussion method some of the disadvantages of the lecture method can be taken care of.

Similarly when lecture-demonstration method is combined with a well directed discussion (interaction), it may prove to be a successful technique of teaching science.

In our schools lecture method and lecture-demonstration method are most commonly used. If we add "discussion" or "interaction" into it, these methods may come out to be much more effective,

There may be 4 types of interactions.

(i) Teacher-Learner Interaction (TLI)
(ii) Learner-Learner Interaction (LLI)
(iii) Teacher-Material Interaction (TMI)
(iv) Learner-Material Interaction (LMI)

When teacher is lecturing, TLI may be initiated. When children are discussing in small groups, like tutorials, LLI may be initiated. When teacher is demonstrating, he is using some teaching aids (material) he can use TMI along with TLI for more effective teaching.

When children are doing some experiments in small groups, LMI will be of better use along with LLI and TLI.

Programmed Instruction Method

Programmed Instructional Materials as discussed in the elsewhere, provide self-learning units. Such units may prove to be very useful when our science teachers are heavily loaded, and they do not have time to interact specially those students individually, who really need them.

There are some topics in every field of science (Physics, Chemistry and Biology) which the students can leam on their own if programmed learning units are available on these topics. But in our country programmed" learning units are not available in the market. So the only choice remains that some innovative science teachers should write some programmed units on selected topics to be used by their students. These guidelines may be used when writing programmed units. Such units when written, may be shared by other science teachers in their classes. Self-Learning Modules are as good as Programmed Instruction Materials for self-learning.

Multimedia Package

Like Programmed Instruction, Self-learning modules and Multi-media Packages if available on some topics, may also be given to students to cover part of syllabus on their own. Multimedia packages can also be developed by teachers. Such packages once developed may be used again and again. This is Multimedia Package Approach of teaching.

Individualised Instructions

Not all students are alike, but we teach them the same thing by the same method. In a classroom there are students of different science background. Most of them perhaps do not have aptitude for science, if they have a choice perhaps they will not offer science. But we are to teach the same science to all of them, and we usually use the same method to teach all students, without taking into consideration their individual differences.

Usually we can classify our students in three groups — average, below average and above average. When we teach science we assume some pre-requisites or entry behaviours of our students, we assume that this much they already know, and men we start our lesson. When we do so, we take into consideration only the average students, and forget about the below and the above average. The result is that only the average students are satisfied and the below and the above average are frustrated. The only solution remains that some individualised instruction and some other self-learning materials be developed and used to satisfy all the students.

Programmed Instruction is one way of individualised instruction. Self-learning modules, slide-tape programmes, and multi-media packages are some other means. Though such materials are not available in the market, yet they can be developed by some innovative teachers for the use of their students. Then their materials can also be shared by other science teachers in their classes.

4

Approaches in Vogue

Modular Approach

Use of self-learning modules in teaching is another form of individualised instruction. This is called Modular Approach of teaching and learnmg. If self-learning modules are available on some topics, they can be given to students as assignment for self-learning. Teachers can also develop such modules on some topics. Such modules once developed can be used again and again.

Teacher-centred versus Child-centred Approach

Teacher Centred Approach (TCA). If we observe classrooms, we find it is the teacher who speaks most of the time, and the children either given no opportunity to speak or a very little opportunity to speak — ask questions or interact. This is a Teacher Centred Approach of Teaching.

Example. In a study about 1000 classes were observed (I-XII) in all subjects and in all types of schools, and it was found that on an average 95 per cent of the time teacher was speaking and 5 per cent of the time the children were speaking. This is an example of Teacher Centred Approach of Teaching.

Lecture Method and Lecture Demonstration Method are Teacher Centred Approaches of Teaching. Teacher Centred Approach is a very effective method for teaching skills (processes). Reading a thermometer, reading a spring balance, preparing gases like hydrogen, oxygen and carbon dioxide, salt analysis, volumetric and gravimetric exercises, setting up a microscope, making a slide and seeing it through a microscope, setting the experiment for photosynthesis etc., are all skills. Until a child perfectly learns a skill, the teacher is very much involved in telling the child "what to do" and "how to do." The teacher has to use Teacher Centred Approach. Cooking; sewing; driving a scooter, a motor cycle or a car; repairing; playing musical instruments; dancing etc., are all skills. Teaching each of these skills, a teacher is needed who teaches these skills by Teacher Centred Approach.

Example. Reading a thermometer is a skill. According to a study children and even teachers not taught this skill by Teacher Centred Approach, generally read the thermometer wrong. If the reading was 46°C, they read 40.6°C. Then came the teacher to teach this skill. He pointed at 40 and asked "What is the reading?" The child said "40°C". Then he pointed at 50 and asked "What is the reading?" The child said, "50°C". Then the teacher asked, "How many marks are there between 40°C and 50°C?" When the child failed to answer, the teacher himself counted — 1, 2, 3, 4, 5, 6, 7, 8, 9,10. Then the teacher asked "How much is one mark?" Then the child replied "1°C." (This is actually the least count of the thermometer which the child was not knowing, and therefore he read 40.6°C instead of 46°C). Then the teacher asked, "How many marks is the mercury above 40°C"? And the child counted, "1, 2, 3, 4, 5, 6." Then the teacher asked, "Now tell, what is the reading of the thermometer?" And the child again counted, "41, 42, 43, 44, 45, 46," and then said," Thermometer reads 46°C and not 40.6°C".

Now look at the approach, teacher used to teach the child to read the thermometer correctly. In this approach the teacher was more involved than the child, and therefore this is Teacher Centred Approach. Reading a thermometer is a skill. Therefore Teacher Centred Approach (TCA) should be used to teach skills (processes) to the child.

Child Centred Approach. Some innovative teachers themselves speak less in the class, and give opportunity to their children to speak more. Here the science teacher acts as moderator (leading and moderating discussions) and a guide (helping slow learners). This is Child Centred Approach. In teaching science by Lecture Method or by Lecture-Demonstration Method, these innovative teachers involve their children in interaction and question-answer sessions that even their lecture and Lecture-demonstration become child centred. Inquiry Approach, Problem Solving Approach, Laboratory Method, Scientific Method, Project Method and Investigatory Project Method are Child Centred Approaches.

Example. A teacher is teaching a concept "Air has weight" by scientific method. It involves "*weighing*" by a spring balance, which is a *skill (process)*. The teacher teaches the skill (process) of weighing to the children by Teacher Centred Approach before he teaches the concept "Air has weight."

Then he starts the lesson with a:

1. ***Problem.*** Does air has weight? (This is TCA). Then children formulate their own

2. ***Hypotheses.*** (i) Yes, (ii) No. (This is CCA). Then children (as already know the skill of weighing or reading a spring balance) test their hypotheses themselves with an experiment.

3. ***Experiment.*** weighing an empty football bladder, and the same football bladder full of air. (This is CCA). Then they themselves draw the conclusion.

4. ***Conclusion.*** that air has weight. Hypotheses "yes" is right, and hypotheses "*no*" is wrong. (This is CCA).

Here step — 1 is Teacher Centred as teacher asks the question or poses a problem. Steps — 2, 3, 4 are Child Centred. Therefore Scientific Method is 25 per cent teacher centred and 75 per cent child centred. Thus as a whole Scientific Method is Child Centred Approach (CCA).

Note "weight" is a concept and "weighing" is a skill. When skill of "weighing" already taught by the teacher to the children by Teacher Centred Approach, the concept of "weight" is to be taught by Child Centred Approach. Do not tell to the child "air has weight," let him find out himself whether or not "air has weight" by the Child Centred Approach (CCA).

Remember

1. Teach skills (processes) by TCA, and
2. Teach concepts by CCA.

Activity Approach

"Believe nothing because you have been told about it. Don't believe what your teacher tells you merely out of respect for the teacher."

Who said this? When this question is put to science teachers in seminars the reply is 'some scientist'. Actually it is the statement of Lord Buddha.

Many times teachers teach and children do not understand. This is because children are conditioned in accepting and memorising what teacher tells them, without questioning and understanding.

In science there are many facts, principles, laws, concepts and skills, which children memorise without understanding. Have you ever thought why is it so?

Cognitive Development of Children. There are three types of children:

1. *Formal operational* — They can understand science without activities.

2. *Concrete operational* — They can understand science only if they do activities by their own hands.

3. *Pre-operational* — They can understand science if they do activities repeatedly by their own hands.

This is the way Piaget categorised the children. These are the children's cognitive stages of development.

Example. Siddiqis worked with Piaget at Florida State University (USA) in 1970 when he came as a Visiting Professor. He went to the neighbouring schools to demonstrate how children at these cognitive stages look at things, think and response. There it was found that only 5 per cent children at primary level (I-V) were at formal operational stage, the remaining 95 per cent children were either concrete operational or pre-operational.

By using Piagetian tasks, Siddiqis conducted Research Studies on 1206 Primary school children in Delhi from all type of schools during 1975-77. The average interview time with each child was about 15 mmutes. So it took about 300 hours to complete the task. It was found that only 4.4 per cent children at primary level (I-V) were at formal operational stage. In Class V formal operational were 9.4 per cent, concrete operational 69.3 per cent and pre-operational 21.3 per cent.

Even at Upper Primary Level (VI-VIII) a good number of children will be at c.oncrete operational stage. This shows that specially at primary and upper primary levels, if children are not involved m doing activities or get first-hand observations, the concepts do not become clear. They may memorise and recall without understanding. When the concepts are not made clear m lower classes, their cumulative effect is seen in higher classes. Other than this there are new concepts at secondary and senior secondary levels which can be clarified through activities or relevant demonstrations.

Science is Doing

Generally m our schools, science is taught by giving Lectures, and sometime by demonstrating few experiments. Children are not really mvolved m doing activities by their own hands. Teachers should also leam a lesson from the following saying:

"I heard and I forgot,

I saw and I remembered,

I did and I understood "

This is not just a saymg. As hypotheses these were tested by Siddiqis and they were found correct.

If our objective is that the child may remember the content for sometime. Lecture Method may be relevant without even using Audio-Visual Aids. If the objective is that the child may remember for longer duration. Lecture will not work. But Lecture-Demonstration will be more effective. Care should be taken that every child is able to observe what is being demonstrated using all the 5 senses (see, touch, smell, taste, hear).

But if the objective is that the child must understand then doing is the only method for pre-operational and concrete operational children. Lecture and Lecture-Demonstration are not going to work. The children will have to be mvolved in doing activities by their own hands.

Thus Activity Based Science-Teaching is the only way of teaching science, if we want our children to learn science. Learning science is understanding science, and not just memorising.

Sample science Activities for primary, upper primary and secondary classes have been given. Some of the activities from this list may be selected according to the science topics to be taught by you in various classes. These activities may be demonstrated by you, or may be done by your students by their own hands, in science classes. These activities will make science teaching quite interesting and learning science by Activity Approach will be a fun for students.

Process Approach

Another important aspect of Activity Based Science Teaching is Teaching with Process Approach.

"If you will teach content, then who will teach science" D.S. Kothari. Science is not just content. Science is content plus something. That something is Process. If our stress shifts from content to process, content will automatically be included and much more meaningfully.

American Association for the Advancement of Science (AAAS) has identified 13 science processes — observing, classifying, using numbers, measuring, using space-time relationships, communicating, predicting, inferring, defining operationally, formulating hypotheses, interpreting data, controlling variables and experimenting.

If we teach science through process approach, it automatically becomes activity based. If a child leams science through process approach, he leams lot of science on his own. Thus Process Approach is one of the best ways of teaching science, as it motivates the children, and they get involved in doing activities.

Certain competencies are to be developed in children while teaching science like spirit of inquiry; objectivity; courage to question; problem solving; decision making; investigating; developing scientific attitude or temper; using scientific method; reducing all sorts of prejudices based on sex, caste, religion and language etc. " These are also the objectives of NPE — 1986. These competencies may be developed in children through Process Approach of Teaching Science, more meaningfully.

Although one has to devote a little more time when teaching science through Process Approach, but teaching-learning process becomes more interesting and effective. There are teachers who use Process Approach for teaching science in their classes, and for their children learning science is fun.

Environmental Approach

Use materials (like plants, animals, human body, living-non-living, natural-manmade, wind, hails, snow, dew etc.) and phenomena (like rains, lightning, day and night, seasons, dispersion, rainbow, photosynthesis *etc.)* of the environment around you (like family, house, neighbourhood, school, earth, sky, human body etc.) as teaching aids, when teaching science. Involve students in discussions based on what they observe in their environment in and outside classroom.

Make an exhaustive list of materials and phenomena available in your environment. Add more items whenever you see some more, in your list. Classify them according to the topics you teach in science, and use them again when teaching science. Your students will enjoy learning and you will enjoy teaching science by EVS approach.

Use of Different Methods

About 1000 Science teachers from 250 Schools of the country (12 states) were oriented in Teaching of Science in the 'In-service Teachers Training' workshops during (1997-2000) conducted by D.M.N. Siddiqi.

Himachal Pradesh

1. Kangara   2. Mandi   3. Chandigarh

Punjab

4. Bhatinda   5. Jallandhar

Haryana

6. Hissar   7. Ambala

Bihar

8. Ranchi   9. Patna

Uttar Pradesh

10. Brij Vihar

Rajasthan, Gurarat

11. Padma Biriani

Andhra Pradesh, Tamil Nadu, Karnataka

Hyderabad

Delhi

13. Delhi SCERT, Delhi DIETs, Municipal Corporation Delhi (MCD) Science Centres and Research & Training Institute.

All the 22 Methods were tried out. The followmg 11 methods were found most effective. When teachers taught, children also learned (understood).

Child Centered Approach (CCA) — for teaching Science Concepts.

Teacher Centered Approach (TCA) — for teaching Science Skills or Processes.

Scientific Method — Problem, Hypotheses, Experiment, Conclusion.

Process Approach — observing, classifying, using numbers, measuring, using space-time relationship, communicating, predicting, inferring, defining operationally', formulating hypotheses, Interpreting data. Controlling variables and experimenting.

EVS Approach — Our Body, Our family. Our House, Our Neighbourhood, Our School, Our Earth, Our Sky.

Discussion or Interactive Approach

(i) Teacher — Child Interaction (TCI)

(ii) Child — Child Interaction (CCI)

(iii) Teacher — Material (Teaching Aid) Interaction (TMI)

(iv) Child — Material Interaction (CMI)

(Improved) Lecture — add 6 [(i), (ii)]

(Improved) Lecture — Demonstration — add 6 [(i), (ii), (iii), (iv)]

Self-Learning Methods

> Self-Leaning Modules

> Programmed Learning Technique, (now is becoming old, but still effective)

> CDs (Computer Discs)

> Multimedia Packages (Printed Material, Audio-Tapes, Videotapes, CDs, Internet, Internet etc.)

Concrete to Abstract Approach. **Direct purposeful experiences. Contrived experiences. Dramatic participation, Demonstrations, Field trips or Ecursions, Exhibits, Motion pictures and Television, Radio recordings and still pictures. Visual symbols and Verbal symbols.**

Activity Based Teaching Approach

What do we mean by UNDERSTANDING ? **This QUESTION was asked by a good number of children learning Science at various levels. Their answers are summarised below:**

I feel, I understand Science because:

1. state it in my own words.

2. give its examples.

3. recognise it in various guises and circumstances.

4. see connections between it and other facts or ideas.

5. make use of it in various ways.

6. foresee some of its consequences.

7. state its opposite or concourse.

Strengths, Weakness And Suggestions For Further Improvement. The participating science teachers gave their feedback for the teachers training programmes. This is summarised below :

- We leamt several new techniques for teaching of science which we were not taught in out B.Ed. Programme. Now we are better equipped for Activity Based Science Teaching. When we will use the methods we have learnt here in out science classes, our students will hopefully understand better and enjoy science more.
- (Improved) Lecture and (Improved) Lecture - Demonstration seem to be more effective than just Lecture and Lecture-Demonstration methods.
- Now we know that for teaching science Concepts we should use LCA, and for teaching science skills/processes we should use TCA.
- We think that the LLI, the EVS Approach and Scientific Method are the best techniques for science teaching.

Concluding Remarks. Our Science courses are mostly content-oriented. Whenever the courses are updated more content is added. Courses become heavier and heavier while time allotted m the school time-table remains just about the same. Thus, students have to cover much more content in comparatively much lesser time. Moreover classes are crowded and teachers are heavily loaded. Thus inspite of sufficiently available Science equipment for experiments and demonstrations, the content is covered by asking students to read books or giving lectures to cover more content in lesser time without demonstrations and experiments.

Under such classroom conditions we have to devise and use some self-Learning techniques in teaching Science. These along with some other researched methods/approaches LIKE Learner Centred Approach, Teacher Centered Approach, (Improved) Lecture Method, (Improved) Lecture-Demonstration Method, Concrete to Abstract Approach, and Activity Based Teaching Approach will be more effective in science teaching.

Choice of Teaching Approaches

Every teaching method is unique. Different teaching methods are not just a matter of fashion or personal whim. There are grounds for choosing a particular method for a particular situation. A teaching method may prove to be suitable for one situation but completely inappropriate for another.

Our teaching method should be compatible to our objectives. Suppose our objectives are:

1. To ensure that the students obtain the factual knowledge of the subject.
2. To give the students an understanding of the basic concepts.
3. To help the students acquire practical laboratory skills.
4. To promote the interest of the students in the subject.
5. To develop the students' ability to communicate his understanding of the subject in their own words.

If we look at these objectives and choose suitable methods to achieve these objectives, we will see that in order to achieve objectives No. 1 and 2 'lecture method' will be more appropriate, but by this method we will not be able to achieve objectives No. 3

and 4, for which perhaps the laboratory method would be more suitable. The lecture method probably will also be suitable to achieve objective No. 5, if during the lecture notes are not dictated, but students take their own notes.

Teaching Skills in Practice

You learned several methods for science teaching. You also learned how to select particular method or methods for teaching a particular lesson. Now you are to teach science, and all you learned is mostly theoretical. As a practising teacher, you should practise these methods or at least some teaching skills before facing the class. One of the most effective, efficient and dependable methods for developing teaching skills is "microteaching." What is microtenching? How can you use this technique for developing your teaching skills? Answers to such questions might help you to make yourself a better practising teacher.

Microteaching

Practising teachers, when they go to teach in the schools, they face many problems even after completing many theoretical aspects of pedagogy in their course work. Actually teaching is not a simple process. It involves many aspects like class organisation, command on the language, control on the class, probing the students explaining concepts, ideas and so on. The whole idea of microteaching was started at the Stanford University in 1960 by Alien and others. It was initially designed for practising teachers to do practice in teaching in front of their own classmates (it was also recorded on a videotape) before going to the actual classrooms. The feedback given by the peer group and received by the video replay helped the teacher to identify his/her shortcomings and do more practice in identified areas. The idea of the whole process was to bring improvements in one's teaching. Microteaching was found quite an effective process in developing teaching skills in preservice teachers during their training period. Since then it has gained quite a popularity in various teaching training institutes and other training centres. A large number of researches have been done in the field of microteaching and many microteaching centres and research units have been established. Other than preservice teachers training, microteaching is being used for in-service teachers training and in many professional fields like medicine and nursing etc.

As the name indicates microteaching means teaching a short (micro) lesson, for a short time (5-10 minutes); teaching to a small group or may be their own peer group or a small group of students, concentrating on one particular aspect of teaching. The rationale for this approach is that teaching is a complex process involving various aspects, microteaching helps in concentrating on one aspect at a time, therefore reduces the situations to a manageable proportion. The experts and research in microteaching have identified many skills in teaching such as — skill of introducing a lesson, class management and organisation, maintaining students attention, art of questioning, use of chalkboard, lecturing, using the audio-visual aids, reinforcement or encouraging the desired behaviour, explaining things and many more. In microteaching session each skill is practised and mastered individually. Once the various skills have been practised in the Simulated situation the teacher will be able to combine all or some skills of teaching in the real situation of classroom teaching.

Before actually starting any practice in microteaching it is important to orient the trainee teachers with the philosophy and technique of microteaching. This could be done by supervisors or other subject experts, then the skills have to be identified for microteaching practice. *One* way of doing this is to plan and give a regular teaching lesson in simulated situation (in front of the peer group). From this simulated teaching the weak areas of skills can be identified after getting proper feedback, or it can be decided by the subject expert or the supervisor to give practice in some skills which will be more important in teaching, for example, in science teaching, problem solving, inquiry approach and some others can be identified.

The microteaching may be done in the following steps.

Miscrolesson Planning. After deciding on the skills to be developed the first step is the planning of a miscrolesson on the identified teaching skill say introducing a lesson on a selected topic for a short period of time say five-six minutes.

Practice of the Teaching Skill. The-second step is the teaching session where the planned lesson on the specific teaching skill will be delivered to a selected number of classmates who can play the role of that level of students for which the lesson has been developed. The rest of the classmates and the supervisor are observers.

Feedback Session. The teaching session will be followed by a short session where the feedback is given by the classmates as well as by the supervisor. At Stanford University the video-tape was used for the purpose of feedback which was discussed in the class and by actually seeing himself/herself the teacher was able to improve. In some places video-tape records are being used in microteaching sessions. But it involves heavy expenditure therefore it can be avoided.

Re-plan Session. In the light of the feedback received from the students and teachers' the lesson will be replanned.

Re-teach Session. The replanned lesson will be retaught to the same group or roles can be exchanged by the students for about the same time.

Re-feedback Session. The teacher will again receive the feedback from student-teachers (observers) and the supervisor. If needed the same cycle can be repeated to achieve the desired level of performance. Usually there are two cycles but for some there may be three cycles and for others only one cycle is sufficient.

If some sessions of microteaching are planned and arranged in the training colleges for the science teaching, practising teachers will be better equipped and will go to their practice teaching classes with more confidence.

How Should Students Study Science?

(i) You learned several methods of teaching science. You also learned how to select a particular method/methods for a particular topic and situation. You also learned some teaching skills for science class. According to NPE — 1986 "All teachers will teach, and all students will study". Now you will teach science effectively, as you know 'how to teach'. But just teaching is not enough. Your students should also study after you taught them some science. For effective learning, your students should be trained for some study skills, so that they know, how they should study?

(ii) A student should develop and employ study skills in order to derive the maximum benefit from the teacher's talk (lecture) along with T-L Interaction (Discussion) in the classroom, observations and experiments in the laboratory, reading books and journals in the library and doing assignments (homework) at home While some universities abroad have started courses on "Learning to Learn (Development of Study Skills)," at least we should make a beginning.

(iii) "How should I study", should be the objective of every student, you or your student. There is a great deal of literature based upon researches on learning, retention, thinking, cognitive styles, reading techniques, information processing, scheme, metacognition, note taking, problem solving, time management and related subjects. We should take its advantage to get the answer of this question. We should discover the difference between teaching-learning of Science in the School of Today and Yesterday. In order to complete the Today's Science Course, the class contact hours are less compared to the content to be taught, and hence our students are overloaded. Therefore Today's Education should provide an opportunity to students, to learn by reflective thinking, to internalise the concepts and to demonstrate creativity. Besides, Today's Education should encourage and motivate students to leam for themselves (self-learning) and pursue lifelong learning.

*(iv) **Subskills for Learning.*** There are a number of subskills (ingredients of study skills) for learning. Reflective Thinking constitutes the core. Listening (Paying Attention) is "indeed the starting point of studying in the classroom. Likewise, Reading Skills are basic to self-study. Note Taking, Question-Answer Technique, and Communication Skills greatly add to the learning process. Knowledge about Information Processing and Schematisation may enable -to adopt more effective study skills.

*(v) **The Learning Process.*** How students learn, retain and recall information has been the subject of intensive research by cognitive psychologists. The more active the learning is, more easily connections between new information and already existing information are made. More connections facilitate easy recall and longer retention. Meaningful conclusions can by drawn from the findings of the cognitive research studies. Some of them are as follow:

— Readiness to learn and motivation to leam are most essential pre-requisites to all Learning in order to generate your own motivation.

— Objectives of learning *i.e.* the intended capabilities after learning must be kept in view. It saves great deal of time and effort to go by objectives.

— Variation of activity during learning engages you in learning for a longer time,

— Incremental *i.e.* step-by-step learning or learning in small chunks, and self-evaluation during each chunk of learning ensure more permanent learning. Each chunk should have one new idea.

— Thinking while learning ensures your involvement in the process of learning. Mere note taking is not sufficient. Try to understand what you are learning. Recall previous topic. Look for links (connections) between present topic and the previous topic. This reinforces learning on both the topics.

— Memorisation and recall of facts and figures is often aided by remembering cue words, flow diagrams, acronyms etc., *e.g.* acronym VIBGYOR aids in recalling the seven colours of a rainbow.

Sustained research on learning shows that you cannot continue to leam at a stretch. Nor is the rate of learning constant with time. In a classroom, the period of time, for an adolescent, over which the learning is sustained with a reasonable rate of learning *i.e.* attention span of learner is about 20 minutes. So after every 20 minutes the teacher should change the activity for effective learning. They may use different teaching aids, tell a joke, make a mistake, ask a question, give a quiz test etc.

(vi) ***Memorising Facts and Figures.*** Whatever innovations in teaching and learning may take place, one thing is sure you will have to memorise at least some facts and figures. You cannot afford to device equations and think but all possible facts in the examination hall. There are a number of learning strategies for memorising. Some of them are as follows:

— Reviewing, repeating or rehearsing the facts are necessary. Repetition and restatement in your own words help in conceptualising and remembering things.

— Never attempt to memorise what you do not understand. For your understanding explain something difficult to someone else.

— Clustering, categorising and grouping of facts are excellent aids to memory.

— Making acronyms, one words, and analogies may aid recall. Different students prefer different techniques of memorising. You must also have memorised many facts and figures, and so your friends. Share your experiences. What techniques you have used for memorising. Discuss. You can discover your own preferred methods for memorising.

(vii) Questions During Lectures. Lecture Method is not the best method of teaching Science. What, then can you do about it if your teacher decides to use Lecture Method? The least you can do is to ensure you get the message during a lecture. When in doubt, always raise your hand and pose question. If your teacher asks questions during lecturing, raise your hand to show willingness to respond. Do not miss this chance. And when you as a teacher lecture, encourage your students to ask questions. You also ask questions to ensure that your students are understanding what you are teaching. Have a healthy Teacher-Learner Interaction (Discussion) during your lecture.

(viii) Reading Skills. As a science student you are to read a lot. If you develop some Reading Skills in you and then in your students it will help' a lot in learning science.

A reading strategy called SQ3R technique is frequently advocated for effective reading.

S Surveying the subject matter

Q Questioning oneself about the need of reading

R Reading and deriving meaning

R Recalling the previous learning

R Reviewing the salient points

Another method of effective reading is *MURDER* Technique.

M Mood Setting the mood for study doing something relevant and then switching over the study.

LJ Understanding	Making important and difficult ideas.
R Recalling	Material without referring to the text.
D Digesting	Internalising the material.
E Expanding	Knowledge by self-questioning.
R Reviewing	Learning from mistakes.

(*ix*) ***Note Taking.*** There are many good reasons for taking notes while listening to a teacher or reading a book. Note taking promotes listening, thinking, deriving meaning, concentrating, and helps in keeping record for future reference.

Different students adopt different techniques of taking notes. Some students write in the margins of the books, some on cards and others on proper notebooks. Some students write cue words, some half sentences, others make scheme maps i.e. cue diagrams beside key words. One needs not write what the teacher speaks; one may also not write what the teacher writes on the chalkboard or what he shows through overhead projection. One may develop notes in one's own style of adding-on-information in blocks, flow diagrams, schematics etc. After all, one's notes are primarily for oneself. Good note taking is, as much a process of learning as good notes are a product of learning.

It is recommended that. students should use note sheets with adequate margins for future additions, recognition, revision, arrows etc.

A recent malpractice is to photocopy someone else's class notes. It does not work. One's own notes are the best. In your own notes, you can build links to your previous knowledge, you can create your own memory aids — these are more powerful for you than other people's aids, your own notes can concentrate on those things which you find difficult to understand.

(*x*) ***Communication Skills.*** You have a great deal of scope for developing oral and written communication skills in your professional studies. How are these skills acquired?

(a) Skills of Oral Communication. One should learn how to ask a question (Question Skill), how to be precise, how to respond,, how to offer a suggestion, how to propose a solution, and how to speak in public. It is necessary to listen when you speak. One should contribute in group discussions through critical thinking and quick responses. Quite often, someone else has just said what you wanted to say. Why not you? At times, take a lead. Tutorial classes are friendly meetings with free flow of ideas. You should take advantage of your tutorials to develop skills of oral communication in you.

(b) Skills of Written Communication. Assignments and laboratory experiments should be written up independently. While writing, think visuals; draw graphs and other diagrams to convey your thought effectively. Writing is the process of expression of thoughts in black and white. The term black and white' includes written words, figures, tables and the use of desk computers. It is necessary to develop writing skills because you need to write out notes, project proposals and reports, executive summaries, critical appraisals etc. all your professional life. Remember: 'A picture is worth more than thousand words.' So try to put words in a visual form by making effective diagrams.

(xi) ***Problem Solving Skills.*** One of the best ways to leam how to solve a problem is to ask some one else to explain how he proceeded to solve it and why. A heuristic approach to problem solving suggests such strategies as:

— Thinking aloud

— Working backward

— Using trial and error

— Considering other possibilities

— Using means for analysis

— Subgoaling and working by parts etc.

Practice in solving problems leads one to think creatively, to employ different techniques and to arrive at acceptable solutions. Consider the formal type of problem solving that we do in science, *e.g.* problems like 'Prove that. . ./ 'Show that. . .,' etc., in which case the answer is known. In problems like 'Evaluate. . .,' 'Determine. . .,' etc., you have to check your solution by answering some questions to yourself, like:

— Is the answer sensible?

— Does the answer fit in the original data?

— Is the answer unique? Would any other answer fits just as well? If so, how can I decide which is more likely to be correct?

(xii) ***Time Management.*** You are to do co-curricular activities along with curricular activities — assignments, homework, self study. You have to do all this plus a lot more of your own. You have just 24 hours in a day. You cannot increase that. So you are to manage your time. There is no cut-and dried formula for time

management. You are to lay down your own priorities for the work you are to do and complete. It is worthwhile to be regular in homework, and complete your assignments and projects well in tune to avoid undue tension relax. A relaxed mind learns much better. Time for relaxation should be budgeted in the work plan. Make your daily, weekly, monthly and annual work plans, and then stick to the schedules of your plans. This will make your learning a joyful learning.

(xiii) Learning Environment. It is for you to create an environment conducive to your learning. The best environment is that where you as an individual feel motivated and reasonably comfortable to study. Reasonable comfort includes your body posture with no or minimum stress, lighted study comer with fresh air and controlled dust, heat and noise. Concept of noise may differ. Some students can study perfectly comfortably with radio or music deck at full volume, some like it in the background and others cannot bear it at all.

(xiv) Preparing for Tests and Test Taking. Having developed study skills and even after reading and preparing for a test, one may not still score well in a test. This is because Test Taking is a reverse process compared to the acquisition of knowledge. In a test, one has to recall, recognise, manipulate data, compute, analyse and write. Not only this, one has to adopt a strategy of scoring.

(a) Pre-examination Preparation. For pre-examination preparation, complete any outstanding work as quickly as possible, even if this means sacrificing the quality somewhat. Your notes are the most helpful tools for preparation. Organise your notes and highlight the key points. Look at those problems particularly which you do not know well. Answer the questions of the past years question papers. Explaining a concept to someone else makes you understand better. All this will give you a good deal of confidence.

(b) Test Taking. You should know the art of Test Taking to score more. SCORER will help you to score more.

S	stands for	Scheduling the time
C	stands for	Cue words
O	stands for	Ordering of questions to be attempted
R	stands for	Reading between the lines

E stands for Estimation of answers

R stands for Review and Revision.

*(xv) **Relax.*** Relaxation is Basic to good study skills. One can think better and respond better when relaxed. Once you are able to think/ may it be in classroom, laboratory, field or at home, you will be able to grasp the subject. Some knowledge about the process of learning, information processing, note taking etc. discussed here would lead you to better organisation and management of learning.

EXERCISE

1. State five guiding principles when selecting methods for teaching science.
2. How do the vital instincts and senses of a child pay their roles in teaching-learning process?
3. (a) Discuss the weaknesses of a lecture method for teaching science. Defend your answer with some research findings.

   (b) How can a lecture be made more effective in teaching science?

   (c) Write some advantages and disadvantages of a lecture method.
4. (a) What is the difference between a lecture method and demonstration method for teaching science?

   (b) What are the activities a science teacher can do while using demonstration method for teaching science?

   (c) What are the characteristics of a good demonstration?

   (d) What are some key points to be noted by a science teacher when using demonstration method?

   (e) Write some advantages and disadvantages of a demonstration method.
5. (a) What is the difference between demonstration method and lecture-demonstration method for teaching science?

   (b) Write some advantages and disadvantages of lecture-demonstration method.

   (c) How can this method lead to problem solving? .

(d) How can you use the steps of Scientific Method when teaching science by lecture-demonstration method? Illustrate your answer with some examples.

6. (a) What is the difference between demonstration method and laboratory method?

   (b) What is the difference of laboratory work in India and that in USA?

   (c) What are the five kinds of experiments that are usually done in the laboratory? Which of them are done in your practice teaching school?

   (d) What are the objectives of teaching science in the laboratory?

   (e) Write some advantages and disadvantages of laboratory method for teaching science.

7. (a) Differentiate between teacher-centred-teaching and learner-centred-teaching in science. Illustrate the situations in which the two approaches of teaching science should be utilised.

   (b) Name five discovery methods. What steps are common in these methods? Write down advantages and disadvantages of each discovery method.

8. (a) Describe scientific method for teaching science, taking a topic in your field.

   (b) How can the steps of scientific method be taken up when teaching science by lecture-demonstration method?

9. Discuss investigatory project method for teaching science, taking a topic in your field. Compare this method with Scientific method for teaching science.

10. (a) Identify a topic in your field and explain how will you teach by problem solving method.

    (b) Compare this method with scientific method and investigatory project method for teaching science.

11. Identify a topic in your field, and discuss how will you teach by heuristic method.

5

Aims and Objectives of Teahing

For carrying out any activity it is significant to know its purpose. If the purpose is clear, the activity will be carried out effectively. If one knows clearly what is to be achieved the planning will be done accordingly and the work will be carried out properly. Even if it is not carried out properly at least it can be measured or evaluated as to what extent the activity has been successful. This (evaluation) is only possible by comparing the achievement of the activity with its planned purpose, goal or objectives.

In the same way in education or in any particular field of education the identification of goals, aims and objectives is a very important activity. Here the question is what should be the aims and objectives of science education and science teaching? Before knowing the aims and objectives of science education, as a teacher we should also know that aims and objectives of teaching of any subject should be directly related to the educational philosophy and policies. Educational philosophy and policies give justification for teaching various subjects in school including science.

Aims and objectives of science education have undergone many changes because the goals of education are also changing with the changes in the society.

The objectives of science education and science teaching have been stated by various educators, education commissions and committees, and in many different terms. We talk about goals, aims and objectives, etc., sometimes they are used as synonymous terms; and sometimes they are used in different meanings. Before discussing the aims and objectives of science teaching it will be helpful at this stage to distinguish between these terms.

Differentiation

Richard Whitfield of Faculty of Education, Cambridge has described these in the form of a summary (Fig.) showing a chain for the isolation of teaching objectives. This summarised form will give us a clear idea of the various terms the way they are quite often used.

Significant Goals

The first two steps (Fig.) are the goals or aims; they serve to suggest general directions in which our science courses may be steered.

Justification for science in an educational setting Suggests

↓

(1) Aims for science teaching
Translation and selection gives

↓

(2) Objectives of particular courses
By selecting and relating these to specific content and teaching methods, we obtain

↓

(3) Objectives for particular lessons
Some of these at least are amenable to behavioural specification, z e., identifiable in terms of observable qualities of pupils.

Fig.

1. They are general global targets (general objectives) with which we are concerned.
2. They form the basis of the general place of science in the curriculum for given groups of pupils.

Examples

1. To develop interest of pupils in science.
2. To develop inquiring minds.
3. To help pupils to see science in relation to the rest of culture.
4. To prepare some pupils for carriers in science.
5. To help pupils to solve problems

Objectives (Step 3, Fig.)

1. They are the more precise outcomes (specific objectives) for a particular course of teaching or even a single lesson.

2. They are derived from the aims and represent their translation into terms which are tangle in planning a course or series of lessons.

* When objectives written in this form, they are called behavioural objectives.

Examples

1. To develop the ability to formulate hypotheses.
2. To foster the ability to estimate experimental errors.
3. To develop skill in wiring simple circuits.
4. To increase pupils' ability to work as a term in sharing out a complex task.
5. To help pupils describe the structure of human heart.

An objective is an intent communicated by a statement describing a proposed change in a learner — a statement of what the learner is to be like when he has successfully completed a learning experience. It is a description of pattern of behaviour (performance) we want the learner to be able to demonstrate.

In the given examples of objectives some objectives can be achieved by one particular lesson and others can be achieved by many. Such objectives which are very specific in nature and can be achieved by a particular lesson are called *specific objectives,* others which will be achieved by teaching many or even the whole course are called *general objectives.*

In this way, Richard Whitfield explains that the clarification of aims and objectives is what distinguishes the 'professional' teacher from the technician carrying out someone else's orders. The discussion also shows how general aims and justifications for teaching science can be translated into more detailed statements of objectives which affect the choice of curriculum content and teaching methods.

Schemes in Various States

There is hardly any need today to justify the place of science in a scheme of general education for school children. Science is all pervasive. Modern societies exist on the basis of science; science is intimately related to the means of production and means of communication, including transport. Even economics and politics have to depend on scientific factors such as productivity from the land or from industry, the power of modern weapons or the speed of transportation of ground and air forces. In the present situation, therefore, anyone, in any walk of life, must be aware of a certain quantum of science and technology.

The scientific method extends far beyond science. All disciplines are becoming scientific. The method of observation, of making symbolic, graphical or linguistic models, of designing experiments, of applying reason as well as imagination to draw conclusions from data to formulate theories/ the method of keeping an objective view while theories are tested is a method which pervades every discipline. The facts of today may not be the facts of tomorrow, and theories may undergo change, but there can be no going away from the scientific method.

Science should help in reducing obscurantism and all sorts of prejudices based on sex, caste, religion, language or region. By emphasising a rational approach science should help the development of a democratic, secular and socialist state.

The general objectives of science education have a limited utility unless they are spelt out in terms of stage-wise objectives for the guidance of educational planners, administrators, supervisors and teachers. According to Kothari Commission Report (1964-66), NCERT has laid down the following objectives as national objectives of science education in its publication, "The Curriculum for the Ten-Year School — A Framework," for various levels.

(i) Primary (I-V). This is a very crucial stage in the life of a child. The child's spontaneity, curiosity creativity and activity in general should not be restricted by a rigid and unattractive method of teaching and environment for learning. The curriculum should take into consideration the social, intellectual, emotional and physical maturity of the child as well as the socio-economic needs of the community. It will be helpful to identify realistically the basic minimum to be achieved in respect of each and every child and leave enough scope for individual schools to go as far beyond this basic minimum as their circumstances permit. There should be enough scope for flexibility and local adjustments. As far a number of children the primary stage may be terminal, it should be necessary to provide an education to them which prepares them for life and for self learning.

In the primary classes, the sciences should be taught as environmental studies; in Classes I and II as a composite course including both the natural and the social environment, and later on, in classes Ø, IV and V, as two subjects—environmental studies I (natural science) and environmental studies II (social science). One needs not lay down how much of this should be covered in a particular class. The purpose should be not to stuff the minds of children with facts and information, but to sharpen their senses, to enable them observe their environment and to enrich their experience.

Since the environment and the experiences of the children outside the school vary from place to place, the activities provided in the school should also vary so that edifice of knowledge is built not on abstract concepts but also on the solid foundations of experience drawn from the environment of the child. In such a programme a flexible syllabus should be drawn up to cater the needs of all sorts of schools. There is always a criticism that our science textbooks have generally an urban bias. The textbook should not be given so much importance in the learning of science. What is more important at this stage is to provide teachers with guides and prepare them to develop their own instructional material. Reading materials for children should be prepared very thoughtfully so as to motivate them for reading.

The general objectives of science education at primary stage may be stated as follows.

1. The child should learn the method of inquiry in science and should begin to appreciate science and technology in everyday life,
2. The child should develop habits of cleanliness and healthful living and an understanding of the proper sanitation and hygiene of his neighbourhood.
3. The child should learn to cooperate with others and appreciate the utility of working together. Other desirable qualities of character and personality, such as initiative, leadership, honesty should be developed.

4. The child should be able to express himself freely in creative activities and should acquire habits of self-learning.

(*ii*) *Middle (VI-VIII).* At this stage the children become adolescent and this period can become difficult for many children. Problems of adjustment in the family, the school and the society begin to appear. The child becomes a boy or a girl with greater intellectual, emotional, social and physical maturity than the primary school child. Social demands and responsibilities begin to appear. For many boys and girls, this stage is terminal after which they enter life and work. Therefore they should be prepared adequately to face life and develop capacities and attitudes for productive work in which they have to participate.

In the sciences, at this stage, physical and life sciences should be introduced. At the same time/ environmental education, nutrition, health and population education should receive adequate attention so that science is related meaningfully to life. This is the age when work experience should emphasise agricultural and technological processes and tools to help the integration of science, mathematics and technology with production and with the life of the community.

In middle classes (VI-VIII) a number of States and Union Territories have already gone ahead with the introduction of physics, chemistry and biology as disciplines. Some other States and Union Territories could develop integrated science courses upto class VIII; some could also try with groups — physical sciences (including physics and chemistry), and life sciences (including botany, zoology and human physiology). The unit approach, which does not violate the disciplines, and actually brings them closer and provides a more logical and economical procedure, has a great potential and should be adopted. In these classes laws and theories should be gradually introduced, taking care that they are not introduced as dogmas. Pupils should be made to understand that many models are available and one of them is the one they are learning. Open-mindedness and scepticism should be encouraged.

The general objectives of science education at middle stage may be stated as follows:

1. The child should be able to apply the knowledge of science in everyday life.

2. The child should be able to investigate new knowledge in the field of science.
3. The child should develop scientific attitude.
4. The child should learn how to learn a part of scientific knowledge on his own.
5. The child should be able to solve problems around him.
6. To make the child creative.
7. To train the child in science processes.

(iii) Secondary (1X-X). The secondary stage covers the two classes, IX and X. These two classes complete the ten years of general education. After this, there are three possible courses open to students:

(i) They can enter the working force,

(ii) They can take up vocational courses, and

(iii) They can take up higher level academic courses of study to prepare for entrance to the first degree class in the college or university.

The IX and X classes may be terminal for a large majority of students who are to enter the working force. Therefore it is necessary to bring their education upto a standard which will give them the competence to enter life. The Education Commission (1964-66) had thought of a minimum national standard of attainment so that those areas of the country and those sections of the society which are backward could come up and compete fairly with the rest of the people. Thus for maintaining a continuity of the objectives of education from the previous years, it is necessary to pay attention to the academic subjects as well as to the knowledge and skill required for doing socially productive work. These two years are crucial from the-point of view of the development of the personality. While from the onset of puberty in the middle stage there are problems of adjustment which the young child has to cope with. It is at this stage that these become acute and the additional preparation for a transition from the life of a school student to that of a productive person in society has to be undertaken. Therefore it is necessary to give the child some psychological insight into his problems and the knowledge that may help him to understand his own behaviour as well as that of others around him.

The general objectives of science education at this stage may be stated as follows:

1. The student should develop the competence to apply his knowledge to the solution of the problems around him.
2. He should have an understanding of the technological processes in agriculture and industry in use in his surroundings.
3. He should be able to contribute meaningfully to environmental conservation, the reduction of pollution, the development of proper nutrition and health and hygiene in the community.
4. He should be able to help in the development of proper habits and attitudes in the child care and in the improvement of the home.
5. He should acquire the knowledge and skills required for entry into an area of work.
6. He should learn one or two useful trades.
7. It is equally important to give him enough knowledge of the materials, tools, techniques and processes of a job family so that he can enter life with some confidence.
8. Through curricular and co-cumcular activities (science club, science fair, science debate, science essay, science symposium, etc.) he should develop desirable scientific attitude and values like cooperation, team spirit, fellow feeling, leadership, courage, truthfulness, honesty and sincerity.

(iv) Senior Secondary (XI-XII). You will be teaching physics, chemistry or biology or just general science or integrated science. Here is a list of objectives of science teaching as identified by a group of science teachers (in a workshop at SCERT Delhi) teaching science (Physics, Chemistry or Biology) to senior secondary classes (XI-XII). Some of them may also fit in the lower classes (middle or secondary). You may or may not agree with all the objectives. You might like to add some more adjectives to this list. Thus this list of objectives of science teaching may be a guideline for you to identify some objectives which you will like to achieve at the end of your lesson, unit, course or programme. These objectives are listed below:

1. To give students up-to-date knowledge in science.
2. To develop their curiosity to learn science.
3. To train them in scientific method of learning.
4. To orient them to apply science and technology in agriculture, medicine, research and industry.
5. To develop in them the competency to apply scientific knowledge to the solution of the problems around them.
6. To enable them to contribute meaningfully to the conservation of environment, the reduction of pollution, the development of nutrition, health and hygiene conditions in the community.
7. To enable them to help in the development of proper habits and attitudes in child care and in the improvement of the home.
8. To enable them to reduce all sorts of prejudices based on sex, caste, religion, language or region.
9. To sharpen their senses to enable them to observe their environment and to enrich their experience, rather than to stuff their minds with facts and information.
10. To make them aware of these aspects of science that are environment based and life centred.
11. To train them in the use and maintenance of science equipment.
12. To make them creative.
13. To develop in them the mental faculty of open-mindedness, making them understand that there are many models of experimentation that are possible.
14. To prepare them for change and create in them confidence for facing problems of the future.
15. To enable them to formulate and test hypotheses.
16. To enable them to investigate the scientific phenomenon rather than just verifying known conclusions.
17. To enable them to investigate the scientific laws, principles and facts etc., which they can do by laboratory experiments.

18. To enable them to believe and remember scientific laws, principles, and facts etc., discovered by others and in the textbook.
19. To train them in science processes in order to discover some of the science content.
20. To involve them in learning processes as far as possible instead of treating them as passive listeners.
21. To build proper base for professional and higher science courses.

Objectives of Education

Once a teacher decides to teach his students, he plans several activities for a successful lesson. First he decides the topic, secondly he prepares objectives to be achieved, then he decides a relevant methodology to achieve the identified objectives. Finally he plans to evaluate student's performance.

Objectives are identified and written in various different forms. Some teachers believe that their students should "really understand" others desire that their students should know some scientific laws, facts and principles. Some desire that their students should "internalise knowledge," and still others want that their students should grasp the core or essence or comprehend. Do they all mean the same thing?

To clarify such confusions and help all teachers, administrators, professional, specialists and research workers who deal with curricular and evaluation projects, an attempt was made to build a taxonomy (or classification) of educational objectives. You will be familiar with biological taxonomies. These taxonomies are very helpful in communicational accuracy, better organisation and interrelation of various living things. Also in chemistry you will be familiar with classification of elements in periodic table.

The idea for developing a taxonomy or classification system was formed at an informal meeting of college examiners attending the 1948 American Psychological Association convention in Boston. After considerable discussion it was .agreed upon that a theoretical framework which could form a common frame of reference could be used for better communication among examiners. The theoretical framework might best be obtained through a, system of classifying the goals of educational process.

For developing this taxonomy certain organisational principles were developed. It was agreed that the taxonomy should be an educational-logical-psychological classification system. Thus *first* importance should be given to educational considerations. *Secondly* the taxonomy should be a logical classification for which every effort should be made to define terms as precisely as possible and to use them consistently. *Finally,* the taxonomy should be consistent with relevant and accepted psychological principles and theories, and value judgments about objectives and behaviours should be avoided.

Following this initial meeting at Boston in 1948, a series of meetings were held up till 1953 by the group of college and university examiners, where a threefold division of educational objectives was developed: *Cognitive affective* and *Psychomotor.* It was found that most of the objectives stated by teachers as well as found in the literature, could be placed rather easily in one of the three major domains or classifications. The three domains are separately discussed below.

According to (Bloom's) Taxonomy of Educational Objectives, the objectives can be classified into three domains:

1. Cognitive Domain (remembering)
2. Affective Domain (feeling)
3. Psychomotor Domain (doing)

Examples. Given below are listed some objectives of Nutrition Education in the three domains.

(i) Cognitive Domain (Knowledge and Intellectual Skills). To help the children to:

1. understand the need for adequate food and that proper nutrition is essential for physical and mental development, health and happiness.

2. become aware of the foods available in the locality and need to produce more food,

3. become aware of the ways in which food can be prepared and make attractive, tasty and nutrition in eating.

(ii) Affective Domain (Attitude). To help the children to:

1. take interest in selecting, and in liking to eat different groups of food.

2. feel the necessity of producing more food and take interest in kitchen gardening.
3. take interest in finding out what kinds of food are available in the locality.
4. become convinced of avoiding waste of food at all levels.

(iii) Psychomotor Objective (Skill). Children:

1. select and eat proper combination of food.
2. do not eat without washing hands, but wash hands before and after eating and develop similar hygienic food practices.
3. participate in food production at home and in school.
4. explain the kinds of food available in the locality.

Objectives : Cognitive

Cognitive objectives were further classified into six categories—knowledge, comprehension, application, analysis, synthesis, and evaluation.

Knowledge. Knowledge is defined as the remembering of previously learned material. This may involve the recall of a wide range of material, from specific facts to complete theories, but all that is required is the bringing to mind of the appropriate information. Knowledge represents lowest level of learning outcomes in the cognitive domain.

Examples. Knows common terms, knows specific facts, knows methods and procedures, knows basic concepts, knows principles, theories and structure.

Comprehension. Comprehension is defined as the ability to grasp the meaning of the material. This may be shown by *translating* material from one form to another (words to numbers), by *interpreting* material (explaining or summarising) and by establishing outcomes go one step beyond the simple remembering of material and represent the lowest level of understanding.

Examples. Understands facts and principles, interprets verbal material, interprets charts and graphs, translates verbal material to mathematical formula, estimates future consequences implied in date, justifies procedures and methods.

Application. Application refers to the ability to use learned material in new and concrete situations. This may include the application of such things as rules, methods, concepts, principles; laws and theories. Learning outcomes in this area require a higher level of understanding than those under comprehension.

Examples. Applies concepts and principles to new situations, applies laws and theories to practical situations, solves mathematical problems, constructs charts and graphs, demonstrates correct usage of a method or procedure.

Analysis. Analysis refers to the ability to breakdown material into its component parts so that its organisational structure may be understood. This may include the identification of the parts, analysis of the relationship between parts, and recognition of the organising principles involved. Learning outcomes here represent higher level of intellectual skills than comprehension and application because they require an understanding of both the content and the structural form of the material.

Examples. Recognises unstated assumptions, recognises logical fallacies in reasoning, distinguishes between facts and inferences, evaluates the relevancy of data, analyses the organisational structure of a work (art, music, writing, project report).

Synthesis. Synthesis refers to the ability to put parts together to form a new whole. This may involve the production of a unique communication (theme or speech), a plan of operation (research proposal), or a set of abstract relations (scheme for classifying information). Learning outcomes in this area stress creative behaviour, with major emphasis on the formulation of new pattern or structures.

Examples. Writes a well organised theme, gives a well organised speech, writes a creative short story (or poem or music), proposes a plan for experiment, integrates learning from different areas into a plan for solving a problem, formulates a new scheme for classifying objects (or events or ideas).

Evaluation. Evaluation is concerned with the ability to judge the value of material (statement, novel, poem, research report) for a given purpose. The judgments are to be based on definite criteria. These may be internal criteria (organisation) or external criteria (relevance to the purpose) and the student may determine the criteria. Learning outcomes in this area are highest in the cognitive hierarchy, because they contain elements of all of the other categories, plus conscious value judgments, based on clearly defined criteria.

Examples. Judges the logical consistency of written material, judges the adequacy with which conclusions are supported by data, judges the value of work (art, music, writing) by use of internal criteria, judges the value of work (art, music, writing) by use of external standards of excellence.

Objectives : Effective

Affective domain objectives deal with interest, attitudes, values, appreciation and adjustment. These objectives describe behaviours ranging from students merely being aware that a given phenomenon exists to behaviours where they are increasingly willing to attend, respond to phenomenon with a positive feeling, attach values with it and at some point conceptualise their behaviours and feelings. Finally they organise these conceptualisations into a structure. This structure grows in complexity as it becomes his life outlook.

This shows a process by which a given phenomenon or value passed from a level of bare awareness to a position of some power to guide or control the behaviour of a person.

Affective domain objectives were further classified into five categories intended to be hierarchical in order.

Receiving (Attending). Receiving is to orient the learner to learn. This is the first step that he is willing to learn what is being given to him.

The category of receiving has three different levels, the lowest level is the awareness or being conscious of something. The next point is that he is willing to receive and then he is attentive when something is given to him.

Examples

(i) The students are aware of scientific activities in the school.
(ii) They are willing to take part in scientific activities.
(iii) They attend activities arranged by science club.

Responding. Responding level comes after the learner has given his attention. Responding includes behaviours like compliance and willingness to respond and getting satisfaction by responding.

Examples

(i) Students respond to the questions asked by the teacher.
(ii) Students raise hands to answer questions every time a question is asked by the teacher.
(iii) Students feel happy after answering the questions correctly.
(iv) Students take pleasure in explaining scientific phenomenon to others.

Valuing. The abstract concept is an important element of behaviour. At this level individual is not motivated by the desire to comply or obey but he is motivated because of his own valuing or assessment and commitment to the underlying value. The value system has slowly accepted and has come to be used by the student at his own criteria of worth.

Examples. Students have faith in the power of reasoning and methods of experimenting and discussions.

Organisation. When the learner develops certain values, he encounters situations for which more than one value is relevant. In such cases he is able to organise the values into a system.

Examples. Students develop a plan for doing some scientific activities and school work at home.

Characterisation by a Value or Value Complex. The individual acts constantly in accordance with the values he has developed.

Examples. Students develop a code of behaviour based on scientific attitudes.

The Domains

It is really hard to compartmentalise human behaviours clearly in terms of cognition and affect. No teacher or curriculum developer really intends one entirely without the other. There are many researches which demonstrate that cognition and affect can never be separated.

It is also noticed that the interest arises from increased information about something. According to Burner, some workers have felt that it is the process of problem solving and discovery in learning that brings about increased motivation for the subject and therefore develops interests and attitudes. Their view is that it is not much what is learned, but how it is learned which will determine the affective objectives that will be attained at the same time as the cognitive objectives.

Thus you learned about the aims and objectives of science teaching. As a science teacher you should distinguish between "aims" and "objectives" and "general and specific objectives" of science teaching. You will be teaching science at various levels — middle, secondary or senior secondary. Now you can identify objectives of science teaching at various levels. Now you know that the objectives of science teaching can be placed into three domains — cognitive, affective and psychomotor. As a teacher, for your science lessons, you can take objectives from each domain. Identify only those objectives which you feel you can achieve. They should be compatible to the cognitive level of students and the existing classroom conditions. If objectives are written in behavioural terms, teachers know what exactly they are to teach, students know what exactly they are to learn, textbook writers know what exactly they are to write and paper setters know what exactly they are to ask in examination.

Exercise

1. Why is the identification of objectives in science teaching important? Discuss.
2. What is the difference between "aims" and "objectives" of science teaching? Illustrate with examples.
3. Differentiate between "general objectives" and "specific objectives" of science teaching.
4. Why do we teach science?
5. State general objectives of science education at primary level. Can they also be the objectives at middle, secondary and senior secondary levels?
6. State general objectives of science education at middle stage. Can they also be the objectives at secondary and senior secondary levels?

7. State general objectives of science education at secondary level. Can they also be the objectives at middle and senior secondary levels?

8. From the list of senior secondary (XI-XII) objectives of science teaching, identify the objectives which can be achieved at:
(a) middle level, (b) secondary level, (c) senior secondary level.

9. What are the three domains of educational objectives? Give at least three examples for each.

10. Write the six categories of educational objectives in the Cognitive Domain. Explain each category with examples.

11. Write the five categories of educational objectives in the Affective Domain. Explain each category with examples.

6

Advancement of Science in India

In our country Science is witnessed to be taught from very early days. If we look at the development of science in India, we find that very early in her civilisation India developed a great interest in mathematics and Ayurveda. During British Empire introduction of modern science in India was extremely slow, and the development of science in India was greatly accelerated after independence

Historical Background

Before the rise of modern science in Europe, around the 17th century, the level of advancement in sciences (astronomy, mathematics, medicine, biology, metaphysics, etc) achieved by ancient and medieval societies in the old world did not differ appreciably from one cultural area to another. In India the development of sciences is as old as her civilisation itself. Her peculiar geographical position enabled her to become the natural meeting ground of many nations and cultures and, in consequence, played an important role in the transmission and diffusion of ideas very early in her civilisation, India developed medical and alchemical practices of the Ayurveda. In mathematics, India developed a great interest and aptitude and made notable contributions to the number theory, the decimal place value, algorism, trigonometry and algebra.

Advent of Modern Science

In the beginning of the nineteenth century people with varying degrees of scientific background (medical men, naturalists and engineers) started coming to India from Europe, at first in search of services under local princes and chieftains and later on to man the scientific surveys and establishments set up by the government. These men framed in European institutions and laboratories, spent the best part of their lives in India and left an excellent record of their work in various branches of science.

Despite such long contacts, introduction of modern science in India was extremely slow. There were many causes of this delayed reaction. The European scientific world in India was limited to field sciences and not to basic sciences that depended on mathematics and laboratory work. Indian fauna and flora attracted the attention of European naturalists from the seventeenth century, Modern zoological researchers in India had their beginnings in random and scattered observations by the naturalists on elephants, fishes, serpents, molluscs, birds and mammals.

First Medical College

The Colonial Government adopted from the beginning a policy of secrecy and exclusion of Indians from Government scientific work. For technological jobs not considered of military importance, restrictions against the employment of Indians were relaxed as they could be employed very cheaply. As an example of the low salaries to trained and qualified Indians/ the order of the Governor-General dated 28th January 1835, establishing the Calcutta Medical College, regulated that "as inducement for pupils of a respectable class to enter the Institution, the pay of the Native Doctors, who shall have been educated at the College, and have received the certificates of qualifications, shall be Rs. 30.00 p.m. rising to Rs. 50.00 p.m. after 14 years of service, whereas an European Assistant to the Superintendent of the college shall draw a staff salary of Rs. 600.00 p.m. in addition to his registered pay and allowances." Calcutta Medical College established in 1835 under a number of capable teachers, became an important institution, for the study of anatomy, physiology and medicine (along with surgery), as well as of chemistry, botany and natural philosophy.

First Research Institution

Indians asked for Western Education in Science from the Government. The Colonial power agreed to create facilities but with miserly financial provision just sufficient to train a few clerks able to operate in English in Government offices and European

Commercial houses, and not to enable the native people to pick up treasures from European science. So the hard way of working for science began. Mahendra Lal Sircar (*born* in 1833), an M.D. of the Calcutta Medical College, clearly saw that science would never develop and strike deep roots in this country under foreign tutelage and that Indians themselves must come forward to raise funds and found institutions for the training of scientists and organisation of research. In 1876 Dr. Sircar himself founded India's first research institution, "The Indian Association for the Cultivation of Science," completely under Indian Management and control with finances derived from private subscriptions. In the first half of the twentieth century the association developed into an important centre for research in the physical sciences - in optics, acoustics, scattering of light, X-rays and magnetism; and C.V. Raman performed his Nobel Prize Winning Experiments in its unassuming laboratories, *i.e.* western India. Jamshedji Tata a businessman, prepared plans for a similar institution for technical and scientific education and research which finally took the shape of "The Institute of Science" at Bangalore in the beginning of the twentieth century.

First Science College

The Educational Despatch of 1854 paved the way for University education. In 1857 the three Universities of Calcutta, Bombay and Madras came into existence, but they came out just as examining bodies with powers to grant degrees. The actual teaching and academic work were left to the colleges. Fortified by the University Act of 1904, which empowered Universities to appoint professors and lecturers, to hold and manage educational endowments, and to erect, equip and maintain libraries, laboratories and museums, Asutosh Mookerji, Vice Chancellor of Calcutta University took the initiative in establishing the, first University College of Science. Undaunted by the Government's refusal to provide funds for the creation of professorships and other facilities, Asutosh obtained princely endowments from Sir Tarak Nath Palit and Sir Rash Behary Ghosh, who had amassed enormous amounts of money and property in the legal profession, and established a number of chairs in Chemistry, Physics, Applied Mathematics and Botany. According to the terms of the endowment, professorships could be filled only by Indians, a clause which further irritated the Government firmly entrenched in the view that only Europeans were suited for such high positions. This University College of

Science, although starved financially all through, produced a group of physicists and chemists who received international recognition for their scientific developments and institutions staffed by high salaried Europeans and maintained and patronised by Government funds cut a sorry figure.

National Science Policy Resolution (1957)

The development of science in India was greatly accelerated after independence (August 1947). In 1950 the Government of India appointed a Planning Commission for preparing a blueprint of all-round economic development. In 1954 the Indian Parliament accepted socialism as a political goal. Declaring these objectives, fullest emphasis was laid on the development of science and technology on all fronts. In 1957, the Government took one step further in adopting a National Science Policy Resolution that envisaged the cultivation of science and scientific research in all its aspects, assured an adequate supply, within the country, of research scientists of highest quality through an intensive programme of training, promised the availability of conditions and an atmosphere of academic freedom in which the creative talent of men and women would find full scope in scientific activity. The resolution thus reaffirmed the Government decision to encourage science and develop a healthy scientific community as a sound basis after a balanced economic development.

Science Education in Independent India

- In the beginning of twentieth century science was not a school subject in our country. The Report of the Secondary School Commission 1953, recommended the teaching of General Science as a compulsory subject in the high and higher secondary schools.
- The All India Seminar on the Teaching of Science in Secondary Schools (1956) dealt with almost all the problems facing the inclusion of General Science as a Core Subject for the Higher Secondary Classes - syllabus, apparatus, teaching aids, textbooks, science clubs, science museums, examination techniques etc. It suggested a uniform system of science teaching for the entire country, suited to its needs and resources.

- Indian Parliamentary and Scientific Committee (1962) studied the allied problems of science education in schools like
  - growth of school population,
  - shortage of qualified science teachers,
  - accelerated achievement in science,
  - demand for increase in technically trained manpower,
  - growing importance of science in the affairs of mankind, and
  - changes in the processes and goals of science.
- UNESCO Planning Commission (1963-64) worked on the problems of science education in India and suggested ways to improve it. As a follow up programme, Department of Science and Mathematics Education of the NCERT took up the pilot project of preparing new disciplinary science curricula at middle (VI-VIII) level -text books (Physics, Chemistry, Biology), teachers' guides, science kits, kit guides, teacher training films and evaluation material. This Disciplined Science Programme was changed to Integrated Science Programme in mid-eighties.
- In 1970 under UNICEF Assisted Science Education Programme (SEP) Primary "Science is Doing" Programme was developed by NCERT, which was used in primary schools throughout the country. This Programme was a package of classes I and II Science Syllabus, Class III-V Science Texts, Teachers Guides, Primary Science Kit, Kit Guide, and Teacher Training Films. This Programme was changed to EVS Programme in mid-eighties.
- Kothari Commission (1964-66) recommendations were implemented in 1975 when Science for All (SFA) was introduced as a part of general education during the first ten years of schooling. With this 10+2+3 education scheme started with an additional year of schooling, in the country. First Disciplined Science Course (Physics, Chemistry, Biology) was introduced at secondary level (IX-X). This was changed to Disciplined Science A-Course (Physics, Chemistry, Biology) and Integrated Science B-Course. Students had an option either to take Science A-Course or to take Science B-Course. This again changed to just one Integrated Science Course for all. At +2, Senior Secondary

level (XI-XII) Disciplined Science Course (3 different science subjects - Physics, Chemistry, Biology) started from the very beginning of 10+2+3 education scheme.

- Then in 1986 the National Education Policy Document (NPE-1986) came out (Chapter 23). If some one asks, "What is new in this new education policy (NPE-1986), "Implementation" perhaps will be the right answer. Much emphasis has been given to quality pre-service and in-service teacher education in the policy document. For this District Institutes of Education (DIETs) and Institutes of Advance Studies in Education (LASEs) were established throughout the country for Elementary and Secondary Education respectively.

Science in Twenty-first Century

India is now engaged in a broad spectrum of scientific research, both fundamental and applied, in Government, Universities and Private Research Establishments. In recent years there has been extraordinary success in developing new polymers, ceramics, composites, superconductors, nanomaterials, smart materials and biomaterials. Biotechnology, Genetic Engineering and Biomedical Research are some other fields in which India has started entering.

AIDS (Acquired Immuno Deficiency Syndrome) poses a threat to India as a large number of people are infected with HIV (Human Immunodeficiency Virus). There are no drugs today for AIDS. The problem which has dogged anti HIV drugs is that resistant mutant forms of virus are formed within mere weeks. Lot of research work is to be done in search of a vaccine against HIV.

Per capita consumption of energy in India is very low compared to developed countries, and even that we are unable to afford. In the years to come when we have already entered twenty-first century, we will need much more energy. The major effort in next decade would have to be through an increase in the production of coal and a search of new reserves of oil. We should also give due emphasis to new technologies for solar energy and hydrogen energy. India is also to expand its nuclear power programmes. Nuclear energy could play an important role in meeting our bulk energy requirement. Our expertise in the field of nuclear power technology as well as related research areas, is an asset for us.

For all this we need huge amounts of funds, as scientific research has become costly. If we compare the funds available for scientific research in India compared to some other developing countries, India has a very gloomy picture. South Korea had planned to increase its R&D spending to over 5 per cent of its GDP by year 2000. China had planned to increase its R&D investment from 0.5 per cent to 1.5 per cent of GDP by the year 2000. Unfortunately India's R&D expenditure has come down to 0.89 per cent of GDP from 1.1 per cent earlier. We need to realise that in order to be able to do competitive scientific research and development we have to bring our R&D expenditure to at least about 1.5 per cent of GDP and focus our efforts on a few selected programmes and projects.

Our scientists want people to support them and understand their needs, and they are to inform people about science, why science is needed, what they are doing and why. They (our scientists) are to build up partnership with public, industries, politicians and bureaucrats. They need informed friends of science at all places.

When changes which affect our future, are happening and will happen at such a rapid rate, and are based on science and technology, it is necessary that our scientists be more close to decision making.

In the existing state of scientific advancement and development of resources for research, the rate of scientific growth of developed countries is likely to continue to be faster than that of the developing countries like India. Science has become deeply involved with defence and big industry, with the result that big sciences like atomic energy, space, etc., has been and probably will remain concentrated in super powers, In nuclear, space, computer and few other sciences, developing nations like India are already at the mercy of super powers. To be self-sufficient we are to change our science curriculum right from the school stage. We are not just to teach science but also scientific method. We are not just to teach science content but also science processes, the ways in which scientists advance their knowledge and solve problems. Science should be presented to students as a way in which they can conduct an inquiry into the nature of things as well as a body of information built up by other people. The science processes are being neglected and the school science has been concerned almost exclusively with the content — the body of information. Science is not just content. Science is content plus science processes. If we want to advance in science like other developed countries, science processes should be given due importance like science content in school science curriculum, and students should be encouraged to become personally involved in solving problems and in discovering some science for themselves.

EXERCISE

1. What was the position of science education in ancient India?
2. "During the British Empire introduction of modern science in India was extremely slow." Discuss.
3. Discuss very briefly how the development of science was greatly accelerated after independence.
4. Discuss the role of the curriculum developers when science is developing so fast in our country.
5. "Knowledge of science becomes double every decade." What should be the role of our science teachers in this context?
6. How should our school science be related with the scientific research when we are entering the twenty-first century? Discuss.
7. Explain the progress in school science education in the first fifty years of our independence (1947-97). Are you satisfied with this? Discuss.

7

Behaviour and Objectives

If you are keen in making lesson plans which may help you in achieving your identified objectives, they (the objectives) should be clearly stated. If objectives are not well defined, it is impossible to evaluate a student, a lesson, a unit, a course or a programme efficiently, and there is no sound basis for selecting appropriate material, content or instructional method. Unless the teacher (or programmer) himself has a clear picture of his instructional intent, he will be unable to select test items or frame questions that clearly reflect the student's ability to perform the desired skills or demonstrate his acquisition of desired information. With clearly defined objectives, the student knows which activities on his part are relevant to his success.

A meaningfully stated objective is one that succeeds in communicating to the reader the writer's instructional intent. It is meaningful to the extent it conveys to others a picture (of what a successful learner will be like) the writer has in mind. For example, if you provide another teacher with an objective, and he then teaches his students to perform in a manner that you agree in consistent with what you have in mind, then you have communicated your objective in a meaningful manner.

Useful Words

The best statement of the meaningful objective is the one that excludes the greatest number of possible alternatives to your objective. There are many needed words which are open to a wide range of interpretation. To the extent that you use such words, you have yourself open to misinterpretation, consider the following examples of words in this light.

Words Open to Many Interpretation — In order to understand, to really understand, to appreciate, to fully appreciate, to grasp the significance of, to enjoy, to believe, to have faith in, etc.

Words *Open to Fewer Interpretation* — to recite, to write, to identify, to differentiate, to solve, to construct, to list, to compare, to contrast, etc.

What do you mean when you say that you want a learner to know some thing? Do you mean that you want him to be able to recite, to solve, or to construct? Just to tell him you want him to know tells him little — the word can mean many things.

Though it is all right to include such words as 'understand' and 'appreciate' in a statement of objective, the statement is not explicit enough to be useful until it indicates how you intend to sample the 'understanding' or 'appreciating. Until you describe what the learner will be doing when demonstrating that he 'understands' or 'appreciates' you have described very little if you want him to do at all. Thus, the statement that communicates best will be one that describes the terminal behaviour of the learner well enough to avoid misinterpretation.

Observable Behaviour

The most important characteristic of a useful objective is that it identifies the kind of *performance* that will be accepted as evidence that the learner has achieved the objective. The way to write an objective, that meets this requirement is to write a statement objective, that meets this requirement is to write a statement describing one of your educational intents and then modify it until it answers the question, "What is the learner doing when he is demonstrating that he has achieved the objective?" If the answer of this question is "YES" the statement of the objective will include the "Observable Behaviour" which the learner will be showing when he is demonstrating that he has achieved the objective. The objective written in this manner is called Behavioural Objective. As for example 'to be able to solve quadratic equation' or 'to be able to repair a radio' are behavioural objectives which include the observable behaviours 'solve' and 'repair' respectively.

Let us see another objective. 'To develop an appreciation for music.' Now ask the same question "what is the learner doing when he is demonstrating that he has achieved the objective?"

1. Does he sigh in ecstasy when he is listening to music?
2. Does he buy a stereo system and records?
3. Does he correctly answer 95 per cent multiple choice questions on the history of music?
4. Does he write an essay on five musical instruments?
5. Does he say 'Oh Boy! It's too much.'

For every question the answer is No. It is not a behavioural objective.

Conditions Stated

To state an objective that will successfully communicate your educational intent you will sometimes have to define terminal behaviour further by stating the conditions you will impose upon the learner which he is demonstrating his mastery of the objective. Here are some examples:

1. Given a list of
2. Given any reference of learner's choice
3. Without the aid of references
4. Given a standard set of tools
5. Without the aid of tools
6. Without the aid of calculator.

As for example in the behvaioural objective 'Given a list of 35 chemical elements, the learner must be able to recall and write the valencies of at least 30/ 'to recall and write' is the observable behaviour and 'Given a list of 35 chemical elements' is the condition. Similarly the behavioural objective 'Given a linear algebraic equation, the learner must be able to solve for the unknown without the aid of references,, tables or calculating devices' has both — the observable behaviour as well as the condition.

For conditions you should ask yourself questions like these:

1. What the learner will be provided?
2. What will the learner be deprived?

3. What are the conditions under which you will expect the terminal behaviour to occur?

Very often, a good way to explain to the learner the conditions under which he will be expected to perform is simply to show him some sample test.

Example

(Behavioural objective stating observable behaviour and condition). The student must be able to demonstrate his understanding of the rules of logic by correctly solving problems of the following type:

Which of the following statements is illustrated by the diagram below:

(a) All animals are birds

(b) Some birds are animals

(c) All birds are animals

(d) No birds are animals.

Answer, (c)

Criterion for Choice

'What is it you want the learner to be able to do' gives the Observable Behaviour, and 'how will you want him to be able to do' given Criterion of acceptable performance. In order to include Criterion of acceptable performance in the statement of objective, indicate 'what the acceptable performance will be' by addition of words that describe the criterion of success.

Examples. (Behavioural objectives having criterion)

1. The student must be able to correctly solve at least seven simple linear equations within a period of 30 minutes.

Behaviour : Solve

Condition : within 30 minutes

Criterio : atleast 7

2. Given Human Skeleton, the student must be able to correctly identify by labelling at least 40 of the following bones; there will be no penalty for guessing (list of bones inserted here)

Behaviour : Identify

Condition : Given a human Skeleton

Criterion : at least 40

Condition and Criterion for Observable Behaviour

In order to test whether the statement of objective consists of *observable behaviour, condition* and *criterion,* the following questions may be asked:

1. Does the statement describe what the learner will be doing when he is demonstrating that he has reached the objective? (Behaviour)

2. Does the statement describe the important conditions (given or restriction or both) under which the learner will be expected to demonstrate his competence? (Condition)

3. Does the statement indicate how the learner will be evaluated?

Does it describe at least the lower limit of acceptable performance? (Criterion)

These are the 3 items for stating Behavioural Objectives.

Three Items

How can you write the behavioural objective having all the three items behaviour, conditions and criterion?

1. Identify the terminal behaviour by name, you can specify the kind of behaviour that will be accepted as evidence that the learner has achieved the objective.

2. Try to define the observed behaviour by describing the important conditions under which the behaviour will be expected to occur.

3. Specify the criteria of acceptable performance by describing how well the learner must perform to be considered acceptable.

Although each of these items might help an objective to be more specific, it will not be necessary to include all the three in each objective except observable behaviour.

Summary

1. A statement of instructional objective is a collection of words or symbols describing one of your instructional intents.
2. An objective will communicate your intent to the degree you have described what the learner will be doing when demonstrating his achievement and how you will know when he is doing it.
3. To describe the terminal behaviour (what the learner will be doing):
   (a) Identify and name the overall *behaviour* act.
   (b) Define the important *conditions* under which the behaviour is to occur (given or restrictions or both).
   (c) Define the *criterion* of acceptable performance.
4. Write a separate statement for each objective; the more statements you have the better chance you have of making clear your intent.
5. If you give each learner a copy of your objectives, you may not have to do much else.

Specific Objectives

When stating objectives in behavioural terms, some keywords (called behavioural terms) are used. In the cognitive domain there are six categories of objectives — knowledge, comprehension, application, analysis, synthesis and evaluation (Chapter 3). The teachers should practise in writing behavioural objectives in all these categories. For convenience behavioural terms for each category are given below:

Knowledge—define, describe, identify, label, list, match, name, outline, reproduce, select, state.

Comprehension—convert, explain, extend, generalise, give example, infer, paraphrase, predict, rewrite, summarise.

Application—change, compute, demonstrate, discover, manipulate, modify, operate, predict, prepare, relate, show, solve, use.

Analysis—break down diagrams, differentiate, discriminate, distinguish, identify, illustrate, infer, outline, point out, relate, select, separate, subdivide.

Synthesis—categorise, combine, compile, compose, create, devise, design, explain, generate, modify, organise, plan, rearrange, revise, rewrite, summarise, tell, write.

Evaluation—appraise, compare, conclude, contrast, describe, discriminate, explain, justify, interpret, relate, summarise, support.

Items for Test

When objectives are clearly defined and stated in behavioural terms, it is easy to develop test items (for multiple choice test items) for evaluation. Teachers should practise in constructing test items for identified objectives stated in behavioural terms. Some sample test items developed on some behavioural objectives are given below:

SAMPLES TEST ITEMS

Topic : Structure of an Atom

Behavioural Objectives

1. The students will identify the definition of atom with 100 per cent accuracy.
2. Given a list of material objects such as proton, positron, electron and neutron the students will identify the names of the particles of an atom with 100 per cent accuracy.
3. The students will write, how weights of electron, neutron and proton are related (weight of neutron is approximately equal to the weight of proton and weight of electron is negligible compared to the weight of proton and neutron) by memory with 100 per cent accuracy.
4. The students will write the charges of electron, proton and neutron (negative, positive, neutral) by memory with 100 per cent accuracy)
5. Given a diagram of atomic model the students will label the parts (shells) and necleus with 100 per cent accuracy.
6. Given the number of protons and electrons in an atom the students will write the charge of that atom with 100 per cent accuracy.

7. The students will write the position of protons, neutrons, and electrons in the atom by memory with 100 per cent accuracy.
8. Given the number of protons and neutrons, the students will write the atomic weight of the element.
9. Given the number of electrons or protons in an atom, the students will write the atomic number of the element.
10. Given the number of particular shell (1st, 2nd....last, next to last) the students will write the maximum number of electrons in that shell with 100 per cent accuracy.
11. Given the atomic number and atomic weight of an element the students will write the number of electrons in various shells and the number of protons and neutrons in the nucleus with 100 per cent accuracy.

Test Items

1. The smallest unit of elements is a/an

   (a) electron (b) atom
   (c) molecule (d) proton

2. The atom consists of all the following except

   (a) electron (b) proton
   (c) positron (d) proton

3. The weight of neutron is approximately equal to the weight of

   (a) electron (b) proton
   (c) twice the proton (d) none of them

4. The weight of an electron is

   (a) equal to the weight of neutron
   (b) equal to the weight of proton
   (c) negligibly small
   (d) more than the weight of proton or neutron.

5. The charge of a proton is

   (a) positive (b) negative
   (c) neutral
   (d) sometimes negative and sometimes positive

6. A negatively charged atomic particle is

   (a) proton (b) electron

(c) neutron (d) nucleus

7. A neutral particle of an atom is

(a) electron (b) proton
(c) neutron (d) nucleus

8. 'A' represents

(a) shell (b) nucleus
(c) both a and b (d) none of them

9. 'B' represents

(a) shell (b) nucleus
(c) both a and b (d) none of them

10. If an atom has 17 protons in its nucleus and 17 electrons in the shells the charge of the atom is

(a) positive (b) negative
(c) neutral (d) none of them

11. The nucleus of an atom has

(a) protons only (b) neutrons only
(c) neutral (d) none of them

12. Which of the particles are found outside the nucleus in an atom?

(a) neutron (b) electron
(c) proton (d) none of them

13. An element has 11 protons, 11 electrons and 12 neutrons. The atomic weight of the element is

(a) 11 (b) 12
(c) 22 (d) 23

14. An element has 8 electrons, 8 protons and 8 neutrons. The atomic number of the element is

(a) 8 (b) 16
(c) 24 (d) 36

15. An atom has 8 electrons. The number of electrons in its 2nd shell will be

(a) 2 (b) 6
(c) 8 (d) 18

16. The atomic number of an element is 17 and its atomic weight is 35. All of the following statements are correct except

    (a) the nucleus will have 17 protons and 18 neutrons
    (b) the nucleus will have 18 protons and 17 neutrons
    (c) the first shell will have 2 electron
    (d) the third shell will have 7 electrons.

Answers

1. (b)	2. (c)	3. (b)	4. (c)
5. (a)	6. (b)	7. (c)	8. (b)
9. (a)	10. (c)	11. (c)	12. (b)
13. (d)	14. (a)	15. (b)	16. (b)

EXERCISE

1. What do you mean by a "meaningfully stated objective"?
2. Write down words:

   (a) open to many interpretations

   (b) open to fewer interpretations.

   What is the harm if we use words open to many interpretations, in stating our educational objectives?
3. What is the importance of:

   (a) behaviour

   (b) condition and

   (c) criterion in writing a behavioural objective?
4. Write down behavioural terms for stating specific objectives in the six categories of the cognitive domain.
5. (a) Recognise a topic of a lesson in your field. Write five behavioural objectives to cover that content, which you can feel you can achieve at the end of the lesson.

   (b) Write a multiple choice test item for each objective.

8

Educational Technology

Before, five centuries, when the first book was printed, no longer did students need to cluster at the feet of their teachers to listen and memorise what was read to them from a precious, laboriously produced hand-written manuscript. The printed book was a form of automation, a kind of teaching machine. Each student could have his own copy of the text to study. It seemed that the teacher has been permanently replaced, but the teacher increased in importance. His function changed. Relieved of the chore of reading to his students, now he had time to counsel and to explain and expound, to interpret and correlate the mass of information and knowledge that books made available to all.

For centuries the teacher's chief job has been that of presenting information and testing students to see whether they can remember it on cue or.not. But now it is clear that assignment of lists of non-functional facts to be studied and remembered is out of place. Changes in a society usually bring changes to its institutions including education. The educational institutions are also affected by rapid increase in number of students, increased mobility of students, increased range of students' abilities and broadend backgrounds. Opinions as to what should be done often contradict each other, but there is a clear demand for action that will enhance the learning of the individual students, the effectiveness of schools and colleges and ultimately the quality of the nation's life.

Today we are seeing the beginning of another forward surge that may prove even greater. The electronic age is changing our traditional notion of education. Since last few decades innovations of all kinds are being experimented and the education has come more and more to understand that learning is an active process. The role of teacher, the role of the classroom, as well as the nature of the learning process itself must be re-examined in the light of new technology, for the sake of the nation's quality education.

The first step towards improving quality would be to free the teacher from much of his daily routine in order to give him time to serve as diagnostician and organiser or manager of functionally varied learning experiences. The second step would be to provide teachers with a large number of teaching techniques and specific curricular material. A third positive step would be the development of teaching material of a highly individualised nature in each subject. Each of these steps could be realised with the widespread use of electronic teaching aids that could take over much of the routine involvement in teaching and also provide better course materials. Classroom teacher then could give more individual attention to their students.

Lot of educators do believe that if technology is properly supported and wisely used, could help meet most of the pressing educational needs and many teaching problems can be solved partly or wholly by the proper use of the rich experiences that can be gained through certain media. In this technological age, therefore, today's teacher should take the full advantage of the existing technological resources for quality education.

Definition

Any definition of Educational Technology must be subject to the concept held by the definer, and this involves consideration of at least two distinct concepts— the physical science or media concept, and the behavioural science concept. Here various definitions of Educational Technology are being given.

(i) The Educational Technology can be defined as the purposeful utilisation, in combination or separately of objectives, techniques, devices, events and relationships to increase the effectiveness of educational process. Educational Technology is fundamentally aimed at improving the efficiency of educational systems by increasing the rate, depth, precision and value of the learning which takes place.

(ii) Educational Technology concerns the systematic use of modern methods of technologies in teaching and learning.

It involves teachers in a variety of roles, some of which are traditional and some still emerging. In this definition special consideration is given to the adaptive role of the teacher.

(iii) Educational Technology is a systematic way of designing, carrying out and evaluating the total process of learning and teaching in terms of specific objectives based on research in human learning, a combination of human and non-human resources to bring about more effective instruction.

Outside the limits of speech, man is dependent upon the tools of his age for his ability to educate or to learn from others. Twenty-first century man has acquired more tools of communication, more power to educate in last fifty years than he ever possessed in the hundreds of thousands of years of pre-recorded history. With the increasing rate of scientific advance and discovery the need has arisen for clarification of new methods of communication and their application. This is the core situatioln with which educational technology has to deal. The greater the pace of change in the world, the more urgent it becomes for us to develop efficiency in the way our young people learn. This is true because education is a bridge between present and future, it is a bridge between what we are and what we may become — as individual, as a nation, as a world. But the test of the value of a new technique for education is not whether learning occurs. Learning is always occurring but we are to test whether the new technique improves the learning rate and depth of understanding as compared with the existing approach.

Educational Technology is still largely a classroom supplement. Teachers now have access to film projectors, slide projectors, tape-recorders. Video Cassette Recorders (VCRs), Video Cassette Players (VCPs) and computers etc. Teaching machines may ultimately prove more effective in a specific learning situation than text and printed material, since they offer greater control over the contingencies involving in learning.

The teacher normally supplements his verbal output with such materials as textbooks, blackboards, maps, posters, slides, overhead projectors, etc. Essentially these devices are limited to the presentation of immobile two-dimensional/orres.

In United States a Commission on Instructional Technology was established long back to determine whether the belief in technology's value for education is justified and whether it is justified to recommend actions to provide for the most effective possible application of technology to American Education. The Commission took 'Learning' as starting point instead of technology. The heart of education is the student learning and the value of any technology used in education must, therefore, be measured by its capacity to improve learning.

Application

Technology will assist and support educational functions. Thus increasing the productivity of the teaching force and freeing them of the multitude of clerical record keeping chores and the elementary task of simply presenting information for students consumption. This can restore the personal touch to the educational process.

But there are many problems in adopting educational technology.

1. Well intentioned resistance to the introduction of technology—some people think that it will dehumanise a very human process.
2. Getting educational research applied—innovaters and leaders have problems in transitioning from research to application. Many successful researches are not carried out towards its application.
3. Scarcity of trained personnel to install/ maintain and supply new methods and equipment.

Few basic principles will affect the successful application of educational technology. The key to success is training and particularly in-service training. The real mass attack on training must take place at school and college level. In-service training needs to be developed on at least at two levels.

(a) At the elementary levels to ensure the elimination of fear and ignorance of the hardware and to show the productive potential in a curriculum situation.

(b) At the advanced level especially in its application to curriculum development.

If educational hardware is going to be used effectively during teaching situations the colleges and schools must be supported by an adequate technical assistance service. Every teacher should take this training in the first few years of his teaching career. Because of the size of turnover of staff in educational institutions, it is essential that in-service training in the handling of technical equipment be continuous until all have learned its use.

Next stage in training could be more advanced, concerned with the techniques of production. One can use this technique in the lecture room situation to take 'Off Air' programmes to enable large groups of students to see a detailed scientific demonstration clearly, or to use it in certain areas of the curriculum.

Significant Hardwares and Softwares

In order to use educational technology we should be familiar with the existing hard and softwares.

Hardwares (Technology in Education): Hardwares include all sorts of teaching machines. Some common ones are listed below:

Projectors

(a) 16 mm film projector

(b) 8 mm/super 8 mm film projector (not being used now)

(c) 35 mm slide projector

(d) Opaque projector (Episcope)

(e) Overhead projector (OHP)

(f) Micro-projector

Tape-Recorders

(a) Spool tape-recorders (not much in use now in educational institutions)

(b) Cassette tape-recorder

Radio Broadcasts

Television

(a) Closed circuit TV/ VCR, VCP

(b) TV telecast

Computers

Softwares (Technology of Education): They include the hand-written or printed materials for effective teaching.

(a) Programmed instructional materials

(b) Self-learning modules

(c) Films, slides, OHP transparencies

(d) Audio-video tapes

(e) Multimedia packages

(f) Computer Discs (CDs)

Now let us discuss these Hardwares and Softwares of Educational Technology very briefly.

Good Projectors

16 mm Film Projectors. A 16 mm teaching film though less flexible than verbal statement or description, is often far more effective. There is much to be learned which is incapable of demonstration. This can be done by controlling the speed of visual presentation, e.g , the flapping of a bird's wing, the unfolding of a petal, the clogging of an artery and the control of spacecraft etc., 16 mm films are available in India in every field of education. In Delhi there are some good resources for such films, like CIET of National Council of Educational Research and Training (NCERT), British Council and United States Information Service (USIS). Educational Institutions can ask for their catalogues and the films can be borrowed. Similar resources can be explored in each state or city. In addition to this some colleges, IASEs and University Departments have their own film libraries. These films are also available in the market for educational institutions to buy.

16 mm film projectors are now very common and most of the educational institutions have these projectors. These projectors make it possible to use 16 mm films (software of 16 mm film projectors) which go along with the lesson. These films can be used as introduction, enrichment or follow-up of the lesson. These films are now being videotaped.

8 mm/Super 8 mm Projectors. 8 mm and super 8 mm educational films in different fields are also available in the market.

They are lot less expensive than 16 mm films. They can also be produced very easily if the school or college is provided with 8 mm/super. 8 mm movie camera. These films shown with 8 mm/ super 8 mm projector are an asset to classroom teaching. The teachers can give their own commentary or it can be audio taped before hand to be replayed whenever these films are used. But now these projectors are not being used in educational institutions.

35 mm Slide Projectors. 35 mm slides and film strips (software of 35 mm slide projectors) because of their characteristic similarities lead to joint treatment. Both are similar materials, both use the same basic principle of projection. Both can be adopted for sound accompaniment. But 35 mm film strips are not being used now. 35 mm slides on different subjects are easily available in the market, which are not very expensive. Such slides could also be made as desired if college or school has its own 35 mm camera. These cameras are getting common these days in India. 35 mm slides projectors project 35 mm slides. These projectors are available almost in every educational institution. Thus they could be used in coordination with classroom teaching. The teaching value of magnified projection has a dramatic impact and there is a further advantage that the class can examine the pictures etc., on the screen as long as desirable.

Overhead Projector. Overhead projector though very often being used in schools and colleges in western world, is not very common in India even now when we are entering twenty-first century. But now it is being manufactured by several firms in our country. Here the transparencies (software of overhead projector) black and white and coloured-photocopied or hand-made can be projected overhead. Thus the teacher can stand in front rather than at the rear of the classroom. These transparencies use transparent plastic material on which instructor writes or draws in the course of the lesson and this appears on the screen and a large class can see clearly what would be visible to only a small group if the chalkboards were used instead.

Micro-Projector. Microscopic slides can be projected by micro-projector and the entire class can see it at the same time. These projectors are either attachments for a microscopic or separate projectors with built-in micro-lenses. They are used much as slide projector but adjustment is more complex and the image is usually not so bright that is why the micro-projectors require complete dark rooms. Micro-projectors are also available for projecting microfilms.

Recording Equipment

Two types of recordings are in general use, those engraved on a disc and those magnetised on tape.

(i) The discs vary in the speed with which they rotate on the machines, because of these variations speed as well as size, the 'play back' machines the 'record-player' must be suited to the requirement of the records and vice versa. This is not being used now in educational institutions.

(ii) The second type of recording made on magnetic tape, involves a totally different sort of play back equipment. The magnetic play back or the 'tape records' can also be used for making recordings. These magnetic tapes could be in a spool or in the form of a cassette (software of cassette tape recorder); both of these involve different machines, the spool tape recorder and cassette tape-recorder respectively. But spool tape- recorders are not being used now in educational institutions.

Most of the colleges and schools have their own cassette tape-recorders or players. They can be used very effectively in classroom teaching by imaginative teachers. For example, instead of giving the same lecture to several classes a day or repeating the same lecture every year, a teacher would be able to devote days or even weeks to the preparation of one outstanding presentation to be audio taped and repeated, and up-dated as often as needed.

Use of Television

TV Telecast. Educational Television programme is another technique for effective teaching. The Educational TV project started in 1961 for Delhi schools. Since then it showed tremendous improvement. Due to the coordination with classroom teaching, this programme proved to be very useful for the students. Teachers knew before-hand what lessons at what date and time will be received on TV and what portions of the syllabus they were to cover in the classroom. Now such TV programmes are not being telecast.

Closed Circuit TV. Due to rapid technical advances, specially in the field of video tape recording the emphasis of closed TV (CCTV) has altered over the past several years and has become a powerful media. For this a TV camera, a Video Tape-Recorder and a TV Receiver are needed. The use of CCTV, rather than films etc., is justified by its facility to be immediate and the fact that it is easier to manage. Close-ups of demonstrations of scientific experiments can be shown very clearly to a big class and to several classes at the same time. Some of the good demonstrations or techniques can be video-taped and shown whenever desired.

But due to its high cost and lack of knowledge for its utility it is not very common in our schools, colleges and universities. Instead TV Educational Video Tapes-Video-Cassettes (software of VCRs and VCPs) are used in our schools with VCRs and VCPs. If will be nice if such equipment is used by us quite frequently.

Use of Computers

Some Uses of Computers. Classroom uses of the computers generally fall into one of three categories. Computers are being used as a direct means of instruction in many developed countries. This use of the computer is often referred to as computer assisted instructions (CAI). Another widespread use of the computers in educational institutions is for calculating and analysing data. A third use of the computer is a device for computer simulated experiments. Other uses of computers in education are scoring of papers, filling up the grade sheets or mark sheets, time table preparation (scheduling), guidance, counselling and curriculum development. Now CDs and Internet are also in use.

Computer is a powerful and evolving tool for managing and sharing knowledge. Today clever software can turn a computer into a television, a canvas, or make it replay images and music, snap photographs, synthesise human speech, organise databases and libraries, and present a combination of animated drawings. Computers and communications are progressively becoming cheaper and faster.

Computers: Distance Medical and Surgical Facilities. Convergence of computers, communication, speech, text and images also presents an extraordinary opportunity in multimedia services and applications. These developments will change the way we live, learn, work, transact cur business and communicate. For example, these techniques could allow doctors to examine patients in another continent and even monitor surgical operations at very far off places.

Computers: Future Attentive Assistants. Scientists are also working on image and pattern recognition techniques that can make computers ubiquitous. Speech recognition would replace the computer keyboard for most of the uses. There are attempts to develop computer systems for recognising faces, expressions and gestures. Such developments would enable us to create smart rooms which could see that people are in a meeting and shield them from interruptions. Such smart rooms would be networked and furnished with cameras and microphones. Thus these rooms could relay information from the room to other interested parties on the network. The computers could also assess what people in the room are saying or doing. Computers could compare the incoming information with models they have stored in memory, and arrive at decisions by tracking people's movement, identifying them and recognising their expressions. Therefore, in future computers will thus be playing the role of attentive assistants.

Internet

(i) ***Present:*** The Internet is a large and global network of computers. Anybody can be a part of this network and share information with its users. The Internet provides access to essentially unlimited sources of information. Internet allows dialogue and exchange of ideas through Electronic Mail (E-Mail). Communication can be carried out at all hours and across large distances.

(ii) ***Future:*** Friendly ways of helping users to find what they want are already becoming available. In the course of time procedures for information quality control will also develop. The Internet will have all the essential features of a massive library system. It will of course take time before Internet possesses a large store of knowledge to rival the best of our libraries. The Internet and its successor technologies will have a profound effect on society.

(iii) ***What India is to do?*** We in India should develop a national information infrastructure, where using phone lines, cables, high speed data networks will allow open access for all to the electronic superhighway of information. All our universities and national laboratories should be connected to this information superhighway, so that researchers cannot only have access to important research journals and other library material but can also collaborate across large distances. The status of libraries in our universities is very unsatisfactory. Unless we do something about it, the research in universities will suffer greatly in quality. Low cost computers and internet connectively could provide a satisfactory solution to this problem. Today many of our higher educational and research institutions have working internet facilities, but many of them are operating at low bandwidth. In the area of software India has a lot of potential. We should now aim at high quality software development for automation, networking, design activities and telecommunications. As of now most of the internet software is imported. There is scope for us to design software for specific applications on the Internet appropriate to Indian needs. We should make every effort to see that India is not marginalized in this rapid race of information technology.

Can Computers recognise the owner? Have you ever wondered about the fact that while you can recognise your computer, your computer cannot recognise you? How would a computer go about recognising its owner?

It would recognise you by:

(i) *The way you speak:* Most PCs today are equipped with a microphone. It would not be too hard to write programmes that can detect and identify voices to a limited extent.

(ii) *The way you look:* This is very difficult and involves having a video camera connected to the PC. The image from the camera would then be analysed to identify the person in front of the PC. This is an active area of research.

(iii) *The way you type:* Just as handwriting is unique, so is the way in which you press the key on a keyboard. A statistical analysis of patterns of key depressions (for how long, how hard and in what order you press keys while typing) can provide good clues to who the user might be.

(iv) *The way you move the mouse:* Hand-eye coordination is fairly unique in human beings. By analysing the way in which you move your mouse, a PC might be able to figure out who you are.

These are some of the ways in which a PC of the future might recognise its owner.

Programmes in Self-learning

Programmed Learning Units. Programmed learning was first associated with teaching machines, and there appears to have been two schools of thought. One was represented by the Harvard Psychologist, Skinner who transferred his theories based on the clinical observation of animal behaviour to the field of learning in the classroom. His programmes were divided into different segments each called a frame. The learner reads the frame and because of its form prompted into making a reply, usually written one and is encouraged to go to the next frame and so on through a series of positive reinforcement. The careful shaping of these stimuli and responses was aimed at securing a carefully prescribed behaviour pattern at the end of the programme. The individual could go at his own pace and learning was secure and certain. The second view, seen at one time to be divergent and the learner should be offered alternative answers. This approach was associated with Crowder. The Skinner programmes were called "linear" and the Crowderian ones "branching."

A programmer, nowadays seeks to arrange an environment within which learning activities appropriate to the programme's objectives are provided. No such guidance is given with a text book.

Adjunct Programming another development can be the link between programmed instruction and a good textbook. It combines some of the progressive features of Programmed Instruction (PI) with the comprehensiveness of textbook. The goal of adjunct programming is to enable the student to learn as efficiently as possible from a good textbook.

What is generally considered an advantage of programmed instruction is the systematic, controlled, and sequential fashion in which content is presented to the learner. In programmed instruction provision can be made for differentiated instruction to accommodate individual differences.

Programmed Learning Units are self-learning programmes. Students tearn on their own with these programmes. Teacher is free to guide those students who really need his guidance.

Self-Learning Modules. Modularization of Instruction is another form of individualisation of instruction and self-learning; Modularization of Instruction is done by selecting, re-arranging or organising material and activities and breaking them into smaller sub-units in order to promote better understanding. The instructions are given in such a way that students know what specific objectives they are supposed to reach. Each sub-unit may have optional activities, from which students choose accordingly, all enabling them to reach the same objectives. Through such instruction the students can direct themselves through learning activities, with minimum assistance from the teacher; *i.e.* they can work at a particular rate that suits them.

Siddiqi developed a Self-learning Module "Man and Environment" and used it in her research study entitled "Development of Self-learning Material for Senior Secondary Biology and Analysis of Its Effectiveness". She found that students who used this module achieved statistically higher than those who did not use the module, and taught by the teacher in a conventional way.

Use of Self-learning Material. You can use programmed learning units and self-learning modules for effective science teaching.

Package in Multimedia

Teaching ideas mainly through one medium, namely, the printed word, is no longer wise either pedagogically or technologically. Taking into account individual differences in the way students learn, it will be wise to use a variety of learning aids assembling them in an integrated form known a multimedia package consisting of (for example) programmed instruction booklets, self-learning modules/ books, slides, tapes (audio/ video), films, transparencies, experiments, CDs etc. The students who do not learn best through reading a text have, therefore, the chance of learning more or better by working with films, slides, tapes and CDs so forth. For the sake of differences in individuals, knowledge should be presented in different forms.

Such packages though so useful, effective, interesting and instructive are not being used in our country. It will be wise to develop some of such packages at least for try-out.

Example. A slide-tape programme is a Multimedia Package. On any topic you can make 35 mm coloured slides (35 mm slides on various topics are also available in the market) by your 35 mm camera. Load your camera with 35 mm coloured slide film. Take pictures. Give the film for developing. You will get a set of 35 mm coloured slides.

Write the commentary for each slide. Audiotape the commentary. Now your Slide-Tape Programme is ready. You can use it again and again in your classroom.

Science Teacher's Role

The goals and expectations of science education change, and with them the curriculum. As the curriculum evolves so must the optimum-role of the science teacher. Today's science teacher is faced with numerous problems of how to teach what is given in his hands. Many science educators believe that the traditional teaching methods which are geared towards inculcating students mostly with factual knowledge, should be revised. Educational technology is here for our rescue. It is important that it should be used wisely as some of the earlier attempts to use teaching machines effectively failed because they were employed as alternatives to the presence of a teacher rather than as extension of his capabilities. It is upto us how best we can use the existing tools in science education. There are several tools as mentioned above which can be used in classroom for effective learning. But these materials are not being used in our educational institutions as effectively as could possibly be. Some of them are not available in the institutions due to their high cost or unfamiliarity of their utility. Some of us are against the use of technological tools with a plea that India's economy cannot afford the use of these expensive machines. But even those machines which are already available in the schools and colleges are also not being used fully. Science education is likely to expand substantially even explosively, over the next few decades and that can be achieved through the application of educational technology. It will be wise if the school and college science teachers should gather to learn the effective use of various technological tools and take with them the ideas which they think are wise and feasible for their classroom teaching.

Developed World Scenario

A report commissioned by the US National Science Foundation

speculates that by the end of twentieth century electronic information technology will have transformed western home, business, manufacturer, school, family and political life. The report suggests that one-way and two-way home information systems, called Teletext and Videotex, will penetrate deeply into daily life, with an effect on society as profound as those of the automobile and commercial television earlier in this century. This proved true. Now the, same is gomg to happen in developing countries like India in twenty-first century.

The study focused on the emerging Videotex industry, formed by the combination of two older technologies, communication and computing. It was estimated that 40 per cent of households in the US will have two-way Videotex by the end of the twentieth century, and this estimation came out true; Videotex system would enable individuals to create their own newspapers, design their own consumer guides. Furthermore this system will bring an increased flow of information and services into the home and at the same time, carry on stream of information out of the home about the preferences and behaviour of its occupants. All this hopefully is going to happen in the developing countries like India in twenty-first century.

Future of Science Education

INSAT-IA was up in space on September 4,1982 with capabilities for telecommunications, metereology and country-wide TV telecasts, but it was declared dead on September 6, 1982. Though it was possible to take this failure rather philosophically as a forerunner of future success, yet it was a serious setback to all our communicational developments. Then INSAT-IB was successfully launched by India on August 30,1983, though INSAT-IC launched on July 12,1988 could not be a success. Afterwards both INSAT-ID launched on June 12, 1990 and INSAT-2A launched on July 10, 1992 were a success. (For more satellites launched by India, see the Table 6.1) We enjoy many benefits of satellite technology. An all-India transmission of TV programmès has been possible through INSAT. The satellites bring to us live programmes in any part of the world. Satellite communication, weather monitoring, remote sensing, and collection of information about planets and outer space are some other applications of satellite technology.

It would be nice if we could produce enough software material for maximum utilisation of INSAT. The developing countries like

India will have to use TV for reaching out the masses in the dark ghosts of illiteracy/ ignorance, disease, poverty and exploitation with a view to providing fundamental education. This is a tremendous task for all educators in general and educational technologists in particular.

It seems that the new media are still quite expensive and their penetration if relatively limited, but future developments hold a promise of considerably cost-reduction and competitive productionization. The cost of computer memory in the developed world for a bit of information was 100 cents in 1954, 1 cent in 1964, 0.5 cent ø 1974 and 0.004 cent in the year 1984. This cost will further decrease in the years to come. In India, the cost of a transistorised radio set has shown consistent reduction inspite of inconsistent price-rise. We do hope that the story would be repeated also a case of TV and Videotex. It is estimated that by 2000, more than six million households would own Videotex in the western world. The developing countries like India would have to chalk out their own plans and priorities in the field of educational technology. In order to do so, we would have to think globally and act locally.

In India, in several States and Union Territories, Educational Technology cells have been started functioning with 100 per cent financial support (for the first 5 years) from the Ministry of Education, under guidance of Central Institute of Educational Technology (CIET) of NCERT in New Delhi. The remaining States and Union Territories will also open similar cells gradually. Hopefully these cells will assist our teachers in effective science teaching using educational technology.

Table. Launching of Indian Satellites

S.No.	*Name of the satellite*	*Date of launching*	*Result*
1.	Aryabhata	19 March 1975	Success
2.	Bhaskara-1	7 June 1979	Success
3.	Rohini	10 August 1979	Failure
4.	Rohini	18 July 1980	Success
5.	APPLE	19 June 1981	Success
6.	Bhaskara-2	20 November 1981	Success
7.	Rohini	31 May 1981	Failure
8.	INSAT-1A	4 September 1982	Failure
9.	Rohini	17 April 1983	Success

10.	INSAT-1B	30 August 1983	Success
11.	SROSS-1	24 March 1987	Failure
12.	IRS-1A	19 March 1988	Success
13.	INSAT-1C	12 July 1988	Failure
14.	SROSS-2	13 July 1988	Failure
15.	INSAT-1D	12 June 1990	Success
16.	IRS-1B	29 August 1991	Success
17.	SROSS-3	19 May 1992	Success
18.	INSAT-2A	10 July 1992	Success

Teacher Training during Service

NCERT organised the first ever interactive satellite based interactive teacher training programme to train primary school teachers on various topics of primary education using INSAT transponder with one-way video and two-way audio technology.

In the first phase the programme was launched in Karnataka on January 7-13, 1996 (7 days) covering about 850 teachers and 80 facilitators and course directors assembled in 20 different district centres (learning ends).

In the second phase, the programme was organised in Madhya Pradesh on August 2-8, 1996 (7 days) covering about 1400 teachers and 170 facilitators and course directors assembled in 45 district centres (learning ends).

The 7 days programmes each for Karnataka and MP had 14 Sessions, each of which were on various topics such as MLL, use of OB materials, multigrade teaching strategies, teaching of Maths, EVS (Science and Social Studies) and Language etc. Each of the sessions was about 3½ hours (2 hours of live interaction and 1½ hours of individual and group activities). Each session comprised of presentation, demonstration and discussion. Participating teachers interacted with panelists through telephone and fax, followed by group activities.

During the 7 days programme of Karnataka about 600 telephone calls and 240 fax sheets were received, and in case of MP about 700 telephone calls and 200 fax sheets were received, altogether about 7000 questions were asked through telephone and fax.

This experiment was highly appreciated by educationists, distance education experts, education administrators and teachers.

Such programmes hopefully will be common in India in the years to come.

Another achievement of this Experiment is the successful networking of various national, state and district level agencies in the implementation of the project.

Organised Planning

What is served to India, is what is cooking in Delhi. What you will get in education is now in included in Ninth Five Year Plan.

Educational Technology in the Ninth Plan is going to take a significant and massive turn. The focus in primary education during the Ninth Plan will have to be on quality because without enhanced, retention and performance of students, universalisation of education will remain elusive. The National Action Plan for continuing education of primary teachers envisages a series of change in the Ninth Plan. The main approach is to develop a training module using multi-channel learning which includes self-learning, action learning, face to face interactive learning and learning through interactive television. The entire multi-channel learning is a capsule model instructional design which is the core of educational technology. Self study materials, which are the basis of self-learning, are semi-structured learning modules. Action learning is conceptualised to be action experience and studies within the schools. Face-to-face interactive learning is proposed to build interactive and problem solving skills among the teachers to interact with the guidance of an expert tutor. The interactive television will bring in an opportunity for primary teachers to interact directly with the experts at the regional, state, and national level

The proposal is to set network in selected national, regional, state and district level institutes through satellite communication. The proposal also includes the setting up of block level resource centres with educational technology facilities for face to face interaction. With block and district level training centres, primary teachers would have access to more than 5500 centres in the country.

The proposed training network will have the capacity of training a few million people every year in the country. In view of both extended capacity of the training system and the need for training the supervisors and teacher educators who play critical role in teachers' performance will also be provided specially designed training modules once every 2 years.

This is for the primary teachers. It is likely that the training network will be extended for upper primary and secondary teachers as well. The universities are not far behind. IGNOU has proposed a network called OPENET interconnecting its study centres, state open universities and other distance education institutes and centres. The proposal is to use VSAT for delivery of courses.

From programmed learning, one way television and radio broadcast and educational technology equipments as teaching aids, India seems to be ready to graduate to satellite communication and computer communication. The new educational technology is likely to sweep the country very fast rather we, the teachers should get ready to receive and respond to this massive change which is bemg conceptualised.

DIET Course

Rationale. With the advancement of science and technology many new developments have taken place in the field of education. The conventional ideas about teaching are proving obsolete and inadequate. With the changing times the expectations from teachers have also increased. A teacher is not only a trainer or instructor in basic skills but he is also an organiser of worthwhile experiences for children. To meet these challenges, a teacher has no option but to adopt new technological aid. With the help of mass media, quality education can be provided to children and adults even in remote and inaccessible areas. The services of competent teachers and subject experts can be made available at any place, without their presence in actual classroom situation. Teacher is now expected to be part of an educational system where in machines, materials and media are important constituents of instructional process. The teacher has, therefore, to understand his roles in the new educational system, and it is for this reason that the present course has been included in the ETE curriculum.

Aims of Technology

On completion of the course, the teacher trainee will be able to

— explain the concept and scope of educational technology and use of E Ò ø teaching-learning process develop skills to use and maintain hardwares.

— develop skills of preparing softwares and making their effective use.

— develop skills of effective use of blackboard, school TV programmes, educational radio broadcasts, educational video programmes develop skills to make use of waste material or low cost material available locally for developing teaching aids.

— develop skills for evaluating effectiveness of various technological aids, media and strategies.

Course Outline **External 40 marks Internal 10 marks**

Tune 45 hrs Unit 1 Introduction to Educational Technology 6 hrs

5 marks Meaning, need and scope of educational technology. Difference between 'Technology of education' and 'Technology in Education'.

Unit 2- Hardware and Software **12 hrs 10 marks**

Hardware

— Effective use of hardwares in teaching-learning process, their general maintenance and safety precautions.

— Television, VCR/VCP, Tape-recorder, Radio-cum-cassette player, overhead projector, slide projector.

Software

— Planning, preparation/development; effective use of charts, maps, flash cards;

— display materials for flannel board and bulletin board, transparencies, slides, audio programmes, slide-tape programme.

Unit 3: Audio-Visual Aids and Mass Media **12 hrs. 10 marks**

— Meaning of A.V. aids and mass media, classification of A.V. aids

— Projected and non-projected aids

— Selection of appropriate teaching aids-Edgar Dale's Cone of Experiences

— Advantages and limitations of A.V. aids and mass media

— Effective use of Educational Television and Educational Radio, pre-telecast and post-telecast activities

Unit 4: Innovative Trends in Educational Technology **15 hrs. 15 marks**

— Micro-teaching

— Simulated teaching

— Team teaching

— Programmed instruction Multi-media package

— Satellite TV transmission

— Computer aided learning

Practical Work: (for Internal Assessment) **07 hrs. 10 marks**

— Any two out of the following:

— Preparation of an audio programme

— Preparation of learning packages in one school subject

— Preparation of any low cost teaching aid.

Excercise

1. Write three steps which can improve science teaching in our schools. What will be the role of educational technology in achieving these steps?
2. What is educational technology? How can it help in science teaching?
3. State problems in adopting educational technology in teaching science. How could they be solved?
4. What are few basic principles of educational technology? How could they help in effective science teaching?
5. Name the hardwares and softwares of educational technology.

6. What is the role of the following for effective science teaching?

   (a) Projectors
   (b) Tape recorders
   (c) Television
   (d) Computers
   (e) Programmed learning systems
   (f) Multi-media packages.

7. What should be the role of a science teacher in the use of educational technology for better science teaching?

8. What is the future of educational technology?

   (a) in the developed world.
   (b) in India.

9. What is the difference between:

   (a) technology in education, and
   (b) technology of education?

10. Discuss the uses of computers in education.

11. What is the scope of self-learning programmes in today's science teaching? Discuss with examples.

12. What is the use of multi-media package in science teaching? Discuss with examples.

13. What is the future of educational technology in India? Discuss.

14. What is the use of Interactive Video Technology? Discuss with examples.

15. What is the picture of educational technology with Ninth Plan? Discuss.

9

Audio-Visual Aids in Use

In an introductory class of audio-visual education from B.Ed. students it was asked some of their earliest school experiences. Following were some of their answers:

(i) "The earliest school experience was when I made things out of plasticine."

(ii) "When in class 3rd we made a model of iglu out of sugar cubes."

(iii) "When I went to see a zoo in my 2nd grade."

(iv) "When we did gardening in a small comer of the school."

(v) "When I played the role of little red riding hood in kindergarten."

(vi) "The puppet show I saw in the school."

Dozens of similar experiences were reported by these (college) students. All these are varied experiences but we see one similarity, they could remember the experiences where they are involved in doing something, when they were active, when more senses were involved. These are some of the experiences where effort was not made to memorise them, on the other hand we do not always remember the facts or concepts that we try hard to memorise. From this we can generalise that learning becomes comparatively permanent when concreteness is there in the experiences. The various experiences help in developing concepts.

The process of building concepts operates naturally from the time a child begins to draw certain conclusions from his experiences and applies these conclusions to new situations. It continues thereafter as he makes new generalisations from new experiences and experiences in which new and old experiences are combined. The overall activity of building concepts, therefore is a realistic definition of Education. Now we can say that two elements are involved in building concepts: (1) Certain amount of concrete experiences, and (2) Combining and recombining these concrete experiences in many ways. When we apply this to classroom teaching, audio-visual aids play a very important role in concept formation and therefore in permanent learning.

The Significance

If we see teaching of science in schools of our country by and large we will find teachers lecturing or even reading out from the books and explaining few things on the blackboard. Some teachers use some demonstrations, charts and models but not very frequently and many a times students memorise things without understanding. Audio-visual aids if properly used help in teaching learning process in many ways (as given below) and can ensure quick and effective learning.

(i) The timely use of proper aids compels attention, develops interest and motivates students.

(ii) They break the monotony of teacher's talk, reduce verbalism, save time (of long verbal explanations) and give a better idea of the real things.

(iii) Audio-visual aids can make learning experiences far more concrete; therefore clarification of concepts, better understanding and long lasting learning are possible.

(iv) Great many teaching problems can be solved partly or wholly by the proper use of rich experiences (through audio-visual aids); therefore they offer great opportunities for improved learning.

The Kinds

Variety of audio-visual aids can be used in science teaching. They can be classified in various ways.

(a) One way of grouping them is as follows:

Visual Aids — charts, photographs, diagrams, static and working models, etc.

Auditory Aids — radio, recordings on tapes, and cassettes.

Audio-visual Aids — films, T.V. etc.

(b) Another way of classifying can be:

Graphic Aids — diagrams, photographs, charts, play cards.

Three-Dimensional Aids — models, specimens, real objects, apparatus, dioramas etc.

Projected Aids — slides, films, etc.

Aids Through Activity — excursions, projects setting and maintenance of aquarium, vivarium, botanical garden etc.

Edger Dale Cone

Some of these aids are more concrete in nature and some of them are comparatively more abstract. Edger Dale has arranged the various audio-visual aids in pictorial form which he called "Cone of Experiences" as shown in (Fig.).

This is a kind of visual aid to visualise and explain the interrelationship of various types of audio-visual material as well as their position in learning process.

At the top of the Cone are verbal symbols which are most abstract and at the base are the direct purposeful experiences which are most concrete form of experiences. This is only a pictorial form where all sorts of aids and experiences are arranged in a Cone. The various bands of the cone representing various experiences and aids, should not be considered as rigid divisions or watertight compartments. They overlap and blend with each other. For example you can be a viewer of an exhibit or a person who made it, you can observe a demonstration or can demonstrate it yourself. It is also not being suggested that the various aids and materials are arranged in the form of their effectiveness but they a e arranged from most abstract to most concrete. As a teacher we should also know that abstract ideas, concepts, or generalisations are not possible without rich meaningful concrete experiences. A science teacher has to pick and choose the aids according to the maturity levels of the students and the topic to be studied. We will discuss the strengths and limitations of each in teaching sciences.

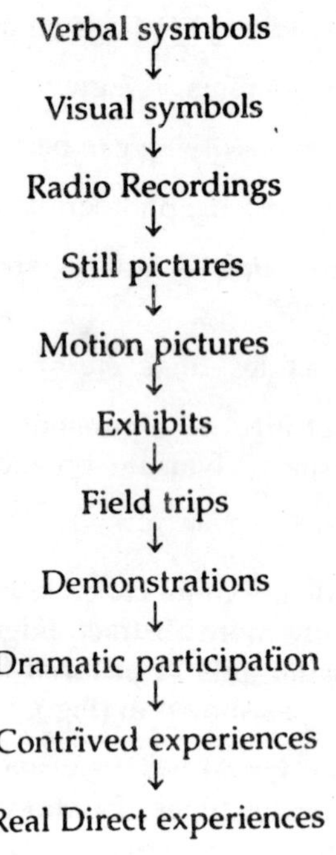

Fig. *Edger Dale Cone of Experiences*

Purposeful Experiences

The base of the Cone of experiences represents "direct purposeful experiences." Here the word 'purposeful' is very important. Every direct experience may not be very meaningful, therefore, it may not be purposeful. We have to see the direct experience in terms to learning outcome. In cases where the real things are too small or too big to comprehend, direct experiences are not very effective and therefore are not purposeful. For example, "structure of atom," "working of a factory," "water supply in a city" etc., can be understood better by some indirect experiences like models, maps or charts, etc.

In teaching science many direct experiences can be given to the students for effective comprehension. Some examples are: observing real flowers, leaves, plants, insects; dissecting animals; taking a walk through woods; going to the seashore and observing marine animals; doing salt analysis in the lab; setting and maintaining an aquarium, etc. In such cases learning is by direct participation.

The science teacher has to decide what direct experiences will be purposeful for his classes and then try to give them as many experiences as possible because direct and concrete experiences soon become associated with abstractions and help in developing more difficult concepts.

Contrived Experiences

What are contrived experiences? Next in the hierarchy towards abstraction are contrived experiences. Examples of contrived experiences are static models, working models, specimens, dioramas, etc. Contrived experiences may differ from the original in size (big things are made smaller and smaller things are made bigger) and complexity. It usually is a simplified and edited version of the real thing, where the unnecessary details can be removed to make the learning clear. For example a petroleum refinery is difficult to comprehend in a real situation but its model will be more meaningful. In the same way models of places where it is difficult or impossible to reach and see can give a clear idea, like models of globe, volcano, parts and systems of the body, bottom of the ocean, view of a forest, polar region, etc. Sometimes we imitate the whole natural habitat in the form of dioramas and keep in museums. Cut-away or half cut models are extremely useful in teaching internal structure of eye, ear, stem, root and automobile, etc.

There are some examples where nobody has seen the real thing, the models are made on the basis of indirect evidences like model of atom, DNA structure. Here the whole concept is developed on the basis of these imaginary models.

While teaching through the models, teacher should give the idea of the real thing, regarding their size and complexity. All models are not correct reproduction of their originals, they are only simplified versions.

Objects and Specimens. Objects and specimens are very common in science laboratories. These are also examples of contrived experiences. We collect rocks from various places. Different kinds of plants and animals are collected; pressing, preserving and sniffing are done for storing and study purposes. The objects and specimens are taken from the real settings. They are samples of real things minus real settings. The specimens are collected and stored so that they are readily available for study purposes. Another. most important advantage of objects and specimens which is not otherwise possible in direct experience is that they can be arranged into groups and classes.

The Participation

This has been placed on the 3rd band of Cone of experiences. Dramatisation means substitute for real experience of reconstruction of the original reality. There are many things we cannot possibly experience at first hand. There is a great value of dramatisation in education. Students can participate in a dramatisation or watch some kind of dramatisation. Both are valuable experiences but participation is much more meaningful and closer to reality than only watching.

The question is "What is the scope of dramatisation in science teaching?" Dramatic acts are quite popular in languages and social sciences. In sciences also the scope is not limited.

The films made on the work of various scientists are only possible because of dramatisation. Such films are quite effective as such experiences are otherwise not possible.

Students of primary and middle classes participate in scientific dramatised act in schools, such activities are also brought to science fairs etc. Some very abstract and uninteresting ideas are taken for dramatisations, for example, different students act as various components of solar system with proper costumes, dialogues, songs, music and dance, and the abstract concepts become clear and leave a long lasting impact on participants and viewers; students act as various petroleum products and explain how they are formed and utilised like coal, petrol, vaseline, synthetic rubber and plastic etc. Functions of vitamins and other components of food can also be taught through dramatisation.

It is also possible to use dramatisation in classroom teaching where costumes are not necessarily required but different students can remember their parts and act out in the classroom.

Interdependence of various components of an ecosystem and balance of nature can also be explained interestingly through dramatisation. An imaginative science teacher can think of many such topics which can be taught more effectively through such activities. Thus dramatisation can become an effective teaching aid in teaching science.

Demonstrations

Demonstrations are quite familiar activities in science classrooms. Their merits and demerits have been discussed at length in the Cone of experiences they have been placed on the fourth band from the base because it is essentially a process of observing. It differs from the first three bands, which are essentially doing. Demonstrations are used to show how something is done or not done. When demonstration is followed by doing on the part of students, it becomes very much meaningful.

Demonstrations are used to clarify ideas, and help to develop skills, processes and attitudes. They are not limited only to demonstrations through apparatus only. They can be used to clarify abstract ideas on the chalkboard, through slides or motion picture also.

Demonstrations can be improved to a great extent if certain points are kept in mind while planning and doing a demonstration.

- Plan all steps of demonstration in advance.
- ❑ Rehearse the demonstration before going to the classroom.
- ❑ Keep the demonstration simple as far as possible.
- ❑ Keep the students involved.
- Make it sure that all the students can see it.
- ❑ Outline various points on the board.
- ❑ Keep summarising various steps.

Excursions

What is Field Trip or Excursion? A field trip or excursion is a planned visit to a point outside the regular classroom. It may be in the school, out in the community or it could be a long trip to far away places. Usually in field trips to places like visits to a factory, observatory, agricultural institute, poultry farms, museums etc., we often see other people doing things. As spectators we are not involved but we directly watch it and get a first hand knowledge. Therefore field trip is an excellent bridge between the work of the classroom and the work of the outside world. The chief difference between a field trip and other educational experiences is that the student get their experiences in the field and not in the classroom.

Because of its nature to be mostly observation it is kept on the 5th band of the Cone of experiences as less concrete than other experiences discussed before. But if the fiel•l trips are planned and arranged in such a way that they go beyond observation, for example of a sea-beach, on a pond where they can also touch, feel and collect things, it becomes a *direct experience* for them. Such a variation in the field trip indicates again how the bands of the Cone interlap and blend into one another.

Importance of the Field Trips. Excursions or Field Trips are of great educational value especially in science subjects. The classroom is a limited place, bounded normally by four walls and meagrely equipped for the task or providing students with worthwhile experiences. The environment outside the classroom has no bounds; it has almost every conceivable situation that a teacher might wish to utilise. In school corridor students may study writing system for supply of electricity to different rooms and laboratories, may determine the power (in watts). On school grounds there may be various types of plants, birds, insects, different kinds of soil, sunshine and shadows, building materials, bicycles, scooters and cars. And just beyond the school boundaries lie the unlimited resources of community.

Contributions of an Excursion or Field Trip. (i) Field experiences are first hand experiences. They arise from direct learning situations. Sometimes they play the same role or even better in the learning of science as do experiments and demonstrations.

(ii) Field experiences tend to be much more meaningful and permit easier transfer of learning to solutions of real life problems.

(iii) Fieldwork if properly organised awakens many interests that classroom work cannot arouse. Fieldwork is the study of actual objects which stimulate more curiosity than to ideas. Out of almost any situation encountered in the field can develop into some challenging problems.

(iv) Fieldwork permits first-hand study of many things that cannot be brought into the classroom because of size and other inconvenience, *e.g.*, it is only outside the class that the students can be acquainted with the flora and fauna of the area.

(v) Fieldwork permits a class to engage in activities that are too noisy or too violent to be used in the classroom, *e.g.*, a model airplane, gasoline engine if demonstrated in the classroom would disturb the other neighbouring classes too.

(vi) Outdoors, students are able to work with large size materials, *e.g.*, an iron piece pipe makes a more impressive lever than a routine stick and erosion is better demonstrated from a garden hose than with a tiny trickle from a yet drawn in a glass tube.

Some Special Experiences of Field Trips. Fieldwork brings students in contact with many objects. The observation and manipulation of objects in the environment are bound to arise questions. Attempts to answer questions give rise to new problems.

Field trips can be used for review and drill. Ideas learnt in classroom can be better fixed in mind in actual situations, *e.g.*, by visiting factories the ideas of running a plant and the products manufactured can be better fixed in students' minds, or visiting a zoological park or a botanical garden, more abstract ideas about animal and plant life can be more clarified to students.

Difficulties Experienced in Arranging Field Trips. Lack of availability of good inventories regarding field experiences, school policies, and transportation problems create hurdles in arranging field trips. Therefore the teacher will have to take a key role if he wants to arrange the trip.

Procedure to Arrange Field Trips

1. Survey of the place of excursion should be taken before going to the field trip, so that the teacher knows beforehand what their students are to see there; or what relevant literature should be studied if places are far away.
2. Objectives of the field trips should be very carefully identified to make a field rip a success. If this is done teacher knows what he is going to teach and the students know what they are going to learn there.
3. Permission from the authorities and parents of students should be taken well in advance.
4. Appropriate activities compatible to the identified objectives should be listed and given as well as discussed with the students beforehand.

5. If there is a need for transport and place to stay they should be arranged in advance.

Preparation of Students/or Excursion

1. It is essential to brief students after arriving at the area. This should be as minimum as possible. A long lecture may deprive the students of an opportunity to explore the place.
2. Students should be divided into small groups appointing a group leader for each group. Group leaders may help in running fieldwork smoothly and quickly.
3. You as a teacher should be aware of the fact that there are slow as well as rapid learners. Activities and responsibilities should be so divided among the students as to be equally shared by both type of students without any feeling that they are slow learners or rapid learners.
4. Students should be made aware that there may be some difficulties like: (a) noise while visiting any working plant in a factory, (b) listening to the guide due to distance while standing around him, or (c) technical language used in explaining particular process; and they should try to solve such difficulties themselves as far as possible.
5. Students may be advised to take notes and draw diagrams, whenever they think it is necessary.

Teacher's Role. The teacher's role is very important for a successful field trip. Some of them are listed below:

1. Watches students closely and gives specific help as and when needed.
2. Recognises student's achievement.
3. Avoids frequent interruption in student's work but occasionally if it is justified.
4. Does not lecture while in field ?
5. Avoids loud voiced comments.
6. Acts as a guide, resource person or consultant.
7. Does the relevant follow-up activities of the trip ?

Follow-up Activities. Follow-up activities are very important in any kind of field trip, it may be a short trip just outside the classroom or a long excursion to various far away places.

Follow-up activities vary accordmg to the nature of excursion. If the field trip is taken just outside the classroom in the school lawns to find the population densities of various species of plants, the follow-up activity will include the pooling up of data collected by each student or each group of students and discussion on the result. If the field trip is an observational trip to places like factories, mills, observatories or hospitals, discussion about what they have learned is important. Field trip can also be taken to study the fauna and flora and collection of specimens from seashore, hill stations or any other places. If such field trip is taken by the students follow-up activities will include pressing of plants, preservation of animals, drying of insects, classification and displaying of material. If proper care has not been taken just after or during the trip (in case of long trips) the materials collected cannot be utilised properly and goes to waste. Sometimes the students and teachers are quite enthusiastic while planning and taking the field trip, but forget about the material after the big excitement or do not do the follow-up activities properly, therefore, the field trip is not as effective as it should be.

In short we can say that follow-up activities should be planned according to the objectives of the field trip. Science teachers should plan their objectives for the field trip well and do the follow-up accordingly for better understanding.

Exhibition

Kinds of Exhibits. There is a big variety of exhibits. Sometimes they are three-dimensional working models, sometimes a series of photographs or photographs mixed with charts, models and real objects. But exhibits are essentially something one sees as a spectator. Usually one is not involved in handling any thing or working with the material. Science teachers take their students to show the science fairs where different kinds of exhibits can be seen. They are also of great educational value. Sometimes they may also influence the attitudes.

When students are involved in making exhibits, it becomes a direct experience for them. Investigatory science projects done by students can be displayed as exhibits. Exhibits can also be used by the science teachers to teach subject matter.

Museum. Museums are places where items and exhibits of knowledge are assembled, protected and studied. In big cities there are public museums of various kinds like art museums, history museums, science museums, and natural history museums etc. Here we are concerned with science and natural history museums. In our country there are not very many science and natural history museums. But if they are available in your cities, advantage should be taken from them.

Mostly Science and Natural History Museums (Science museum in Bangalore, Natural History Museum in Darjeeling and New Delhi) have two functions: (i) presentation and display of the materials, and (ii) to work with classroom teachers on specific curriculum unit. If this facility is given by the public museums, science teachers should take full advantage of such arrangements.

The other kind of museums are college and school museums for various subjects. Biology museums are quite common museums established in some form or the other in many schools and colleges. Museum should not be considered as a collection of various items and objects. It is more than that, it must be viewed with an idea, a process, and an objective. Therefore science museums should not emphasise only on the product of science but due importance should also be given to science processes.

There is a big scope of displaying of specimens and objects collected by students. Models and projects made by students could also be displayed there. In fact development of museum can be taken as one of the science club activities.

Television and Films

Next on the cone towards little more abstraction comes the TV and motion pictures because we are only the viewers of these audio-visual aids. First we will discuss the motion pictures.

Motion Pictures

16-mm Educational Films. It is not possible to learn everything by doing or first-hand viewing. We have to get some of our experiences indirectly, 16-mm films play a very important role in giving this indirect experience. Motion pictures present an abstracted version of the real events omitting unnecessary and unimportant details, they can, sometimes dramatised events so effectively filmed that we feel as though we are present at the reality itself. No other medium has brought so much information and scientific knowledge to the classrooms as the educational sound motion pictures.

There are various kinds of motion pictures. Here we are concerned with the *educational films.* Educational films include *documentary* and *instructional films.* Though some documentary films can be used in classroom teaching but they are especially planned for classroom teaching purposes. On the other hand *instructional films* are specially planned to achieve certain educational objectives and are made in specific subject areas tor teaching purposes. These films can be background films or direct teaching films. They help to promote to achieve a skill, an attitude or to convey certain facts, information, phenomenon or theory. As a science teacher we will be mainly concerned with the instructional films in our areas.

Though we are only spectators before a motion picture but the learning outcomes are quite effective because of certain specific values of motion pictures.

For 16-mm films, 16-mm movie projectors are needed. Now video cassettes of 16-mm films are available, which can be seen on TV. with V.C.P. or V.C.R.

Strengths of Motion Pictures

(a) Motion pictures motivate the students and compel attention.

(b) Movement can very effectively be shown by motion pictures which is not possible in any other aid except direct experience.

(c) It is an edited version of reality, the editing involves manipulation of time, space and by eliminating distractions; it gives relationships of things, ideas and events that might well be overlooked in real life. For example, food web, food chain, etc., can be seen as continuous processes which is not possible in reality.

(d) Time can be controlled in a motion picture with the help of slow motion photography, "movements in animals, insects, flight of birds" can be understood very easily. With the help of time-lapse photography it is possible to see the blooming of flowers, germination of seeds, growths of plants, etc.

(e) Motion pictures can enlarge or reduce the actual size of the objects for better compensation. By means of microscopic lens attachments microscopic organisms like algae, fungi, protozoas, and blood circulation in capillaries etc. can easily be seen and understood by students.

(f) By X-ray cine photography techniques movements of internal organs of animals — action of arms, legs, movement of the heel, swallowing of food, heart-beating/ living movements, etc., can be shown.

(g) Motion pictures can bring past and distant present into the classroom.

(h) With the help of animation techniques motion pictures can show processes which cannot be seen by human eye even with the help of microscope or telescope. For example, behaviour of molecules in solids, liquids and gases, phenomenon of nuclear fission and fusion, etc.

(i) Motion pictures can reproduce the record of events like lunar and solar eclipses, etc. which are not always possible to see. Complicated techniques can be filmed and reproduced when required.

(j) Motion pictures promote understanding of abstract relationship, offer a satisfying aesthetic experience, influence and even change in attitudes.

With so many values, motion pictures not only expedite the rate of learning but they also increase the scope of teaching. This is an important consideration in the field of science where mass of learning and the learning processes are expanding so rapidly that it is to keep hand up with them. Motion pictures enable the teacher to clarify the difficult concepts in less time than with any other technique.

In order to get the most effective use of films or video tapes, the following necessary information and skills should be acquired:

(i) Where to obtain appropriate films or video tapes?

(ii) How to use such films and video tapes in your teaching?

(iii) How to operate the 16-mm film projector, V.C.R, V.C.R.?

School, college and university teachers have to spend some time to find films or video cassettes which they can integrate into their courses. It is possible to find suitable films or video cassettes on various science subjects. Securing catalogues will be important for this purpose.

For an effective use of films or video cassettes, preparation and follow-up are two very important steps to be taken by a teacher. Teacher should select the film or video cassette which goes along with the topic. The film or video cassette should be previewed and important points to be covered in the lesson should be outlined.

It will be advisable to frame few short answer questions. These questions can be given to the students before showing the film or video. During the follow-up activity unanswered questions and other important points should be discussed. Such activities help in coordinating the film or video with the topic. In the absence of such coordination sometimes the film or video becomes a wastage of time and effort.

The next point is to learn to operate the 16-mm projector and V.C.P./V.C.R. which is not very difficult to learn. Ordinarily only a few hours instruction followed by a brief practice results in satisfactory operation. Simple threading and operating instructions are given somewhere on the projector, which should be followed carefully. The possibilities of error should not discourage the teacher but it should be taken as challenge. The thrill of this educational device will compensate for minor disappointments.

Caution to be Observed in Using Films or Videos. Motion pictures may not necessarily be effective for teaching everything. As a teacher you have to be cautious about certain things.

- You have to think about the *effectiveness* of the film or video. If other experiences like direct or contrived are more meaningful, film or video should not be used.
- Sometimes the film or video gives a wrong idea about the *time notion* and *size notion*. It should be clarified to the students by comparing it with a known object or by giving a familiar example.
- If inexpensive devices are available with the *same effectiveness* as motion pictures, then less expensive devices should be used.

- Teacher should see that the film or video is adequate for the comprehension of his/her students.

Television

School T.V. Programmes. Television has all the potentialities of motion picture with a little more concreteness because of the "on the spot coverage" and the nature of the TV programmes, as most of them are specially produced for a particular audience. This is more so for educational TV programmes. In many countries educational TV programmes include series of science programmes.

Educational TV in India. Experimental TV Service was inaugurated on September 15th, 1959. This programme was planned for educational and cultural values of community and designed for community viewing. In the meantime Ford Foundation in India was approached to assist in the development of educational TV. Ford Foundation team of TV experts visited India in February 1960. In 1961 Television was started in India as an educational TV project. The project was launched in close collaboration with the Delhi Directorate of Education and with the financial assistance of the Ford Foundation in 1961.

The educational TV programmes were integrated with the school syllabus based on the principle of direct teaching. Direct teaching implied that the TV programmes were directly related with the school syllabus. They were proposed to help in classroom teaching by bringing into classroom additional resources through the medium of TV. The students were benefited from talented teachers, best and expensive equipment and other audio-visual aids which were not usually available in schools. In the project the teachers were also fully involved from the planning to evaluation. This arrangement of instructional TV was working well in Delhi schools because there was a set prescribed syllabus. In some other advanced countries there is not any set syllabus for all but they have different syllabi choosen by teachers and students. Their educational TV programmes are not strictly integrated with the syllabi.

In Delhi the educational programmes started in General Science, Social Studies, Physics and Chemistry. Later Biology Maths and Geography were also included.

For proper functioning of educational TV and better coordination between Doordarshan and Schools a Television

Branch was set up in 1967 in Delhi Directorate of Education. The TV branch used to divide the syllabus term-wise and week-wise, and select lessons for TV teaching. To ensure close relationship between TV and classroom teaching, a package of a uniform time-table, set examination days and working hours, and a uniform weekly syllabus in the form of a TV booklet was to be distributed to all viewing schools in the beginning of the school session. Such TV booklets used to be prepared for each subject taught on TV. But now we do not have such school TV programmes in Delhi or elsewhere in the country.

This kind of educational TV programme if started again can solve several problems of science teaching in our schools.

Merits

1. It solves the problem of unequipped laboratories to certain extent. Students are able to see effective demonstrations and expensive apparatus which is otherwise not possible for them to see.
2. TV teachers prepare and rehearse a lesson, spend enough time to collect relevant material and up-to-date information.
3. It has all advantages of films plus being a live presentation seems more natural. Only relevant portions of films are shown, along with teacher's explanation and other visual material.

Demerits

1. It is a one way process and students are passive viewers.
2. There is no opportunity for an active participation of the learner during TV lesson.

Better Utilisation of Educational TV. The disadvantages can be removed if some preparation is done and precautions are taken by the classroom teacher.

For effective use of any mass media three things are important: proper reception, proper seating arrangement, carefully planned preparation and follow-up.

Good reception is one of the basic important things for effective viewing. The television branch in Delhi had the responsibility of installing and maintenance of TV sets. The coordination had to be done by the teachers and administration of the school. Classroom teacher was also be familiar with proper handling and minor adjustments of a TV set.

Next important thing is the proper seating arrangements. If a big crowd is sitting on the floor (without any discipline) in an auditorium or classroom, not sure of proper viewing, this kind of arrangement will be a waste of time. The classroom teacher was to see that there was proper seating arrangement.

TV presentation is only one part of the learning procedure. Preparation for the TV lesson or the pre-telecast activities and the follow-up or post-telecast activities by the classroom teacher are equally important without which the TV lesson may not be very much meaningful.

Pre-telecast activities included the preparation by the subject teacher. Preparation varied with class to class and also depended on the topic, the classroom teacher could see the topic of the TV lesson in advance from the TV booklet. During pre-telecast activities his job was to make the students ready to receive the TV instructions. He could ask motivational questions. If some background knowledge was needed it was to be given at this time. The time-table was arranged in such a way that there were about 10 minutes before and after the actual telecast, usually the presentation was of 20 minutes duration, and class periods varied from 35-40 minutes.

After the TV presentation follow-up activities included clarification of points of doubts raised by students. Recapitulation questions could also be asked to see how much they have grasped. With little encouragement by the classroom teacher many activities could be followed by students as continuation of the TV presentation for better understanding.

The TV branch of Delhi also tried to evaluate the lessons. They used to send a printed pad of evaluation check sheets to each school for the constant feedback of TV lessons. If various people connected with educational TV production do their jobs consciously the E.T.V. programmes can be quite effective. You as a science teacher has to play an important role. During your practice teaching you can observe some science lessons on video tapes, evaluate them according to the evaluation check sheet developed by you and give suggestions for further improvement.

Photographs and Radio Recordings

Next stage on the cone of experiences after motion pictures is the number of those devices which can be called as one-dimensional aids. We will take the scope of each in teaching science one by one.

Still Pictures

Kinds of Still Pictures. Various kinds of still pictures can be used in teaching science. They include photographs, illustrations and slides. These visual materials are of great importance in teaching learning situations.

Photographs and illustrations can be used without projection, slides can be projected on the screen with slide projectors. Therefore pictures can be divided into two kinds: (i) unprojected, and (ii) projected.

Unprojected Pictures. Photographs, illustrations and clippings of photographs from magazines and newspapers can be collected for teaching purposes. Pictures give a correct impression of the object or situation and motivate and enrich teaching. It is good to have relevant pictures on the walls of science rooms — pictures of great scientists and some of their apparatus, etc. Pictures can also be used in teaching for motivation, introduction, presentation or recapitulation as the need may be.

Pictures and illustrations with some theme can be displayed on a bulletin board.

Bulletin Board. It is a place for posting "bulletins", as the name suggests. Bulletin boards can be used in many different ways and as an effective "teaching device". Bulletin boards inside and outside the science rooms and laboratories can be used for putting visual materials (pictures, illustrations) with relevant heading and some labelling for supplementing the teaching. It should be of scientific interest and importance. With proper teacher guidance and motivation bulletin boards can provide opportunity of developing creativity, responsibility and interest among • the students. Other than displaying the photographs and illustrations, bulletin boards can also be used for displaying reports of science projects done by students, science news and cuttings from science magazines, collected and presented by them.

Projected Pictures. Projection of visuals have certain advantages. For example, projection magnifies the material, therefore, a bigger group can easily see it. It is somehow motivating, therefore, compels attention.

Different kinds of projectors aroused in classrooms for projecting still pictures. They all are very easy to use, with little planning on the part of the teacher, teaching can be quite effective.

Opaque Projector of Episcope. The opaque projector projects and simultaneously enlarges material directly from original books, magazines, etc. All kinds of written, printed or pictorial matter in any sequence can be projected for teaching purpose. It can also project opaque thin objects like leaves, shells, sample of fabrics, butterflies, moths, etc.

Designs for posters, maps, pictures for displaying on bulletin boards etc., can be projected in the desired enlarged forms and then traced. The opaque projector though has many unexplored possibilities but is not being used much because of its bulk, weight and requirement of a very dark room.

Slide Projector. Such projectors usually project 35 mm slides. It is essentially a simple machine, easy to operate, inexpensive and light weight. It has most of the points of practical importance.

Slides can be shown individually in any desired order.

Slides' Characteristics

(i) Slides are of great value in visual teaching situation, when motion is of little or no importance, for example, in teaching structural details.

(ii) Great variety of visual material such as pictures, charts, graphs, diagrams, maps, tables, anything that can be photographed can be put on a slide.

(iii) Slides are available in black and white and coloured forms on many science subjects covering a wide range of topics and levels.

(iv) Slides are comparatively inexpensive.

(v) Slides require only a slight darkening of the room.

(vi) In some little more expensive projectors the slides can be moved automatically either from a master control or from a synchronising device on a sound track. This arrangement of slide-tape programme is an effective device as the well prepared commentary makes it more meaningful.

Slides in Use

The use of this visual aid will be more meaningful if following points are considered while using them:

(i) The science teacher has to explore if suitable slides are available on the particular topics.

(ii) Second step is the careful preview. The preview helps in deciding on how to use the material to the best advantage. Is it stimulating enough for introduction on the whole lesson could be developed with it or only suited for summarising the lesson.

(iii) Teacher has to think about the purpose also. If showing of motion is necessary for understanding, then slide is not the best medium.

(iv) If teaching involves a series of step by step development, one leading to the next logical sequence the slides are well suited.

Showing slides is only one part of the process. Good discussion and further activities could be developed from it.

The Micro projector. One of the more specialised types of projection equipment is the micro projector. As its name indicates it shows enlarged images of stained sections of microscopic slides or other biological material mounted on microscopic slides so that the bigger group can see it.

The advantages of micro projector are that:

(i) It presents an enlarged picture of the object on the slide for common view.

(ii) It assures the teacher that his students are seeing precisely what he wants them to see.

Some manufacturers make low power projection attachments for slide projectors. Some are simple extensions of a microscope using a more powerful illumination system with a small view screen. This can be easily shown in small groups. But the full scale micro-projectors are quite expensive.

Projectors of any kind are a boon to classroom teachers. These technological tools, if coordinated wisely make the classroom teaching quite effective, because of the novelty of presentation, students become motivated and interested.

Radio and Recordings

Language and Voice Modulation. These are primarily auditory aids. If the speaker on radio or recordings uses simple everyday language with meaningful associations with familiar examples the listening can become quite concrete. On the other hand if the language is difficult without any associations, it could be an abstract thing for listeners. Being only an auditory aid language and voice modulation etc, play a very important role in the effectiveness of these programmes

Values of Radio. Immediately we are able to get the news of important events from all over the world, which is not possible from any other media except vedio or TV. Many events are of great importance for science classes, some of which are mentioned below :

(i) Radio brings reality to the classroom The spectator who describes the events with his tone and description can brings sense of participation amongst listeners.

(ii) Radio programmes if well rehearsed and well presented in the form of stories bring the personal feeling of the actor, different sound effects and voices make them more realistic and meaningful.

(iii) It brings variety to the classroom and helps in teaching

(iv) Though in a well prepared programme enough expenses may be involved but radio being a mass media technology, on the whole it is inexpensive.

Limitations

(i) It is still a one way communication

(ii) Availability and maintenance of radio set may be a problem.

(iii) Radio broadcast timings always do not coincide with the class timings. Provision of radio broadcasts in the school time table is made only in a very few schools.

Educational Radio Programmes in Our Country. Educational broadcasts for schools in the AIR were regular features from the last few decades. These programmes included science lessons for students and teachers at various levels. Teachers' programmes were on content as well as on methodology. Before the board examinations revision lessons on various science subjects were quite popular. These were used to be given by experienced science teachers and educators

The school broadcast was a separate unit of AIR in New Delhi. The unit tried to coordinate between various agencies to improve the effectiveness of the broadcasts. Meetings were held where people were invited from Directorate of Education Delhi, Municipal Corporation Delhi, New Delhi Municipal Council and Delhi University to plan future programmes and give suggestions for their improvement

Radio broadcast schedule in the form of a chart was prmted and sent to the schools in the beginning of the year. Teachers could utilise the relevant broadcast in their classes. Radios and transistors were or could be easily available in the schools. If the teachers are conscious of the radio programmes students can be benefited Pre- and post-broadcast activities improved the effectiveness of the programmes as discussed in TV programmes.

Recordings. All the values of radio can be applied to recordings also. But the disadvantages can be eliminated like timing, administration and one way communication problems. Recordings from many sources can be utilised in the classrooms, like spool-tape records and cassette records.

Advantages of Recordings

(i) Recordings can become two way communication as it can be stopped, discussed and replayed wherever it is necessary, it can be controlled by us.

(ii) Recordings on cassette or spool-tape-recorder can be made in the school also. A commentary can be written and recorded on the available slides in your subject in the school for effective use and re-use.

(iii) Good radio programmes can be recorded and replayed in class whenever needed.

(iv) Scientific talks by eminent personalities can be taped and reproduced in the class.

Visual and Verbal Symbols

Kinds of Visual Symbols. They include the abstract representation of real pictures. Various kinds of visual symbols used in communication are drawings, sketches, diagrams, graphs, cartoons, flat maps, etc. They all can be projected on screen, and can also be shown on the blackboard or on the overhead projector.

Diagrams and charts etc., are part of everyday work for most of the science teachers. Almost all the science teachers use blackboard to show in the structure and happenings of various things in their subjects.

Commercially made charts are available in various subjects. Charts and other graphic aids are also made by various Governmental agencies. Central Institute of Educational Technology (CIET) of NCERT New Delhi develops various kinds of graphic aids for school purposes. Charts are also made in schools by teachers and students and can be utilised in teaching science quite effectively.

Chalkboard. Blackboard now is usually called a chalkboard because of variations in colours. It is one of the very important but quite neglected aid of the classrooms. If it is properly used can become a valuable aid in teaching science.

It should not be taken for granted that you already know the use of chalk board, but the techniques should be learned and practised especially as a trainee teacher.

Importance of Chalkboard

(i) This aid is used with all other aids for better clarification, for example, the main points of a demonstration planning and summarising of a field trip, questions for a motion picture and so on can be written on the board.

(ii) It gives a concrete form to abstract and vague statements and ideas.

(iii) It helps in developing the skill of drawing a particular diagram..

(iv) It is less time consuming and comparatively cheaper.

(v) It can be used for some students activities like quizes, competitions and discussions, etc.

(vi) Some chalkboards can be used for permanent outlines of maps, graphs, tables and other special materials where some filling up can serve the purpose.

(vii) If properly used chalkboard becomes an attractive point and holds students attention.

Effective Use of Chalkboard

(i) Clean the board properly before using it.

(ii) Try to write neat and bold so that it is legible.

(iii) Do not write too much on the board. Start writing from top left hand. Give headings and sub-headings in the written summary.

(iv) If diagrams are used for referring or introduction, they can be made beforehand. If you want the students to draw the diagrams then it should be drawn in front of them and they should be asked to draw side by side. In the same way a complicated process should not be drawn beforehand, but it should be developed before them for clarification and better understanding.

(v) If necessary, some tools can be used to draw on the board.

(vi) Coloured chalks should be used for making complex diagrams.

Overhead Projector. Any thing which is written or drawn on a chalkboard can also be projected by an overhead projector with some additional advantages.

An overhead projector projects material overhead or over shoulder the teacher using it on to a screen behind and above him. They generally have 25 cm x 25 cm writing area which is big enough for writing. What is required to be shown on the screen is written on a glass plate covered with sheet or roll of transparent plastic. Variety of fabrics tipped pens or china marking pencils are used for writing and drawing. Wet cloth can be used for erasing and re-using the sheets.

Advantages of Overhead Projector

(i) It is very simple and convenient to use the machine.

(ii) "Ibis projector unlike any other projectors is operated from the front of the room and the teacher faces class as he or she writes or points on already made transparencies.

(iii) Plastic roll attachment is quite useful. Diagrams, points of the lesson, assignments, tests and similar material can be effectively presented gradually with a minimum of time and effort.

(iv) An important feature of overhead projector is the provision of "overlays" or 'build ups," which have successive layers of transparencies in black and white coloured or both showing cumulative stages of development, sequences and sectional views, which is quite effective in many scientific processes and phenomenon.

Limitations

(i) Though it is not very heavy but a voluminous projector.

(ii) It is quite expensive and needs some planning.

Verbal Symbols

This is the most abstract and one of the most important forms of experience we get and give to our students. Our job as a teacher is to make sure that the various terms, ideas, words, principles and other abstractions used should be meaningful for students. The ideas and concepts which can be translated into verbal symbols come by getting other concrete experiences. Rich experiences gained by students help them to understand the verbal symbols meaningfully and therefore they can read and understand the textbooks also. Ability to speak or read the word does not mean that one also understands the object, process or phenomenon.

If from the very beginning science is taught by reading books or abstraction only, students usually acquire the habit of memorising and accepting verbal formulation given by others. This is no way of teaching science.

Various kind of experiences discussed on the core of experience from direct purposeful experience to visual symbols, all help in the development of verbal symbols meaningfully. Then reading is not only the process of reproduction of verbal symbols but also involves a thinking process, which includes meaning of words.

Textbooks and other reference books provide the most to the students, because all teaching is not possible by any one particular aid or experience. But the textbooks should be written in understandable vocabulary of that level. Sometimes in primary classes the language of science textbooks is much more difficult than the language in the language textbooks of that particular class. Another important aspect is also the style of writing and format. In writing and specially in teaching if references and examples are given from their environment and known things learning will be more meaningful.

Effective Use of Audio-visual Aids

A variety of teaching aids has been discussed in this chapter with some details. It is difficult to select few aids and to say that they are more important than others, or mis should be used more often than others etc. The value of an aid does not depend wholly on its quality itself but it also greatly depends upon the way it is used and the particular time it is used.

The qualities of various aids have also been discussed. No matter how perfect the aid may be, if it is irrelevant to the occasion of its use then it is of little value and an ordinary aid with not too many qualities becomes indispensable if it is used relevantly at the right time. For example, there is film which shows the animals under the sea or life in a desert in relation to their ecology. Neither the materials nor this relationship could be shown in a class by any other media or field trip as effectively as the film could. But always it should not be used as a substitute for other materials of the classroom.

EXERCISE

1. What is the importance of audio-visual aids in teaching science?
2. What are various kinds of audio-visual aids which can be used in teaching science?
3. How will you use the following activities or aids effectively in your teaching? Explain with examples.

(i) Direct experiences
(ii) Contrived experiences
(iii) Demonstration
(iv) Science museum
(v) Still pictures.

4. Identify some places where field trips can be arranged for meaningful learning in your teaching subject. Explain how will you arrange and carry out this activity.

5. What is the importance of 16 mm films? Identify five topics in your teaching subject where films can be effectively used.

6. Discuss the role of the following in teaching science:

   (i) Slide projector
   (ii) Overhead projector
   (iii) Micro projector
   (iv) Opaque projector.

7. As a science teacher how will you utilise educational TV for your classes?

8. How will you use the bulletin boards in your laboratory or classroom?

9. What precautions should be taken while selecting audio-visual aids in your teaching?

10. What audio-visual aids would you like to have in your science laboratory? Justify your answer.

10

Experiments in Innovation

Science education forms an integral part of our school curriculum upto the secondary level in the process of Universalisation of Science Education. The National Policy on Education (NPE)-1986 has laid considerable emphasis on strengthening the science education in the school education system. The current situation of teaching of school science content is as Environmental Studies at the lower primary level (classes I — V). Integrated approach of teaching science is followed at the upper primary stage (classes VI — VIII) and secondary stage (classes IX — X) by integrating all disciplines of Science in a natural fashion. The NPE-86 envisages extension through every effort of Science Education not only to those who are in the formal school system but also to those who have remained outside the system under non-formal and adult education programmes. The qualitative improvement in science education depends on many vital components. The teacher is considered as a crucial factor in the teaching-learning process, developing positive attitudes in the learners for better achievement and the formulation and implementation of science education programmes. The teachers have to discard their traditional methods and usual practices in relying entirely on textbooks. The teaching has to be integrated with environment based on real life situations using local experiences, expertise and resources. The classroom territory has to be expanded over the whole environment so that the activities become supplementary to classroom teaching. If such an approach is systematically implemented with mobilisation of needed resources, it is very much likely that there may be an improvement in our science education at the school stage. Several attempts are being made to improve science teaching in our country, both at the formal as well as non-formal sectors of school education.

Some of the innovative experiences in science education at the school level include Nehru Science Exhibition, Science Museums and Mobile Science Vans, Vikram Sarabhai Science Centre Ahmedabad, Kerala Shastra Sahitya Parishad and Ekalavya Project etc. In such innovative experiences and science activities, the learning is fitted to the abilities and interests of learners as there exists an opportunity for individuals initiative, independent or collective study and creativity. A large number of such activities are organised in India. A few of the major activities are listed and described briefly here.

Nehru Science Exhibition

November 14 is the birth anniversary of Pandit Jawahar Lal Nehru, our first Prime Minister. Children call him Chacha Nehru, as he used to love them much. We celebrate Children's Day on November 14. On this occasion Science Exhibition is also organised by the NCERT. This exhibition is Science Exhibition. To start with, this exhibition used to be organised at New Delhi where Pandit Nehru used to live, when he was our Prime Minister. Now this exhibition is organised in different states. Children from country, from all States and UTs participate in this exhibition. Nehru Exhibition is organised at the national level.

Every year NCERT announces a main theme and sub-themes for Nehru Exhibition. Children make their exhibits on these sub-themes.

Example. **Main Theme: Science in our Environment**

Sub-Themes

(i) Agriculture, Horticulture, Farming and Animal Husbandry.
(ii) Conservation of the Environment
(iii) Health
(iv) Energy Conservation and Needs
(v) Astronomy
(vi) Town and Village Planning
(vii) Machines in the Service of Rural Areas
(viii) Teaching Aids for Science and Mathematics
(ix) Innovations.

This information along with the last date of submitting the entry with the dates of exhibition reaches every school of the country, from States and UTs and from States and UTs to all schools. On information children start working on their projects — static or workin investigatory science projects under the guidance and supervision of the teachers. If a school has a Science Club, it becomes quite active after information under the supervision and guidance of the Science Club.

Teachers' Status

Very often in Nehru Science Exhibition we see some static work or some noble experiments demonstrated by the students with lines and graphs. These are projects but not Investigatory Science Projects. Students should be encouraged and motivated to work on some of science projects, and bring them to Nehru Science Exhibition.

A project may be any purposeful activity. It may be a model working, or experiment.

A project which involves investigation, discovery and finding out which was not known to the student before, is an investigatory investigation is much more than the repetition of a standard Experienced student is to decide what experiments are necessary. He may have to design his own apparatus, if that is not available in the laboratory. He has to search for the appropriate principles, laws, formulae, apparatus and data, and originate a solution to a problem. The student has to behave like a scientist.

Working on an investigatory science project is the way a student can learn science by project method which involves some steps of scientific method like Problem, Hypotheses and Experiment.

Conclusion

Every year more and more investigatory science projects are being seen in Nehru Science Exhibition. It is very encouraging. You should also encourage your students to work on investigatory science projects under your guidance and send it to Nehru Science Exhibition through District and State Science Exhibitions and Fairs.

Museums and Mobile Vans

You must have seen science museums. They are very effective and interesting sources of learning science. What experiences do you get from a science museum ?

Objectives of Science Museum. Main objectives in establishing science museums are:

(i) to help young science learners in understanding concepts of science by play way method.

(ii) to provide a glimpse of past as well as an insight into the future.

(iii) to help schools in their class activities by providing them with a number of equipments and specimens which are otherwise difficult for a single school to procure.

(iv) to arrange extension activities such as field trips, lectures, film shows and exhibitions for the students as well as public.

During the last decade or so, a couple of science museums have been set up in the country including one at Delhi, the Natural History Museum. In Delhi's Pragati Maidan, National Science Centre (National Council of Science Museums) has also been set up few years back. It has several units. 'FUN GAMES' and 'ENERGY' units are very interesting for students. Delhi also has two Primary Science Museums:

(i) Municipal Corporation Children Resource Centre (MCCRC) at R.K. Puram, Sector VI.

(ii) New Delhi Municipal Council (NDMC) Science Centre at Lakshmibai Nagar.

There are good science museums in various parts of the country — Bombay, Bangalore, Calcutta. All these science museums are doing very good Job, carrying out various innovative activities, in science for the improvement of science education. Let us discuss some science museums a little bit in detail.

Nehru Science Centre. The Nehru Science Centre (NSC) is established in Bombay by the National Council of Science Museums. The most important and attractive part of the NSC is a 'Science Park' for children. With green surroundings, the Children's Science Park has exhibited on time, motion, energy, power and work. Also, there are models of railway engines, tram cars, aeroplanes, steam lorries, a windmill and a sun dial. There are birds, animals and fish to acquaint children with nature. While children enjoy the Science Park the most, it also helps them to understand 'what' 'why' and 'how' of the queries, questions and problems haunting their minds.

Nehru Science Centre, Bombay is basically multi-disciplinary in character. Collection of antique exhibits of historic value, presentation of the same through permanent and temporary exhibitions on selected themes, extension activities offering multiple avenues of learning, enjoyment and training to the student community as well as the public, taking science to rural areas through mobile science vans, aiming towards interacting mode of presentation of themes are some of the ways in which the NSC operates. The Science Centre also offers a gallery on 'light and sight'. It presents different principles involved in file process of 'seeing and the vision.' A survey is made of vision, its defects, its importance, its complexities and varieties. Nehru Science Centre also organises extension activities such as science extension in rural areas, film video shows, science seminars for schools, films, video cassettes loan service, amateur weather station, amateur radio classes for children, sky observation programme, astronomical camps, popular science lectures, special science film festivals, aeronautic modelling programmes and training camps for under-privileged children.

Visvesvaraya Industrial and Technological Museums. The Visvesvaraya Industrial and Technological Museum is established in Bombay. It organises various activities and programmes such as motive power gallery (science museum), teacher training, hobby centre, student's science seminars, science quiz, science fair, temporary science exhibitions, science demonstration lectures, mobile science exhibitions, film shows, popular science lectures, etc. The museum has also a regional science centre at Gulbarga.

If you have a science museum at the place where you teach, plan a visit to that museum. If your students go to some places, where there are science museums, ask them to visit them with their parents or if you arrange a field trip to any place, where there is a science museum, take your students there, and see how much science they learn — the science which is not there even in their science books.

Mobile Science Vans. Some science museums have mobile science units, museums on wheel. They are usually sent to the places, where there are no-science museums. They are not as big as a science museum. They do not have as many science exhibits as a science museum has. But even this is a very effective source of learning science for students at upper primary level.

Natural History Museum, New Delhi, National Science Centre, New Delhi and Nehru Science Centre, Bombay have Mobile Science Vans. You try to find out whether there is some science museum, not very far from the place you are teaching, and whether that science museum has the facility of mobile science vans. You can ask such museums to send that unit to your school. If you are successful to bring it, your students may visit the science museum even in their school, and can learn a lot of science.

Sarabhai Centre

For improving the quality of science learning in non-formal system of education, Vikram Sarabhai Community Centre was established in Ahmedabad in 1963. The Centre is one of the pioneer organisations in the country providing a variety of out-of-school activities in science for students, teachers and community. It has a team of highly skilled staff which acts as a nucleus and catalyst for various programmes undertaken by the Centre.

The Centre conducts research and innovative programmes for improving education and community life. These programmes include studies on science and mathematics, environmental studies, integrated science and science learning improvement programmes through enquiry approach, mathematics laboratory, teacher orientation, designing and development of teaching and learning material packages.

The Centre also organises programmes for rural as well as urban community. These programmes are related to the problems of pollution, health, security, population, communication, settlement and values. The Centre is basically a community centre where people come with their children and learn science where interested teachers and scientists experiment new ideas in teaching and learning. The Centre organises science seminars, film video shows, popular lectures, exhibitions, sky-gazing through a telescope, etc. The Centre has a library, laboratories, science museum, workshop, science playground, mass media and A.V. facilities for the community. The Centre provides facilities in rocketry and electronics hobbies to children. In science playground, the children get a glimpse of science through play toys, colour filter towards musical pipes, sand, pits, water pond and evolution pillar.

The centre has also started some small extension centres to the rural areas. A mobile van equipped with a laboratory and A.V. materials tours different villages. Science club activities are organised in rural areas based on emphasis on the environmental awareness.

Shastra Sahitya Parishad

The Kerala Shastra Sahitya Parishad (KSSP) is a voluntary organisation. It was established in 1963. KSSP has around 10,000 members comprising scientists, doctors, engineers, social scientists, teachers, students, workers, peasants and technicians. It has 600 units all over Kerala.

Objectives

1. To popularise science amongst society.
2. To generate science literacy amongst people.
3. To increase community involvement for developing scientific temper in the society.
4. To develop rural technology in the field of energy.
5. To organise health camps, classes and audio-visual campaigns on a wide scale.

Activities. The society has about eight major areas of activities —

(A) Publications, (B) Non-formal Education, (C) Formal Education, (D) Environmental Bridge, (E) Research and Development Wing, (F) Rural Science Forums, (G) Health Brigade, (H) Art and Science.

The details of these activities are as follows.

Publications. KSSP prints a variety of scientific periodicals and books meant for popularisation of science and generation of science literacy amongst the people. These include:

(i) Eureka — monthly magazine for primary classes.

(ii) Sastrakeralam — monthly magazine for secondary School children.

(iii) Sastragathy — monthly magazine for adults.

(iv) Parishad Vartha — monthly bulletin for members.

Non-formal Education. These activities cover a wide spectrum, the main ones being 'Science Campaign' and 'Science Centre.'

Formal Education. KSSP promotes a number of activities aimed at improving science clubs, talent tests and promotion of awareness about the education system amongst the public. The talent tests are:

(i) Eureka Talent Tests — at elementary level.

(ii) Sastrakeralam Quiz — at high school level.

(iii) Sastragathi Talent Tests — at college level.

Environmental Bridge. KSSP was involved m Silent Valley Campaign, Social Forestry Programmes and campaigns against industrial pollution.

Research and Development Wing: Its responsibility is to develop appropriate rural technology in the field of energy, environment etc. A high efficiency *Chulha* (Stove), developed by them has been widely propagated.

Rural Science Forums: KSSP has initiated these forums to prompt villagers to think on their own about their problems and solutions.

Health Brigade: KSSP organises health camps, classes and audio-visual campaigns on a wide scale.

Art and Science: It organises Sastra Kala Jatha and Bharat Kala Jatha.

Ekalavya Project

Ekalavya Science Teaching Project (ESTP) started in 1972 in sixteen rural middle schools of district Hoshangabad in Madhya Pradesh for teaching science through environment based discovery approach. This project was started by Kishore Bharati, in collaboration with Friends Rural Centre, Rasulia with the support of the Department of Education, Government of Madhya Pradesh. A large number of teachers and scientists from various institutions and organisations such as the All India Science Teachers Association, Physics Study Group; Bombay Municipal Corporation;

Gandhi Vidyapeeth, Vedehi, Surat District; Lok Bharti, in Gujarat; The Space Application Centre, Ahmedabad; Universities of Delhi, Rajasthan and Indore; The Tata Institute of Fundamental Research, Bombay; Indian Institute of Technology, Kanpur; NCERT, DAV College of Education, Abohar (Punjab) etc. participated in the development of curriculum, workbooks, science kit, other materials and training of teachers.

In 1978 this programme of science teaching was extended to all the 206 middle schools of District Hoshangabad.

Objectives

1. Implementation of introducing innovations as envisaged in Ekalavya Project within the given framework of the Government school system.
2. Encouraging science teaching through discovery approach in Indian schools.
3. Providing science education experiences through environment.
4. Developing ability among students for applying scientific methods in different situations.
5. Developing scientific attitude (scientific temper) among the students.

Curriculum. Keeping in view the objectives of this Ekalavya experiences the curriculum of science teaching has been on process approach rather than product approach. The process approach of learning science provides numerous opportunities to children to explore scientific phenomena of their local environment. Most of the curricular contents have been taken from their environment. Advanced scientific concepts, such as abstract chemical symbols, theoretical concepts of atomic and molecular structure, and human anatomy etc. have not been included in the curriculum because these concepts are beyond the students direct interaction with the environment.

The selection of curricular content is dependent upon:

(a) relatedness to environment, (b) relatedness to the needs, interests and mental level of the students, and (c) possibility of the application of discovery approach.

Through the above mentioned procedure the curricular contents for classes sixth, seventh and eighth was developed. Some of the examples of the curricular contents for various classes are given below:

Class VI	Kuchh Khel Khilwar
	Samuh Banana Sikho
	Hamari Phaslen aur Samuhikaran
	Vidyut
	Ganak Ke Khel
	Jeev Jagad me Vividhata
	Mini, Pathar aur Chattane
Class VII	Ek Majedar Khel
	Jar aur Patti
	Keeron Ki Duniya
	Phaslon Ke Dushman
	Apni Haddi Pahachano
	Aakash Ki Or
	Taraju Ka Sidhant
Class VIII	Jantuon Ka Jivan Chakkar
	Phool aur Phal
	Paudho me Prajanan
	Vargikaran Ke Niyam
	Jantuon ka Vargikaran
	Gasen

Work Book and Science Kit Materials. In this programme, the workbook is introduced in place of textbooks, which is process based. Principles of science are discovered through experiments. Science Kit is very conducive for discovery approach to science teaching.

Teaching Method. Discovery approach of science teaching is the main teaching method followed in this programme. Students learn science through inquiry approach especially by experimentation, discussion and field trips. The whole class is divided into subgroups of four students each known as a Toli. This Toli pattern is also followed in their teacher training programmes. The students perform experiments in their respective tolies, collect and analyse data and draw conclusions on the basis of the guidelines given in the workbook.

Examination. In this Eklavaya Experience the examination is not based on rote memory or recall etc. Independent observation, data collection, data analysis and drawing conclusions have been given due weightage. It also seeks to test the extent of a pupil's readiness to innovate through physical experimentation.

The examination is conducted to test three basic elements of science teaching, namely, scientific skills, scientific attitude (scientific temper) and understanding of scientific concepts and principles.

EXERCISE

1. When is the Nehru Science Exhibition organised? Who organises it? Where is it organised? Who participate in it? What is the nature of exhibits displayed in it?
2. What is the difference between a 'science museum,' and a 'mobile science unit'? How will you use them in science teaching?
3. Name the science museums you have seen. Where are they located? What did you see in them?
4. Name the city and State where "Vikram Sarabhai Community Science Centre" is situated. What are its activities?
5. What do you mean by "KSSP"? When was it established? What are its activities?
6. What do you mean by "ESTP"? When and where was it started? What are its objectives? What materials were developed under this project?

11

Programmes for Enrichment

There are children not of different ages but also of different abilities in the same class. There are children who are from different socio-economic backgrounds, who have different values and different outlook. There are children who require differentiated educational programme and services beyond those normally provided by the regular school programmes. These programmes can be enrichment programmes and remedial programmes.

Programme for Meritorious Students

Before discussing any enrichment programme it will be desirable to describe the students for whom these programmes are needed — enrichment programmes are needed for gifted children to fulfil their demands.

I. The gifted children have been defined in many ways. One acceptable version in gifted are those who by virtue of outstanding abilities are capable of high performance and are identified by professionally qualified persons. They include all the following:

(a) *Talented.* Those students who may be talented in one or few fields.

(b) *Intelligent.* Students who score high on intelligent test (verbal or non-verbal), they may be with an IQ of 130 or above.

(c) *Creative.* Creative children are intelligent, talented plus they have something extra; they are also productive thinkers.

(d) *Skilled.* They are capable of performing better in psychomotor abilities.

II. The gifted children can be identified by some of their behavioural characteristics as described by T. Renzulli and R. Hartman in their scale for rating behavioural characteristics of superior Students.

A. In their *Learning* characteristics, they:

(i) usually have advanced vocabulary for their age and grade level.

(ii) are keen and alert observers, usually see more to get a more out of a description and films etc.

(iii) read great deal on their own, prefer adult level books.

B. Regarding *Motivational* characteristics, they:

(iv) get easily bored with routine task.

(v) are not easily satisfied with their own speed or products.

(vi) often pass judgement or events, people and things.

C. In their *Creative* characteristics, they:

(vii) display great deal of curiosity, ask questions.

(viii) display a good deal of intellectual playfulness, manipulate ideas *i.e.*, change and elaborate upon them.

D. About their *Leadership* characteristics, they:

(ix) are self-confident with children of their own age as well as adults.

(x) adapt readily to new situations, are flexible in thoughts and actions.

Some Enrichment Programmes for Gifted Students

Some enrichment programmes which are used to fulfil the demands of gifted are described here.

1. *Acceleration.* It means skipping classes, it may be in one subject or more subjects or by some other means shortening the time spent on studies.

2. ***Special Grouping.*** Here the opportunity is given for special education in each homogenous group based on abilities.

3. ***Enrichment Programmes.*** Special academic provision for various students.

Process of Acceleration

One technique used to cope up with the gifted student is accelerating the phase by skipping classes. This technique benefits the individual without changing the actual educational programme. For many years, most of the people, educators and administrators have understood the word acceleration only in terms of skipping ' class or classes. But it has shown results that skipping classes is least desirable method of acceleration. Many emotional, psychological problems may arise in some children when they are not able to adjust in the new peer group. In United States of America some other methods of acceleration are being used successfully. Some such methods are, early admission to primary school, i.e. before the normal age of 6 years, upgraded primary and middle schools, students are allowed to move up for one or two subjects for example a 6th grade child is doing 7th or 8th grade maths or science, students are allowed to take extra load in terms of extra credits in senior classes to be able to finish school early to get early admission in College. The advanced placement programme has become a popular method of stimulating high aptitude students in high schools.

Acceleration does not necessarily work for each gifted child. A thorough knowledge of needs and abilities of the individual is required to accomplish success with minimum personal problems.

Some results of the research studies on acceleration are described here to get a better understanding.

Terman and Odem (1947) suggested as a result of their follow-up study. "It is our opinion that nearly all children of 135 IQ or higher should be promoted sufficiently to permit college entrance by the age of 17 at least, and majority of this group would be better if entering at 16. Acceleration of this extent is especially desirable for those who plan to complete two or more years of graduate study in preparation for a professional career.

Callagher (1966), in summarising research on the topic reported:

"The recent research on acceleration has done nothing to change the generally favourable portrait of these methods for moderately shortening the educational career of talented youth. The advantage of saving a year or two from a long investment in educational time does not seem diluted by social or emotional difficulties."

Reynolds, Brich and Tuseth (1962), in reviewing research on evaluation of early admittance programmes, commented as follows:

"It may be concluded, from the research that early admission to school of mentally advanced children who were within a year of the ordinary school entrance age and who are generally mature is to their advantage. There are few issues in education on which the research evidence now available is so clear and so universally favourable to a particular solution."

As far as we are concerned in India with the present system of education there is not much scope of acceleration except a little early admission to primary classes.

Grouping in Special Manner

Another way of solving this problem is the grouping of students according to their abilities. One of the questions often asked in educational circles is "what is the impact of ability grouping." One of the most comprehensive studies was carried by Goldberg, Passion Just Man and Hagg (1965). The author concluded that merely changing the ability grouping within the class without changing the curriculum or the manner in which the children were taught could not be expected to produce any substantial changes. Goldberg has commented: "Ability grouping is by no means a sufficient condition ensuring greater academic achievement at any ability level. At best, it provides a framework within which enhanced learning may be more effectively planned and executed." Hence to solve the problem of gifted (as well as backward) the ability grouping should be subject-wise with differentiated curricula. For example, in physics, chemistry, biology, maths, there should be at least three types of courses, one for more able in that subject, other for average and the third for below average or the slow learners.

The subject to subject ability grouping in different subjects is only possible if the timetable is made student-wise not section-wise, because a student in higher ability group in one subject may not necessarily be fit for higher ability groups in all the subjects. In American schools the students move from class to class and the subject rooms are fixed. Such homogeneous ability groups are made, and different courses in each subject are being taught, for example, higher ability students are offering BSCS Blue version and low ability students are doing "Pattern and Processes" or some such similar courses of various abilities.

In our country in some schools sections are made according to the ability of the students and also some courses were being offered at various levels. A (higher) and B (lower) level courses in science (physics, chemistry, biology) were being offered in various sections from 1979 at secondary level. The more able students in science were able to offer A-level courses and uninterested and uninvolved average students were able to take B-level courses. Now the Central Board of Secondary Education, New Delhi has proposed again a common course for all from 1984.

There are advantages and disadvantages of this homogeneous grouping. On one hand in ability grouping the teaching can be modified according to the need of the students in a more effective way but on the other hand they get labelled as A and B grade students.

In Delhi, the New Delhi Municipal Council (NDMC) has started several separate schools for talented students called Nav Yug Schools. Here the admissions are given to only gifted children after some testing. But the courses are the same as in other schools.

Various Programmes

Enrichment can be defined as the type of activity devoted to the further development of the particular intellectual skills and talents of the gifted child.

For many years more conscious teachers are using the technique of enrichment for fulfilling the need of gifted child. "Rich" means physical accumulation and "enrich" means richness at the mental level. The question is how should we specially as a science teacher enrich the gifted students so that they will be properly groomed for future.

For any kind of enrichment programmes following preliminaries are important:

(i) Identification and listing of gifted students in your class or classes.

(ii) Identification of modifications or enrichment techniques to be given to bright individuals.

Gifted and talented students when exposed, always accept the challenging situations and if guided properly give very encouraging results. There are some qualities which are found in gifted students, these should be developed to a maximum potential. Some of these qualities are:

- reasoning through complex problems
- abstract thinking
- originality in views and effort
- association and interrelation of concepts
- giving generalisations
- drawing relationships
- curiosity to learn and read
- create new ideas and originate new lines of thought
- have wider interests.

Some or all of these qualities are present to some extent in gifted children but a proper environment is required for their development The task is not easy for most teachers but as a science teacher one should try to take the challenge for helping the students and the society.

Broadly speaking there can be two types of enrichment programmes.

1. *Horizontal, Breadth or Lateral Enrichment Programmes.* In this type of programme enrichment can be given in relating the topic with other related topics. For example, while teaching photosynthesis relation to stoma to and other related metabolic activities can be taken as enrichment.

2. *Vertical, Depth or Intensive Enrichment Programmes.*. In such cases gifted students can be given more intensive, detailed or in depth study of the topic. For example, Kreb Cycle is taught in a

simple way upto X class, the gifted students can be given details of the biochemistry to learn the concept more effectively.

To keep these two aspects in mind the different assignments can be planned for various ability students in a normal classroom. Some teachers in their effort of giving some kind of enrichment programme to the gifted give longer and more extensive assignments of the usual sort. This kind of assignment is not fulfilling the need of the gifted. Some talented students may get disinterested with such assignments. Here the opportunity should be given to explore and do things on their own rather than giving the assignment of the same intellectual level.

In a normal classroom situation this is the least a teacher can do to help gifted as well as backward to give variations in assignments according to their needs. While planning your lesson you should also plan varied assignments for different students. The assignments can be given as options without obvious description of gifted and backward etc.

Although the teachers were always free to plan and give enrichment programmes in the form of special assignments and extra readings etc., this kind of provision was not given in the traditional science curricula.

Special Courses

In developed countries like USA and United Kingdom there has been a strong move from late fifties and early sixties to bring major changes both in content and process of presenting science to elementary and secondary students particularly for the talented students.

Scientists and educationists in the field of physics, chemistry and biology developed various science programmes as PSSC, Chem-Study, CBA, BSCS, Project Physics, ISCS, and Nuf field science series, where they have insisted on curricula that stressed the basic structure of the discipline and the nature of the scientific process. By and large in all these courses provision is made for talented students. The most valuable feature and the new trend in these courses are their scientific integrity and emphasis on science inquiry, experimentation, evaluation of evidences and construction of models and theories. The emphasis on abstract ideas and scientific models exactly fits the needs of gifted students.

The ISCS (Intermediate Science Curriculum Study) was developed at Florida State University as an individualised instructional course where alongwith the main or core course some enrichment and remedial activities are provided in the form of excursions to fulfil the needs of gifted as well as backward students. The enrichment excursions are both in depth and breadth. The science teachers load was reduced with the provision of such built-in activities for gifted (and backward) students.

One of the most important help offered by these new courses to the science teachers was the attention paid to the teachers training and retraining in the manner that the material was to be presented.

In India in our educational system enrichment programmes are more suited for helping the gifted and talented students. We do not have very clear-cut well planned programmes for such students. The science teachers if concerned about their students can help them by identifying the gifted and giving them more challenging assignments.

Self-pacing is another way which can be adopted in science teaching at least for some portions if not for all.

At senior secondary level the investigatory projects according to CBSE, New Delhi if taken seriously by the students and guided properly by the teachers can fulfil the need of gifted student, to some extent.

Some talent search examinations are also being conducted at various levels to identify the gifted and talented.

Talent Search Programmes

1. ***National Talent Search (NTS) Scholarship.*** NCERT conducts NTS contest at the end of three levels to identify talented students. The test is conducted all over the country in various centres on the first Sunday of May every year. The three levels are as follows:

(i) Secondary (Class X)

(ii) Higher Secondary (Class XI)

(iii) Senior Secondary (Class XII)

(NCERT has proposed that from 1985, NTS contest will be conducted at only secondary level, *i.e.*, class X).

Those who compete in written test are invited for interviews. The selected candidates get NTS scholarship till they pursue for science courses including MBBS and Engineering.

2. ***Junior Science Talent Search (JSTS) Scholarship.*** Directorate of Education, Delhi conducts JSTS contest for the students studying in class IX in Delhi Schools. 150 students, who are selected in written test are invited for the interview. The first 100 students are awarded JSTS scholarships of Rs. 240.00 at the end of class IX and Rs. 220.00 at the end of class X.

JSTS enrichment Camps are also organised by the Science Branch, Directorate of Education, Delhi where the students get an opportunity to work in an enriched environment with lot of facilities and expert guidance. They work on investigatory projects, listen to experts in various fields and visit places of scientific interest. Such activities help students in getting motivated to pursue in the field of their interest and help in the development of various scientific qualities.

3. ***Primary Science Talent Search (PSTS) Scholarships.*** Municipal Corporation Delhi (MCD) and New Delhi Municipal Council (NDMC) education departments conduct PSTS contests for the students of MCD and NDMC schools respectively at two levels:

(i) Class IV students, and

(ii) Class V students.

MCD has only written tests. NDMC has written tests as well as oral tests on science practicals (Interviews). Those NDMC students who compete in written are invited for interviews. The selected students get scholarships.

You as science teachers should be in touch with these organisations. Get full information on the above mentioned contests for the talented, prepare your gifted students for these contests, and ask the SCERTs of your state for any guidance in this regard.

Programmes for Mediocres

There are children in science classes who are not motivated to learn science. They are slow in learning than average students, they are weak intellectually and emotionally. They are also called backward children.

Backward Children. Backward children are those having I.Q. below average, usually they are slow in learning. In our normal schools we are mostly concerned with border-line cases.

An acceptable educational defination of backward child is one who is not able to do the work'of one year below. If a VI class child is not able to do V class work he can be considered as backward.

It is also possible that a student is considered backward in one subject and not in others.

The enthusiasm of slow learners tend to be short-lived. Apart from a limited attention span within a lesson, there is a strict limit to the length of the time that a teacher can spend on any topic before it loses appeal. It is easier to teach those who want to learn science than it is to teach those who do not. This will be a challenge to teach science to slow learners. This challenge should be taken by science teachers not as a burden but with pleasure.

I. D.S. Robertson of Jordentiff College Education Glasgow has listed some skills and qualities to be developed in slow learners. They are as follows:

(i) The ability to communicate in speech and writing and to read with understanding.

(ii) The ability to make measurement and do calculations.

(iii) Capacities for thought, judgement, discrimination and enjoyment.

(iv) Responsibility for their work.

(v) An understanding of the physical world and the society in which they live.

(vi) A vocabulary for discussion of current events and issues in science.

(vii) An appreciation of the importance of personal relationship and the value of co-operative effect.

(viii) An ability to find out scientific information for themselves.

(ix) An awareness of the variety of ways in which leisure time can be used.

(x) Self-confidence, self-respect, and as realistic an idea of one's own capabilities and potential as is possible.

Virtually all these qualities can be fostered within the teaching of science, and it is thus important that one should think of education through teaching rather than of teaching science as an end in itself.

The same objectives could well be achieved through a study of different topics in science. When choosing science content to meet these objectives, the following questions should be kept in mind by the teacher.

(i) Is the material relevant? In other words, will the pupils see the material as useful to them either at the time they are in school, or after they have left school.

(ii) Is the material capable of being presented in an interesting way?

(iii) Is the material within the pupils' powers of comprehension.

Remedial Programme. Special programmes are needed for above average and below average students both to cope up with their needs.

Special Grouping. As discussed in the case of gifted special grouping according to the abilities of slow learner has been identified as an effective way, if special curricula are also given to them. Even if special programmes for slow learners are not available, at least the teacher can develop a teaching style which will be more effective for slow learners.

Many special curricula in sciences have been developed in USA and United Kingdom where stress is on experimentation and the materials are tailored to their unique characteristics and needs. The content covered is comparatively less, and more real experiences are given. Science is studied in its social context including problems of society related to various science subjects.

BSCS has developed a special curricula for below average students "pattern and processes".

Another programme developed for educationally uninvolved students is "Ideas and Investigation in Science" (Biology and Physical Science).

In our country we do not have special ability grouping and special curricula for slow learners in regular schools. The A and B level science courses (CBSE) discussed above are for above average and average students respectively, and there are no special courses for slow learners, and even these two courses merged in 1984.

Remedial Programmes. Like enrichment programmes for gifted students some remedial programmes are also designed for slow learners. Programme instruction works very well with slow learners because of self-pacing. Therefore, special curricula developed for slow learners also include simple programmed materials.

In most of the Indian schools there is provision for a remedial period in the beginning or at the end of the school hours. Very few teachers are using this period for actual remedial work. Many a times teachers use this period to cover the course or to revise the course in a full class. This period should be utilised only for actual remedial work for the few students who have been identified as slow learners and actually need teacher's help.

Role of the Teacher. The teacher has to be patient with slow learners, they need care and love. They develop hatred if they are not properly cared as they are emotionally weak.

Students can learn more if the teacher makes the learning "Child Centred" as far as possible. The students should be allowed to become active agents in the educational process.

A warm but firm hand, and a real concern is required for slow learners. The teacher should praise the slow learners frequently. The teacher should help the students to achieve success. This will encourage them to work hard, and they will devote more time in studies. Thus they will be able to learn just about the same devoting more time what average students learn in less time.

EXERCISE

1. How will you identify the following types of students in your classes?

   (a) Slow learners.

   (b) Gifted and talented students.

2. What provisions can be made for the gifted students in your science classes?

3. How will you give academic help to a slow learner in your class?
4. Select one topic from your subject area. Write three assignments one for gifted, other for average and third for slow learners on that topic. Give justification how the assignments are suited for the three categories.
5. After becoming a teacher in a school, how will you use the remedial period provided in the school time-table.
6. What abilities should be developed in talented students? Suggest some activities or procedures to be used to develop some identified abilities.
7. In what way a science club can help the gifted students?
8. Discuss some National and State level programmes for the talented students.
9. What will be your role as a science teacher that your gifted students can compete in some science talent search programmes?

12

Instruction in a Programmed Manner

Percentage of our science teachers (Physics, Chemistry and Biology) have good background in their respective subjects, and they take interest in teaching and trying out new science programmes. Even in the schools which have enough science equipment and the science labs are well equipped, the lecture-demonstration method is the one most commonly used, as our science teachers are heavily loaded and they get a very little or sometime even no time for planning their lessons during school hours. Our schools have usually 8 periods of 30-40 minutes duration. Regular teachers also work as substitute teachers (where in America if a teacher is on leave, a substitute teacher is invited from outside to teach his classes) during their planning periods besides their teaching 6-7 (out of 8) periods daily, six days a week (where in Western countries schools work five days a week), and Sunday is the only holiday.

Our textbooks are written in a traditional way. If our science teachers could have well sequenced programmed materials, it would be a great help to them, as mentioned above, they are heavily loaded. Also if the programmed materials provided activities of 20-25 minutes duration, students would have more opportunity to do the experiments themselves even in smaller periods. So well sequenced programmed materials would be more useful for teachers to teach and for students to learn than the materials now available.

Definition

Let us look at some of the definitions of programmed instruction.

(1) Cronbach describes a programme of instruction as follows: "A programme is a pre-arranged sequence of explanations and questions. A programme whether for a brief unit or for an entire course, is a carefully planned progression of ideas, beginning with elementary notions and working upto relatively complex theories or applications.

(2) According to B.F. Skinner a programmed instruction is simply a matter of breaking the material to be learned into easy steps, arranging steps in logical order with no gaps, making sure the student understands one step before moving to another and then incidently, making sure that he is successful.

(3) According to Espich and Williams a programmed instruction may be defined as a planned sequence of experiences, leading to the proficiency, in terms of stimulus response relationships. By this definition a programme is an educational device that causes a student to progress through a series of experiences, which lead to the students proficiency. The experience here is student's own experience in the learning process, not just the teacher telling. Planned sequence determines what experiences and in what order should occur. What is the student supposed to be able to do after completing the programme? How well? How quickly? All such questions implied in leading to proficiency in terms of stimulus-response relationships refer to the basic behavioural science concepts on which programmed instruction is based, and which are taken into consideration when a programme is written.

Psychology of Behaviour

No one knows for certain how or why programmed instruction works, but it is generally agreed that basic behavioural psychology is somehow involved. At least the originators of programmed instruction attributed its success to some basic tenets of behavioural psychology.

The results of the change in behaviour called learning are observable or measurable. All behavioural changes of students as a result of learning may be of three types: (1) Psychomotor; (2)

Cognitive; and (3) Affective (Chapter 3). (1) and (2) are comparatively easier to measure than (3).

In any teaching situation for effective learning the best method is:

1. Present the stimulus to the student.
2. Help the student to make the desired response to the stimulus by giving him clues, by leading him towards it, or by telling him the response itself.
3. When die student makes the desired response to the stimulus, immediately reinforces that response.

Programmed instruction takes advantage of the basic human drive for success. The programmer guides the student toward making the correct response. He then shows or tells the student that he has given the desired response — that he has been successful. Each time he makes the correct response, he is positively reinforced by being told that he is correct, his drive for success is satisfied. Each time his drive for success is satisfied, the probability increases that he will make the correct response to the given stimulus in future situations.

The Advantages

The programmed instruction does have a number of advantages over conventional methods. It allows for individual rates of learning and it gives immediate reinforcement of correct responses. According to Burner the technically most interesting features of automatic devices are that they can take some of the load of teaching of the teacher's shoulders. For this time the teacher can be used by his students who need him and whenever they need him. According to James this type of teaching is very frustrating and tiring but extremely rewarding. When science teachers have worked as long at individualized instruction as they have to make grouped instruction workable, the rewards may be proportionally increased.

Theory and Practical Integrated

In teaching science, a continuing area of concern to educators has been the problem of integrating laboratory experimentation with instruction in scientific theory. The need to individualize course content for students is also recognized. Programmed instruction may offer one solution to both of these difficulties. If the science curriculum can be programmed so that individual rates could be dealt with more effectively, and if laboratory material can be developed which enable students to conduct experiments effectively on an independent basis, laboratory experi mentation may be integrated more satisfactorily into the typical science course.

A summary of the subject area in which programmed instruction has been used reveals that these areas which require laboratory activities are rare. Cowan indicated that there were no auto-instructional materials available in physics that provided students with laboratory experiences Cowan and Siddiqi developed and used such materials in their research studies.

Prefect Programming

Hundreds of good science textbooks are available in the market They are not designed to teach but to convey information to the student. In a programme a programmer determines for a student, what he should and what he should not assimilate. In a programme, the student is guided along a path and given those experiences that will cause him to learn those things. No such guidance is given with a textbook Adjunct programming can be a link between programmed instruction and a good textbook. It combines some of the progressive features of programmed instruction with the comprehensiveness of textbooks. The goal of adjunct programming is to enable the student to learn as effectively as possible from a good textbook.

An Adjunct Programme may be one of two types (1) The text itself is kept intact and the programme is supplied as a separate unit, or (2) sections of the textbook are extracted vibration and used in the programme as the basic information. The most popular procedure as used by Cowan and Siddiqi is to leave the textbook intact. Their programmed materials which they developed for the PSSC Physics Text, provide a very good example of adjunct programming. They used these materials in their research studies. Students using the auto instructional materials studied from the same text, worked the same problems, viewed the same films, and performed the same experiments as regular physics students. Cowan did not use a qualified physics teacher in the classroom to direct their studies. The use of auto instructional materials prepared for this study evidently provided a good physics programme, as students using these materials were able to demonstrate as well in achievement as those not using these materials but taught by a qualified PSSC physics teacher. In Siddiqis study students of experimental group used the auto-instructional materials under the guidance of their physics teacher, while, the students of the control group did not use such materials, they were taught by their teacher in a conventional way. The experimental group demonstrated statistically higher mean level of achievement in PSSC physics.

What Students Say about Programmed Instruction (PI)?

Siddiqi developed an Adjunct Programme for PSSC physics. It was student self-directed study guide m PSSC physics. Here are the comments (unedited) of some of the students who used it.

Strengths

1. "Students can do whenever they want to do. If we do not understand anything now, we can do it some other time."
2. "When you learn on your own, you are more apt to remember it."
3. "Student learns more if he goes on his own rate. In conventional classes superior students get frustrated. They want to go ahead. Slow students don't understand. Teacher stops the whole class. With these materials superior students also have an opportunity to go ahead. Every student is able to go on his own rate, not waiting for anybody, not trying to catch up with anybody."
4. "Teacher gets more time, when he can go and help other students. He goes to the student who has problems, and not to the student who does not have any problem; so he does not waste his time. Teacher's time can be put to better use. We do not need the teacher all the time. We only use him when we need him. Teacher can enrich the student more when he talks individually."
5. "PSSC text was easy to understand with these materials. Text was too complicated, and the guide made it simplified."
6. "Guide has more hints to do labs than does the lab manual."

7. "Self-tests were good. When I missed something, I went over it and it helped me very much to learn physics."

Weaknesses

1. "These materials were unable to motivate those who were not self-motivated to use these materials."
2. "This approach did not work for lazy students. Some students need a push and without a teacher always available to keep them working they have a tendency not to study. It's hard for some people to pace. It requires more discipline to work on your own."
3. "This approach is good for those who want to learn by this approach. If the student is the type who cannot go on his own, this approach is not good; he should (probably) be taught by the conventional method."
4. "Sometimes a student is isolated by this approach — text guide, problems, lab, text, guide; that's all he has to work with."
5. "Physics is such a hard subject that you have to have more teacher help."
6. "I did not like it too much, because I am lazy by nature."

How Teachers Feel about Programmed Instruction (PI)?

Teachers who taught the students using programmed instruction materials also pointed out some strengths and some weaknesses of mis approach of teaching.

Strengths

1. "These materials are excellent for |hose who have difficulty with PSSC physics."
2. "These materials enabled some students to achieve what they were unable to achieve without them."
3. "These materials developed in students an attitude of doing independent work, which they will need when they will go to College and University."

Weaknesses

1. "Only those students who feel responsibility learn more by this approach."

2. "These materials are not good for slow learners."
3. "Some students go behind and behind not because they were not capable to move but because they were lazy. Some students can read but they don't want to read. There is a problem of keeping the student motivated."
4. "This approach is more time consuming. Some students took more time to finish the same material."
5. "When working on their own only half of the students use their time effectively while others use their time doing something else."

Concluding Remarks of Students and Teachers for PI

The conclusion of a group of students regarding the autoinstructional material was: "With autoinstructional materials, the text, and a teacher to explain, the self-study would be most practical and best for students."

In general most of the students and teachers liked the programmed instructional materials and this approach of instruction. They pointed out individualisation, independence, self-pacing, self-evaluation, and better use of teacher's time as some of the major strengths of this type of instruction. More than half of the students and teachers liked individualised instruction. They reported that using this approach for instruction, the teacher got more time to interact with individual students. They pointed out that the PSSC Physics Students Guide made PSSC Physics easier for the students. They also pointed out that this approach of instruction was best suited for superior students. More than half of the students liked the idea of moving according to their own pace, but the teachers did not like this idea very much, as it was hard for them to cope with their students, when different students were doing different things in the same period. Most of the students and all the teachers pointed out that lack of self-motivation was the main weakness of this type of instruction.

Programmed Instruction Unit Development

Some of you as a science teacher will like to use programmed instruction materials in your science classes. Usually programmes are not available in the market. Though developing programmed instruction materials is a time consuming job, yet some of you will like to develop some programmed instruction units. It will be a good project for your instruction.

Before developing programmed instruction units, it will be nice if you learn how to develop them. One such programmed unit "Structure of an Atom" is given here as a Sample. You go through it, and after that we will discuss, how it is developed.

A Sample Programmed Unit

Structure of an Atom
(A Programme Unit)

Instructions to Students

This is not a test. This is a Programme designed for you to learn the Structure of Atom.

In this Programme you will find numbered paragraphs.

These paragraphs are called Frames. Read each Frame carefully and answer the questions given after each Frame.

Check your answers from the Answer key given at the end of the programme.

Frame 1. Matter is made up of very small particles called atoms. The smallest particle of matter is........

If answer is correct go to Frame 2, otherwise Repeat Frame 1.

Frame 2. Atom is made of various particles called electrons, protons and neutrons. Electrons are negatively charged particles. Protons are positively charged particles. Neutrons have no charge, that is, they are neutral.

Complete the following sentences:

(a) The positively charged particle of an atom is.....

(b) An electron has ...... charge.

(c) A neutral atomic particle is called.......

If answers are correct go to Frame 3 otherwise Repeat Frame 2.

Frame 3. Check the statement below that is true. A proton is:

(a) positively charged.

(b) negatively charged.

(c) neutral.

(d) sometimes positive, sometimes negative.

If answer is correct go to Frame 4, otherwise Repeat Frames 2 and 3.

Frame 4. Check the statement below that is true. A neutron is:

(a) positively charged.

(b) negatively charged.

(c) neutral.

(d) sometimes positive, sometimes negative.

If answer is correct go to Frame 5, otherwise Repeat Frames 2 and 4.

Frame 5. Check the statement below that is true. An electron is:

(a) positively charged.

(b) negatively charged.

(c) neutral.

(d) sometimes positive, sometimes negative.

If answer is correct go to Frame 6, otherwise Repeat Frames 2 and 5.

Frame 6. The weight of a proton is approximately equal to the weight of a neutron, and the weight of an electron is so small compared to the weight of a proton or a neutron that it can be neglected.

Check the statement below that is true.

The weight of a proton is approximately equal to the weight of:

(a) electron.

(b) neutron.

(c) each of them.

(d) none of them.

If answer is correct go to Frame 7, otherwise Repeat Frame 6.

Frame 7. The charge of an electron is equal and opposite to the charge of a proton. If the charge of an electron is -4 units, then the charge of a proton should be:

(a) –4 units

(b) +4 units

(c) more than 4 units

(d) less than 4 units

If answer is correct go to Frame 8, otherwise Repeat Frame 7.

Frame 8. If the charge of a proton is $+x$ units, the charge of an electron should be.......

If answer is correct go to Frame 9, otherwise repeat Frames 7 and 8.

Frame 9. An atom can be assumed to be spherical in shape. At its centre there is a very small space (compared to the atom as a whole) containing protons and neutrons. This space is called nucleus (Fig.).

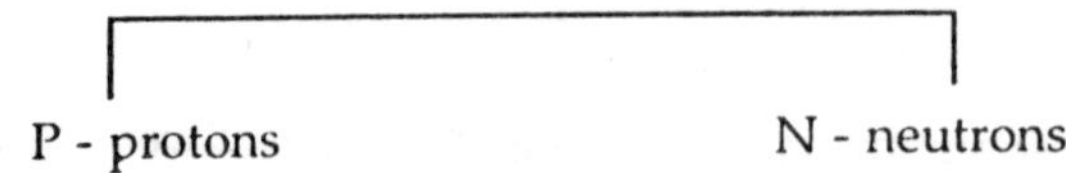

Fig.

Check the statement below that is true. The nucleus of an atom contains:

(a) protons only.

(b) neutrons only.

(c) protons and neutrons both.

(d) none of them.

If answer is correct go to Frame 10, otherwise Repeat Frame 9.

Frame 10. Around the nucleus some hollow spheres of different sizes can be assumed. The space between any two of such hollow spheres is called a shell (Fig.).

∇ — boundary of first hollow sphere.

Δ — boundary of second hollow sphere.

Fig.

Check the statement that is true.

(a) A is a shell.

(b) Λ is a shell.

(c) Both A and Â are shells.

(d) None of them are shells.

If answer is correct go to Frame 11, otherwise Repeat Frame 10.

Frame 11. As the number of electrons is equal to the number of protons and the charge of an electron is equal and opposite to the charge of a proton the atom as a whole is neutral.

Example—Sodium atom has 11 electrons and 11 protons. If charge of an electron is — x units, the charge of a proton will be $+x$ units.

Charge of 11 electrons = $-11x$ units.

Charge of 11 protons = +11x units.

Therefore total charge of sodium atom is equal to −11x plus +11x = 0.

Complete the following statements:

(a) A neutral atom has 40 electrons, then it should have.......... protons.

(b) If an atom has 10 electrons but only 9 protons, then the atom...... neutral (will be, will not be).

If answers are correct go to Frame 12, otherwise Repeat Frame 11.

Frame 12. Nucleus has protons and neutrons. Around the nucleus there exist electrons in various spherical shells.

Complete the following statements:

(a) Electrons exist in the.........

(b) Protons exist in the..........

(c) Neutrons exist in the. ....

If answer is correct go to Frame 13, otherwise Repeat Frame 12.

Frame 13. In a particular shell the electrons are assumed to be moving in various circular orbits. The total number of electrons in all the shells of an atom is equal to the number of protons in its nucleus. This number *i.e.* the number of protons or electrons in an atom, is called atomic number.

(a) Sodium has 11 protons in the nucleus. The total number of electrons in all the shells of sodium will be........

(b) The atomic number of sodium is.......

If answers are correct go to Frame 14, otherwise Repeat Frame 13.

Frame 14. The atomic number of oxygen is 8. What will be the number of protons in the nucleus, and the number of electrons in the shells?

(a) Number of protons is......

(b) Number of electrons is.......

If answers are correct go to Frame 15, otherwise Repeat Frames 13 and 14.

Frame 15. The sum of the number of neutrons and protons is equal to the atomic weight of an atom.

Example. Oxygen has 8 protons and 8 neutrons. Thus the atomic weight of oxygen is 8 + 8 = 16.

Sodium atom has 11 protons and 12 neutrons. Check the statement below that is true. Atomic weight of sodium is:

(a) 11

(b) 12

(c) 23

(d) 1

If answer is correct go to Frame 16, otherwise Repeat Frame 15.

Frame 16. Nitrogen atom has 7 protons and 7 neutrons. The atomic weight of nitrogen is.... .

Frame 17. The atomic weight of hydrogen is 1. It has 1 proton, then the number of neutrons in hydrogen atom is......

If answer is correct go to Frame 18, otherwise Repeat Frames 15,16 and 17.

Frame 18. The number of shells in an atom may vary from 1 to 7, that is the number of shells in an atom cannot exceed 7, though it can be less than 7 i.e. (6, 5,4,3, 2,1) depending upon the total number of electrons in a particular atom.

The number of electrons present in each shell is governed by 2 rules. *Rule 1*—The nth (n is the number of shell) shell cannot have more than $2n^2$ n electrons.

Example

For the first shell $n = 1$

therefore $2n^2 = 2. f = 2$

It means 1st shell cannot have more than 2 electrons (if the atom has more electrons they will be in the other shells), though it can have less than 2 (if there are not enough electrons in a particular atom).

For the 2nd shell $n = 2$

Therefore $2n^2 = 2 .2^2 = 2 .4 = 8$

It means 2nd shell cannot have more than 8 electrons though it can have less than 8 (as explained above).

According to this rule, there should not be more than:

(a)..... electrons in 3rd shell.

(b)...... electrons in 4th shell.

(c)..... electrons in 5th shell.

(d)..... electrons in 6th shell.

(e)..... electrons in 7th shell.

If answers are correct go to Frame *19*, otherwise Repeat Frame 18.

Frame 19. Oxygen has 8 electrons. According to the above mentioned rule write down the number of electrons in different shells.

Shell 1.......

Shell 2.......

Shell 3.......

If answers are correct go to Frame 20, otherwise Repeat Frames 18 and 19.

Frame 20. The atomic number of chlorine is 17. Write down the number of electrons in different shells.

Shell 1.......

Shell 2.......

Shell 3.......

Shell 4.......

If answers are correct go to Frame 21, otherwise Repeat Frames 18, 19 and 20.

Frame 21. *Rule 2*—Last shell cannot have more than 8 electrons in an atom, and the last but one shell cannot have more than 18 electrons. Complete the following statements:

(a) An atom has 5 shells. The number of electrons in its 5th shell should not exceed......

(b) The number of electrons in its 4th shell should not exceed........

If answers are correct go to Frame 22, otherwise Repeat Frame 21.

Frame 22. The atomic number of sodium atom is 11 and its atomic weight is 23. Write down the number of the following items of a sodium atom.

(a) Electrons...........

(b) Protons.........

(c) Protons and neutrons........

(d) Neutrons..........

(e) Electrons in 1st shell........

(f) Electrons in 2nd shell..........

(g) Electrons in 3rd shell...........

(h) Electrons in 4th shell...........

If answers are correct go to Frame 23, otherwise Repeat Frames 13-22.

Frame 23. The atomic number of carbon is 6 and its atomic weight is 12. Complete the carbon atom by putting at proper places the number of electrons, protons and neutrons.

If answer is correct congratulations, you learned what we wanted to teach you through this programme. If not please repeat Frames 13-23.

ANSWERS

Frame 1

Atom

Frame 2

(a) proton

(b) negative

(c) neutron

Frame 3

(a) positively charged

Frame 4

(c) neutral

Frame 5

(b) negatively charged

Frame 6

(b) neutron

Frame 7

(b) +4 units

Frame 8

X units

Frame 9

(c) protons and neutrons both

Frame 10

(b) B is a shell

Frame 11

(a) 40 protons

(b) will not be

Frame 12

(a) shells

(b) nucleus

(c) nucleus

Frame 13

(a) 11

(b) 11

Frame 14

(a) 8 protons

(b) 8 electrons

Frame 15

(c) 23

Frame 16

14

Frame 17

0

Frame 18

(a) 18

(b) 32

(c) 50

(d) 72

(e) 98

Frame 19

shell 1=2, shell 2=6, shell 3=0

Frame 20

shell 1=2, shell 2=8,

shell 3=7, shell 4=0

Frame 21

(a) 8

(b) 18

Frame 22

(a) 11

(b) 11

(c) 23

(d) 12

(e) 2

(f) 8

(g) 1

(h) 0

How was it Developed?

In developing this unit the System Approach was used. The System Approach (Fig.) has the following steps:

1. Identify problems and state terminal objectives.
2. Conduct task analysis.
3. Describe entry behaviours of students.
4. State sub-objectives in behavioural terms.
5. Develop evaluation instruments.

6. Determine instructional sequence.
7. Select appropriate media and instructional procedures.
8. Develop instructional materials.
9. Conduct formative and summative evaluation.

Terminal Objective

Given the atomic weight and atomic number of an element the students will find out the number of protons and neutrons in the nucleus and the number of electrons in the various shells of the atom.

Analysis of the Job

Hierarchical methodology (Fig.) was chosen for the programme Structure of an Atom. There is an ordered relationship between sub-skills which ultimately help to learn the terminal objective. The simple things are given first that makes the basis for more complex concepts.

Entry Behaviours

The assumed entry behaviours for this programme were the following:

1. Knowledge of some common elements such as oxygen, hydrogen, nitrogen, carbon, sulphur, sodium, chlorine etc.
2. Simple addition, subtraction, multiplication and division.
3. Knowledge of positive and negative charges.
4. Basic skills of reading, writing, generalizing, and following directions.

Behavioural Objectives

Behavioural objectives were prepared in such a way that they were consistent with each task in the task analysis.

All the behavioural objectives contain an observable response, important condition under which the behaviour will be evaluated, and the criterion for satisfactory performance.

Instruments for Evaluation

The test was made to test all the eleven behavioural objectives. It contained 16 test items. There were one or two test items to test each behavioural objective. All the test items are multiple choice tests and seems to be appropriate to test the task required in the behavioural objectives. The language used in writing test items was kept easy enough to be understood by the students.

This test was used as a Pre-Test, in which the items are sequenced m the same manner as they would appear in the programme (in the Sequence of Tasks and Behavioural Objectives). The same test can also be used as Post-Test (though a separate Post-Test is preferred), whose items should be scrambled, so that they are not in the same order as in the programme. In the multiple choice questions the order of correct responses was random.

Sequence for Instructions

The frames were constructed in the same sequence as shown in the task analysis. The frames were sequenced in such a way that by completing all the frames the terminal objective might be achieved by the students.

Medium in Vogue

The strategy of linear programming was chosen. The self-learning unit was an instructional programme, having enough practice frames.

Material for Instructions

A Programmed Instruction Unit Structure of an Atom was developed.

Programme Evaluation

Formative Evaluation. After writing the programme and the tests (pre-test and post-test) one IX class student was selected for one-on-one evaluation. This student was of an average ability. Two copies of the programme were prepared, one for the student and other for the programmer. When the student was using the programme, the programmer noted down his reactions and suggestions, which seemed to be important in revising the programme. The following feedback was received from one-to-one evaluation.

1. There was smooth flow or material in the programme, that is, the arrangement of the frames was logical.
2. At some places difficult language was used.
3. The programme needed more practice frames.
4. Frame No. 18 was not well explained, cue and prompt were also needed in this frame.

The programme was revised according to the feedback received from one-on-one evaluation. Then the programme was tried out on a small group consisting of five IX class students. Each student was given pre-test, the programme and the post-test. Before starting the programme the group was told about the programme and the importance of the criticism. They were also asked to write any suggestions if they have. They all took 40-55 minutes to complete the programme. Finally they were interviewed by the programmer and were asked to give their suggestions. The programme was further revised according to the feedback received from small group evaluation.

Simmative Evaluation. The revised programme was given to the target population, (150 IX class students) after giving the pre-test. There were few students who asked questions when going through the programme, but when they were asked to read the matter again they seemed to understand it. All of them were able to complete the programme in time (about 2 periods of 30 minutes duration). Post-test was given the next day.

The pre-test and post-test gain shows that 72 per cent of the students achieved 80 per cent or more objectives. The majority of the students used in the summative evaluation programme showed enthusiasm in working with the programme. Many of them said that they liked the new system of instruction and wanted to have more programmes like this. The vast pre-test to post-test gains exhibited by most of the students generated a great deal of excitement and confidence. This fact alone made the whole project a worthwhile experience for the students.

More About This Unit

Constructed Response Frame. As the word Constructed implies, no choice are presented to the student in a Constructed Response Frame. He does not select one response from many, as in the

Discrimination Frame. Instead, the student constructs his own response each time. That is, he supplies the answer from his own knowledge.

The response the student constructs can take many frames. He may be asked to write or supply a word or statement, draw a diagram, or perform any other type of over action requiring a response from within his own repertory.

Examples. Frames No. 1, 2, 8,11,12,13,14,16,17,18,19,20, 21,22 and 23. The Constructed Response frame is basically a two-part structure, the set frame and at least one *practice frame.* It may be desirable to have several practice frames with each set frame.

Set Frame. Whenever the response asked for is found in the data portion of the frame, it is known as a set frame. The student may never have seen the desired response prior to reaching this frame, but he is able to supply this response simply by deducing it from the data within the frame itself.

Examples. Frames No. 1, 2,11,12,13,14,16,18 and 21.

Practice Frame. The set frame is followed by a practice frame. The practice frame gives the student a chance to practise what he has learned in the set frame.

Examples. Frames No. 8,19, 20, 22 and 23.

Discrimination Frame. As the name implies, this construction technique is used to teach student to make discrimination. A student who has been taught to make fine discriminations through the use of Discrimination Frame sequence will find that he can go beyond the programme material and approach the subject matter from any direction. For example, if taught a definition by Discrimination Frame Sequence, he will be able to define it when given the term; if given the definition, he will be able to name the item; if physically possible, he will be able to illustrate it.

Examples. Frames No. 3,4,5,6, 7,9 and 15.

Baboon Frame. In this frame the student is asked to make a choice from among four answers: Choice A, Choice B, both A and B, or neither A nor B.

Examples. Frame No. 10.

Some More About Baboon Frame

Basically, the BABOON Frame Sequence consists of three frames similar in purpose to those of the Constructed Response Frame Sequence. The first frame is a set frame; it contains enough information to enable the student to come up with the correct response when asked to respond. This frame is followed by a practice frame; here the student is asked to demonstrate, with a little prompting. In the final frame, the minimum amount of stimulus is presented to the student and a maximum response is called for.

Examples

1. A Trapezium is a figure with four sides, two of which are parallel. Place a check mark (^) before the correct statement below check only one Answer.

.... A. Figure A is a trapezium.

.... B. Figure Â is a trapezium.

.... C. Both Figure A and Figure Â are trapeziums.

.... D. Neither Figure A nor Figure Â is a trapezium.

B. Figure A is a trapezium.

2. Place a check mark (^) before the correct statement below. Check only one answer.

Fig. A *Fig. B*

(A) Figure A is a trapezium.

(B) Figure B is a trapezium.

(C) Figure A and Figure B are trapeziums.

(D) Neither Figure A nor Figure B is a trapezium. D. Neither Figure A nor Figure B is a trapezium. 3. Define "Trapezium" and draw two figures. A trapezium is a figure with four sides, two of which are parallel (or words to this effect). The example figures that you have drawn should match this definition.

Programmed Units Categorised

Linear Programme. In linear programmes, all of the students are normally required to take all of the frame.

Example. The self-learning unit, "Structure of an atom" is a linear programme.

Linear Programme strategy was used in writing this Programme due to the following reasons:

1. The topic was new for most of the students for whom it was developed, and they were needed to be provided with a lot of practice.
2. The topic of the programme was of such nature that the subject matter involved ascending order of complex skills to be learned/ therefore it was felt that all the students should be required to take all frames.
3. The type of learning task necessitated mostly constructed response answers.

Branching Programme. The word branching suggests any deviation from the straight line, A Branching Programme allows for greater differences in student abilities.

The Branching Frame Sequence Technique. "Systematics" is given in Appendix I-1. This technique presents the student with remedial information/ if necessary and permits him to take steps that are as large as his capabilities allow. A particularly adept student may go through a programme in a minimum number of steps, whereas his less able cohort may require twice that number to learn, the same amount of material. The Branching Programme offers the student alternate paths from which to choose, and the path he takes depends upon the response he makes in each frame.

Units for Practice

Hence now you know how to develop a programmed instructional unit. Identify some topics in your field, on which you feel good programmes may be developed. Develop, evaluate and revise programmed instructional units on these topics, and share these self-learning units with your fellow teachers.

EXERCISE

1. What is the need of programmed instructional units in effective science teaching?
2. What is programmed instruction?

3. What are the bases of Behavioural Psychology for learning through programmed instructional materials?
4. What are the advantages of programmed instruction?
5. What is the scope of integrating science practicals with theory in programmed instructional materials?
6. What is adjunct programming? What are its two types? Discuss how adjunct programming can help in better science teaching.
7. Write some strengths and weaknesses of teaching or learning science through programmed instructional materials.
8. Write down the steps for developing a programmed unit using system approach.
9. What do you mean by:

   (a) task analysis, and (b) entry behaviours? Illustrate your answer with examples.
10. Distinguish between:

    (a) formative, and (b) summative evaluations.
11. What are:

    (a) Constructed Response Frames, (b) Discrimination Frames, and (c) Baboon Frames. Illustrate your answer with some examples..
12. Differentiate between:

    (a) linear, and (b) branching programmes. Illustrate your answer with examples.
13. Identify a topic in your field. Using all the steps of system approach, develop a programmed unit on this topic.
14. (i) Go through the following PI Units:

    (a) Structure of Atom.

    (b) Systematics.

    (ii) Write down the strength and weaknesses of each.

13

Individual Level Instructions

No two individuals are resemble. In a class there are students of varying science background, interest and science learning capacities. Some are slow learners and some comprehend the things very fast. They have different reading abilities. Some can read the books for hours, while some do not want to read for so long. These differences are there because of different social and cultural backgrounds of students and also because of some psychological factors. Students are also different in cognitive and psychomotor skills and processes. Individual differences loosely defined as intelligence are not recognised in a traditional system.

When a teacher in a traditional set up plans a lesson, these individual differences are not usually taken into consideration. The teacher assumes some pre-requisites of the lesson taking into consideration only the average child. In such situation for slow learners it is hard to understand what the teacher teaches, while for some fast learners the lesson becomes boring, as they already know most of the things and also learn fast. Therefore, above-average students get frustrated, they want to go ahead, slow students do not understand and the teacher gets worried about it. One way of solving this problem is that the instruction is individualised, so that superior students would also have an opportunity to go ahead. Eventually every student is able to go his own rate, not waiting for anybody, and not trying to catch up with anybody.

Socrates could interact with each of his pupils, man to man. He had an advantage of working with a few-selected students. But since Socrates' day, instruction has been directed toward education of masses. Now the aim is to lift the whole of masses out of the dark pit of ignorance.

With the increasing failure of teachers to communicate with individual students in large classes, it has become apparent that some other mode of instruction is needed to meet the demands of both the students and the learning process. According to Tyier a very necessary resource is a place where children may be taught individually or in small groups. There is an urgent need to devise learning situations in which only one or a few children are involved in order to understand the processes of learning more clearly and fully. Individualised instruction can make it possible for each student to learn what is most appropriate for him personally.

Individualised instruction is not new. It has been used for decades, even centuries, for a too far advanced child, or a child who had unusual motivation in a certain direction and wanted to move rapidly. It is, however, a relatively new experience when we teach the entire class in a formal educational setting individually, under the direction of a teacher.

Individualised Instruction Programmes are a boon to teachers who are attempting to alleviate problems of large classes, extreme variation in student backgrounds and abilities, ever expanding fields of knowledge, and greater need for coverage of material by students. They help students become more responsible for their own work. They relieve the teacher of some of the busy schedule of the conventional class. Individualised Instruction Programmes make the teacher free from usual classroom duties and provide time for the teacher to give individual attention to the student who really needs it.

Individualised Instruction can make it possible for each student to learn what is most appropriate for him. It is rightfully expected that the new science teaching approaches like individualised instruction will result in increased learning and in the development of more positive attitudes towards science. The idea behind individualised learning is very sound, but it will remain an idea and ideal unless it will represent ways of accommodating and satisfying the individual needs within the organisational framework of formal education.

Individualisation Bases

There are many approaches to individualisation. For any kind of individualisation in practice certain bases are important.

(i) The main load of information transfer is carried by printed material, therefore, it should be written very clearly.

(ii) Proper instructions to follow the instructional material should be given in the beginning.

(iii) The objectives of the study should be given very clearly so that the learner knows what is to be expected. It is better if objectives are given in behavioural terms.

(iv) The textual material should be written in a simple and understandable language. Topics should be divided into sub-topics or sub-units. Proper guidance should be given to do activities etc., if any.

(v) Self-evaluation questions should be given after each topic.

(vi) The role of the teacher should not be of direct teaching but of proper guidance and help to the students who need it.

Individualised Learning Procedures

Some of the procedures or mechanisms that have been used as individualised learning in formal educational programmes are reviewed briefly.

Programmed Instructions. The best known educational innovation of this century that is associated with individualisation is programmed learning. Provision of self pacing is very helpful for most of the learners. The breaking of subject matter in small steps and reinforcement by questioning makes it quite effective for most of the learners. Linear, branched and adjunct programming are all used quite effectively in making any programme individualised.

Individualised Instructional System. This is one of the model developed for individualised instructions for college subjects by Keller. The scheme is called "Keller Plan" or Personalised System of Instruction (PSI).

Keller Plan included large-chunk programming (different from programming mainly in the size of the frames). Many other similar schemes have been developed, they are called Individually Prescribed Instruction developed at the University of Pittsberg.

Individualised Instructions Through Computer. An important aspect of educational technology is the use of computers in teaching-learning process. In many developed countries computers are being used for giving individualised instruction, various names are given to these as Computer Aided Instruction, (CAI), Computer Assisted Learning (CAL), Computer Managed Instruction (CMI). They all follow the same basic structure. Because of its great speed of operation a computer can handle large number of students simultaneously, say 200 or more and they can be at different points in the curriculum. The student sits at the terminal device which could be an electric typewriter. Messages can be typed out by the computer and the student can enter his responses on the keyboard. It could also be a TV. screen where visual image is conveyed to the students and the keyboard again can be used to give responses. Student also receives information through audio messages from type written messages or visual displays ranging from graphics to complex photographs.

With such available devices individualised instruction in many subjects can be offered to the students of various levels.

Independent Study. Independent study is one of the various ways of Individualised Instruction. Independent study is not really new. It has been used for decades, even centuries, for a too-far advanced child, or a child who has unusual motivation in a certain direction and wants to move rapidly. It is however, a relatively new experience when we refer to entire classes of students working independently for external examination, under the guidance of their teacher, and yet given the opportunity to work at their own individual rates to accomplish what they know is expected for them in the way of objectives of the course.

In the recent years, science educators and psychologists of the stature of Schwab, Butts and Piaget have been advocating the necessity of devising independent study programmes in science.

Individualised Instruction Programmes

If we go into the literature, we find many individualised instruction programmes in science at various levels, developed and tried out in United States and other developed countries at school level. Here are some of the examples.

1. Mini Courses for undergraduate Biology at Purdue University.

2. A Self-Designed Science Curriculum as Rossford Junior High School, Rossford, Ohio.

3. Student-Designed Curriculum in Earth Science at Burbank Junior High School m Boulder, Colorado.

4. Individualising Science with Behavioural Objectives at Sahuaro High School, Tucson Arizona.

5. CAI Programme in Chemistry at the University School of Florida State University.

6. Junior High Earth Science at the Wilson Laboratory School, Mankate State College, Minnesota.

These are some of the many school level Individualised Instruction Programmes in science developed and used in their science classes by some innovative science teachers.

7. ISCS Project: Probing the Natural World. At the national level the Intermediate Science Curriculum Study (ISCS) developed a Junior High Curriculum (Class VII-IX) "Probing the Natural World/' at Florida State University. In this programme individualisation of rate of instruction has been achieved to a high degree. Some individualisation of content has also been accomplished through remedial, and enrichment units called "excursions."

8. HPP Multi-media Approach: The multi-media approach developed by Harvard Project Physics (HPP) is another individualised instruction programme at national level. It gives the student a number of options as to the actual learning experiences he will have in each of the six general units of subject matter around which the course is organised.

9. FSU School individualised Instruction Programme: This is a programme for grades VII-XII presented at the 1971 NSTA Convention at Washington D.C. It reported the efforts of the science faculty at the University School of the Florida State University toward individualising instruction. Craig, Parker, Summerlin, and Bolin the science teachers of the University School have done a wonderful job in individualising Life Science. Chemistry and Physics.

10. FSU Teachers' Initiated Projects (TIP): National Science Foundation (NSF) funded Department of Science Education of Florida State University for concluding a Summer Institute in individualising science programmes (Teachers Initiated Projects "TIP") in which selected science teachers from all over the United States worked on projects in the summer of 1972 to individualise science programmes for their respective schools. In this institute the participating teachers developed units in Physics, Chemistry and Biology according to their own needs, and a group of five Biology teachers (including Najma Siddiqi'), developed and Individualised Biology Course for High School Students. The Biology course was divided into the following ten units:

(i) Basic Unit of Life

(ii) Micro-Organism

(iii) Evolution

(iv) Ecology

(v) Anatomy Physiology Part I

(vi) Anatomy Physiology Part II

(vii) Biogenetics

(viii) Reproduction and Development

(ix) Genetics

(x) Animal Behaviour

Each unit was divided into many sub-units and well defined objectives were given for each sub-unit. To achieve these objectives variety of activities were suggested like specific reading from various available textbooks, work sheets, audio-visual material like slide/film strip, tape programmes, 16 mm films, film-loops and laboratory exercises. They could do the activities of their choice to achieve the objectives. After completing one or more sub-units students could take individual tests to see their progress. After completing the whole unit students were expected to take achievement test on the unit.

As for the setting of the room it was quite different from a traditional setting. Most of the material required by the students (except the one which could not be stored) was available in the room like glasswares, chemicals, other equipment, various textbooks, work sheets, tape-recorder, aquariums, vivariums etc;

Everything was marked and stored at a set place from where students could get the material without disturbing the teacher.

This individualised instruction programme in Biology utilising the various available Biology materials worked well in few Tallahassee (Florida) schools. It was quite successful in teaching biology concepts to different ability students. Some students were able to cover all the 10 units in one year, there were some who hardly could finish four thoroughly. This also helped in improving attitudes towards biology. The students enjoyed the personal relationship with the teacher and the teachers were able to give special guidance to each student to help him/her progress well. Another important observation was that slow learners and above average students were more benefited by this individualised programme.

11. PSSC Individualised Instruction Programme: Cowan and Siddiqi (Nasim) (Appendix 1-3) also tried to make PSSC Physics individualised. Cowan developed a set of auto-instructional materials for PSSC Physics at the University of Texas in 1962. These materials, in the form of an adjunct programme, were used later by his students as a study guide in his 1964 research study. Cowan did not use qualified physics teachers in his experimental classes. Students using the autoinstructional materials studied from the same text, worked on the same problems, viewed the same films, and performed the same experiments as students in the control schools but without having a qualified physics teacher present in the classroom to direct their studies. Teachers working in the experimental classes had no background in physics and were acting as adult supervisors. Cowan found that there was no significant difference in the mean level of achievement between students using autoinstructional materials and students not using such materials but taught by a physics teacher in a conventional way.

Since Cowan did not use qualified physics teachers in his experimental classes, there was no one to see how far the students were able to move in performing the suggested PSSC activities. There was no one to guide the students in solving the immediate problems.

Siddiqi (Nasim) revised Cowan's PSSC physics autoinstructional materials (for the revised PSSC physics 2nd edition text) at Florida State University in 1972 and used them in his research study with a different kind of set up. The students of the experimental group were asked to work individually or in small groups, and were allowed to interact with their physics teacher whenever necessary. Students were required to submit some assignments (as instructed in the auto instructional materials) to their teacher for correction.

The experimental and control groups covered the same content of the PSSC text, therefore the same standardised PSSC achievement tests were used for both the groups.

During visits to experimental schools, Siddiqi (Nasim) observed that most of the students were actively engaged. They were reading the text along with programmed materials. They were following the directions given in the programmed materials and working on their own, doing the labs and solving the problems. Whenever needed, they were also interacting with the teacher individually or in small groups. Not all the students however, were behaving like this. Some of them were not doing anything except sitting quietly, or talking about unrelated events or copying other students notes and assignments.

The experimental group achieved statistically higher than the control group. If achievement is accepted as a criterion for measuring the effectiveness of the Individualised Instruction Programme, on the basis of the results reported in this study, such individualised instruction materials used to teach PSSC physics were more effective than the conventional method of teaching. Similar material could be developed and tried out in other science subjects and at various grade levels.

Scope and Sphere

In many countries of the Western world individualisation of instruction in science is becoming quite popular to accommodate differences among individuals, so that the teaching may be made more meaningful and effective for all the students. As discussed earlier individualisation is done by single teacher for his/her own class, or by group of teachers together for their classes and some programmes have been developed at national level also for commercial use. In some such programmes individualisation is of pacing only, *i.e.*, all individuals will cover all the content but they will proceed at their own optimum rate. On the other hand in most other individualised instructional programmes students can select the content from a given set of content according to their background, interest, need and capabilities. In other words attempts are made to match educational programmes to individual's need and goals rather than the other way round. This is possible in these countries because the educationists and authorities are trusting the teachers and the teachers too have proved their worth. Also the classroom teacher is not very tightly bound to a set and fixed syllabus, he has the option to choose one and even develops his own syllabus for the subject, gives his own examination and even different examination to different students.

In India we have a fixed syllabus to cover and common external examination is given to secondary and senior secondary classes. Though in primary and middle schools, in most of the States and Union Territories there is no external examination but still most of the teachers are not utilising the freedom to bring any flexibility in curriculum to make the teaching more learner centred. Under the present situation it does not seem possible to give such individualised learning where students can pick and choose the content and material according to their interest and abilities. But individualisation in terms of pacing is possible to a certain extent. Most of our science teachers are not conscious of these new approaches in teaching. Very few try this approach of individualised instruction once in a while in their classes. There are many problems also. Developing individualised instructional materials is a time consuming job, it also needs expertise and experience. Our teachers are much loaded perhaps do not have time and expertise to develop such materials. If opportunity is given to them they will surely like to use such materials in their science classes.

(i) Some Innovative teacher educators have developed some individualised instruction material for teaching science. Siddiqi (Najma) of University of Delhi has developed two self-learning Biology units for class XI based on the syllabus prescribed by Central Board of Secondary Education (CBSE), New Delhi.

1. Unit 1 Systematic.

2. Unit 2 Man and Environment.

These units were used in about 10 Delhi schools on an experimental basis during 1982-83.

(ii) Mathur of NCERT has developed a set of 21 self-learning units for class XI physics based on the prescribed syllabus of CBSE, in a series of workshops in which a number of experienced physics teachers participated. This set of self-learning units is a package for Individually Guided System of Instruction (IGSI), for the use of students learning class XI physics with individualised instruction approach. These units cover the entire class XI physics syllabus.

Unit 1 Scalars and Vectors

Unit 2 Measurement

Unit 3 Applied Mathematics and Kinematics

Unit 4 Laws of Motion

Unit 5 Projectile Motion

Unit 6 Work, Energy and Motion

Unit 7 Impulse and Momentum

Unit 8 Circular Motion

Unit 9 Rigid Body Rotation

Unit 10 Kinetic Theory of Gases I

Unit 11 Kinetic Theory of Gases II

Unit 12 Thermodynamics I

Unit 13 Thermodynamics II

Unit 14 Radiation

Unit 15 Surface Tension

Unit 16 Fluid Dynamics

Unit 17 Electricity I

Unit 18 Electricity II

Unit 19 Electromagnetism

Unit 20 Applied Electromagnetism

Unit 21 Astronomy

NCERT has asked SCERTs of various States and Union Territories to try out this individualised instruction programme in some of their schools.

There are topics in every course which are not very interesting to teach or in some topics lot of drilling is required, some such portions can be selected by the teachers and similar individualised instruction material in all science subjects and at all levels can also be developed by some innovative teachers or groups of teachers, which can be shared by other teachers in their science classes. We should give a try to such innovative ideas.

EXERCISE

1. What is the need of individualised instruction in science teaching?
2. Discuss the following individualised instruction programmes:
   (a) ISCS Project: Probing the Natural World
   (b) HPP Multi-media Approach
   (c) Teachers Initiated Projects (TIP)
   (d) PSSC Individualised Instruction Programme.
3. Identify a topic of your choice in a subject of your field. Develop an individualised instruction programme for your science class.
4. Programmed Instruction is one way of individualised instruction. Discuss.

14

Planning the Lessons

If any activity is well planned in advance comes out to be successful, so is the classroom teaching. If a teacher plans his lesson beforehand, he knows what he is going to teach, how he is going to teach, what teaching aids he is going to use, what questions he is going to ask, what questions students might ask, what objectives he is going to achieve and how he is going to evaluate that he has achieved his identified objectives. The answers of such questions make a lesson plan. For a beginning teacher it (lesson plan) may be a detailed script and for an experienced teacher it may be a small package of some teaching points in the written form or just in his mind. For a science teacher a lesson plan comes out to be very effective and economical.

It is advisable for a science teacher to select and organise in a logical sequence, the suitable material for classroom instruction. Where should he start today's lesson with respect to where he ended yesterday? If yesterday's lesson ended with the completion of a demonstration showing that certain solutions under given conditions conduct electricity, how should he develop his lesson today? Should the demonstration be repeated at the very beginning of the lesson? Should the students be asked to tell what they observed yesterday? Should the same apparatus for conductivity of solutions be placed on the demonstration table. Should the teacher state the conclusions drawn, yesterday? Should the basic generalisations be asked from the students?

When teaching a certain lesson, what questions should the teacher ask? Should the teacher answer all the questions raised by the students, or the students leave the classroom with some questions unanswered? When the teacher is lecturing or demonstrating, should the student note down all the information, applications or uses?

There are several possible answers to the above questions. The teacher should give serious thought to such questions when developing his lesson plan, in order to arrive at an efficient and economical approach to teaching. The format of the lesson plan and the actual written material in it are not of great importance. The significant factor is that the lesson plans provide the science teacher with the opportunity of checking which of the suggested teaching methods are potentially most effective for achieving the identified objectives of the lessons.

Lesson Plan : Features

The important features of what a lesson plan should contain are:

(i) Why should we teach this lesson (Objectives)?

(ii) What should we teach in this lesson (Content)?

(iii) How should we teach this lesson (Methods)?

(iv) How should we know that students have learned what we taught them (Evaluation)?

Objectives. In listing objectives for a particular lesson, careful thought should be given to such categories as understanding factual information and its application as well as developing: (a) problem solving skills, (b) scientific attitude, (c) critical thinking, (d) interest in science and (e) values. It is unlikely that objectives covering all categories be attempted in one lesson. Some of these objectives like developing scientific attitudes or problem solving skills may be attended over a long period of time after several lessons. Such objectives should be written as general objectives. When developing lesson plans, the teacher should write only those objectives (as specific objectives) for which he is quite sure, that he would be able to achieve at the end of that lesson. Sometimes some student-teachers write quite a number of objectives in their lesson plans, perhaps to impress their supervisors, while only few of them they probably achieve.

Content. The teacher should take up only that much content, which he feels he will be able to cover in the limited time. In introducing a lesson, especially when a new unit is being taught for the first time, the teacher should attempt to stimulate, motivate and generate student's interest in the topic. Student's past and present experiences can serve an effective approach to new units.

Other ways of launching content with the ultimate aim of motivating students to learn a particular topic may be: (a) giving special homework assignments that require research, (b) survey conferences, (c) investigations, (d) special readings, (e) experiments, and (f) observations. The teacher may also bring in or ask students to bring in new articles (from magazines, journals or newspapers) of contemporary importance and relate such reports with the content of the lesson as well as with the needs and interests of the students and the community. Students may also be encouraged to bring in various supplementary material pertaining to the topic of the lesson. In short the teacher should utilise all these means for the selection of content and should not limit himself only to the textbook.

Methods. There are several methods of teaching science. Now when the teacher has identified the objectives of the lesson and selected the content to be covered, this is the right time to select an appropriate method of teaching the lesson. He should choose the method/methods which best fits/fit in the lesson. The teaching method should be compatible to the cognitive level of students, identified objectives and existing classroom conditions (number of students, size of the classroom, duration of period, availability of apparatus for classroom demonstrations and experiments, and other audio-visual aids etc.). There are several audio-visual aids for teaching science. The teacher can select some appropriate audio-visual aids from those available and improvise or make some on his own which best fit in the lesson. It should be noted that only appropriate-audio-visual aids should be used in the lesson, and those too if they are actually needed. Sometimes mostly student-teachers use so many audio-visual aids in one lesson, which make the lesson more confusing instead of interesting and clarifying the difficult ideas. This should be avoided. The appropriate audiovisual aids may be used to introduce the lesson as well as during the entire lesson.

Evaluation. This part of the lesson plan helps the teacher to determine to what degree learning occurs during the lesson. Several key questions asked by the teacher (during the lesson or at the end of the lesson) and the kinds of responses obtained from the students will enable the teacher to evaluate the degree of learning. Students' questions will also give the teacher some insight into the nature of difficulties that some students might have. A summary which elicited from the students at strategic places during the lesson as well as at the end of the lesson will also provide the science teacher with an evaluation of the teaching-learning process.

Questioning as an Art

The art of questioning is also critical when teaching a lesson of science. We should not underestimate the importance of questioning skills increasing or diminishing student participation. We ask questions for a variety of reasons.

(i) To obtain feedback about the level of understanding in the class.
(ii) To know what they already know.
(iii) To promote thinking.
(iv) To draw attention to something.
(v) To provide the student with an opportunity to verbalise his ideas in a coherent way.
(vi) To give opportunities to praise and encourage a student, and
(vii) To act as a measure of class control etc. etc.

To meet this variety of purposes requires many forms of questions, some of greater subtlety than those which have one simple, factual, and correct answer. To promote thinking requires more open ended questions, i.e., those having more than one acceptable answer.

In addition to questions and students' oral responses, evaluation in the course of a period may also be made by observing the students working at their seats or those who may be asked to come to the blackboard. When students are in the science laboratory careful observation of their work habits will also reveal the nature of their learning. A science teacher can observe a student's error at the board, at the desk or in the laboratory and correct the mistake promptly to prevent a block to learning the major and minor ideas of the lesson.

Learning Stimulated

In addition to the four criteria suggested above for lesson planning, the science teacher should be conscious of some other important points when he is just about ready to teach. Why should these students desire to learn the solution to the problem or understand the scientific principle? Psychologists often refer to *motivation*. How does the teacher motivate the students to learn each lesson? The teacher can set the stage for learning by presenting an inspiring demonstration, a series of experiments, and questions or problems in which the students can become involved or in which they can identify themselves with specific situations.

Students interests, needs or experiences can serve as the spring-board for introducing the lesson. Some teachers may begin with their own personalised experiences, the showing of a film or slides, or having a student or group of students bring in and discuss a science project. There are some typical ways in which the science teacher attempts to stimulate learning with the hope that the students will be motivated to learn. Here lies the need for flexibility in the lesson planning. Some students may actually assist in the planning of instruction if given the proper opportunity. Such students should be more strongly motivated to learn the basic ideas of the lesson under the guidance of the science teacher, so that they could assist their teacher in the classroom when teaching science to the entire class.

Various Steps

There are many types of lesson plans. The Hebertian steps provide us with the best, basic lesson plan Hebertian steps of a lesson plan are as follows:

1. Preparation
2. Aim
3. Introduction
4. Method (Presentation)
5. Application
6. Recapitulation (Revision and Conclusion).

Preparation. However knowledgeable you may be, and however certain you may be of what you wish to teach, you must plan how much and by what method you propose to teach for a successful lesson.

Time must be your first consideration. Very often the bell rings when the lesson is just half completed. Duration of period should be divided into three parts — time for teacher's activities, time for students activities, and time for recapitulation.

Secondly, you must plan your lessons in terms of the specific objectives for the lesson identified by you, *i.e.*, what you wish to achieve in a 30-40 minutes period at your disposal.

Thirdly, you must plan your lesson according to the cognitive level of your students, taking into consideration their age (maturity level) and aptitude.

Fourthly, you must well prepare yourself for the lesson asking yourself a few questions like these. Do you have the requisite knowledge and background for the lesson? Can you perform adequately the skills you propose to teach? Have you considered the way you will start and proceed for, your lesson?

Fifthly, you must prepare all the materials and teaching aids necessary for the lesson, asking yourself a question. Have you arranged these materials (specimens, charts, illustrations, maps, diagrams, models etc.) in a sensible manner so as to achieve sequence and unity in your lesson.

Sixthly, you must ensure that your students are prepared before the lesson starts with everything necessary for the lesson.

It has been seen infinitely that more lessons are ruined by neglect of these simple preparations. It would be advisable that a sound teacher should consider himself as a stage manager who must have all that is necessary in the way of effects, scenery and properties available at the precise moment that they are needed so that a smooth production is achieved.

There is, moreover, a vital psychological aspect to this question of careful preparation. Students react quickly to efficiency. If they are obliged to behold daily a fumbling an ill-prepared teacher they will speedily lose respect for such a person. On the other hand the daily spectacle of business-like preparation on the part of their teacher will earn their admiration, and incidently, their polite attention.

Remember

Prepare your lesson.

Prepare yourself.

Prepare your materials and teaching aids.

Prepare the material and aids for your students.

Aim. Following a successful preparation the teacher must state clearly the aim of the new lesson. (The aim may further be subdivided into some general and specific objectives which are going to be achieved during the lesson.) The students must know the purpose and objectives of the lesson. If they know clearly what they are supposed to achieve, then their thought processes will follow more easily the teacher's exposition, explanation and steps of the lesson.

Remember

A class of students without an aim is like a leaderless army.

The students must know where they are going.

The aim of the lesson must be stated clearly and emphatically.

Introduction. If the lesson has been sensibly prepared, the teacher will have taken pains to plan a suitable introduction. The introduction should not only set the atmosphere or mood for the lesson, but it should gather together the students and focus their concentration on to the subject in hand. To prevent initial in attention, attention should be paid to two aspects of the introduction stage of your lesson — social introduction and subject introduction.

Social Introduction. You should greet the students courteously and discuss with them the exciting things they have been doing. Be human and sociable with them for a minute or two and gradually calm them down by friendly conversation.

Subject Introduction. After this brief social introduction, you should introduce them to the nature of the present lesson. This is perhaps best achieved by reminding them (by questioning) of the ground covered in the previous lesson on the subject, or activity in hand. Educationally it is vital to proceed from the firm base of the 'known' before attempting to explore the territory of the 'unknown.'

This can be achieved by putting the new knowledge which is linked up with their previous knowledge gained in the previous lesson or from everyday experiences. In order to develop curiosity for learning, the teacher should make the students realise that their knowledge is incomplete and a lot of new knowledge is still left to be acquired by them. Thus you may involve the following steps:

(i) testing their previous knowledge;

(ii) asking short reflective questions enabling students to realise their ignorance of numerous scientific facts and create interest therefore in learning the new subject matter;

(iii) using audio-visual aids; and

(iv) performing interesting demonstration relevant to the topic of the lesson.

Remember. Introduction is the bridge between the previous activity and the present activity.

Introduction creates the new mood for the new lesson. a Introduction is necessary to prepare the minds of the students for me new topic of activity. Introduction is the process of rallying the minds and bodies of children to face a new experience.

Method (Presentation). You have learned several methods of teaching science. You should practise all the methods in your practice teaching taking into consideration the: (a) objectives of lesson, (b) cognitive level of students, and (c) classroom conditions.

When teaching science it should be kept in mind that students' activities are predominant than the teacher's activities. Remember it is the student's lesson, and not your lesson. Restrict yourself to a brief introduction, statement of aim and a short, thought-provoking exposition and explanation and then employ to the full all the senses of the students (as for as possible) — the hands (learning by doing), the eyes (learning by seeing), the ears (learning by hearing), the mouth (learning by saying), the nose (learning by smelling), and the tongue (learning by tasting). Only at the end of the lesson you should use your voice emphatically to summarise the lesson. If your students find out things themselves and reach solutions by constructive reasoning there will be infinitely more satisfaction for them than if they are constantly 'told' by you.

Thus, after the students are prepared to receive the lesson, and the teacher has clearly stated the aim of the lesson, he should start the lesson, and the students should get the new ideas and knowledge. Here the teacher should draw out the maximum from the students by asking suitable questions. The lesson should proceed with the actual participation of both the students and the teacher. It can be made more interesting and concrete by the use of the suitable audio-visual aids and experimental demonstrations.

The new ideas and knowledge to be given to the students should be related as far as possible with their previous knowledge. This is a very important point to be kept in mind when mtroducmg new scientific principal and generalising some new scientific facts.

Finally the students are in a position to generalise what they have learned so far. Answers to some relevant questions now asked by the teacher, he will be able to draw out various scientific principles/ conclusions and formulae. Thus, the students receive the new knowledge and the teacher acts as a guide for them.

Remember. Your methods of teaching should a make the students think a make the students. Do a make the students. See a make the students. Say a make the students hear.

Application. In order to develop interest and satisfaction among students for the subject they should be made familiar with the use and application of various generalisations in daily life and conclusions drawn out. The new knowledge thus gained by the students becomes more meaningful and permanent for ever. In former'times application merely consisted of the students proving by stereotyped exercises that they had learned what teacher had taught them. The very words 'test' or 'exercise' explain this former conception. Without denying the value of this practice, we find that application has, to the progressive teacher, a much wider significance. As we have decided,, it is vital that the teacher employs an interesting, imaginative and lively method of presenting his subject matter, it is equally vital that such a presentation be matched by an interesting, imaginative and lively application.

Remember. Knowledge and skills must be applied and practised if they are to be lasting benefits to your students.

Minimum of presentation, maximum of application.

Match an interesting presentation by an interesting application.

Recapitulation (Revision and Conclusion). "Teach little, revise more" is an excellent slogan for a teacher. It is not correct to imagine that more than sixty per cent of anything you teach for the first time will be observed by the students. For this reason, you must reinforce what you have taught by causing the students 'to see, say and do ' the things you have presented to them orally.

Revision is essential to any piece of teaching and without it the ablest presentation will only be partially successful. You must revise as you teach and you must revise as you have taught.

It is vital that no lesson should be concluded without an emphatic summary of what has been taught. At least five minutes must be allocated by the teacher in the lesson plan for this purpose of hammering home what has been taught, by a systematic review or recapitulation of what has been achieved.

Here the knowledge imparted to the students is tested by asking some relevant questions. This is a way of revising the lesson by question-answer technique. This also enables the teacher to find out whether the students have followed what he has taught them, and whether or not the method of teaching is effective.

This summary should be first drawn from the students by questioning and then repeated with vehemence by the teacher as he points to the main items summarised on the blackboard. Revision is thus oral, aural and visual. The teacher speaks and illustrates and the pupils hear and see.

Remember

Revision, Revision, Revision.

Now Summarise and Revise the Stages of Your Lesson Plan.

You have *prepared* your lesson thoroughly.

You have stated your *aim* clearly.

You have *introduced* it humanly.

You have employed an interesting *method.*

You have devised an imaginative *application.*

You have *revised* your lesson decisively.

Lesson Plan Models

Some lesson plans are given in Appendix A as SAMPLE. You can go through them before making your own lesson plan.

Planning the Units

Planning a Unit is similar to lesson planning. A Unit may have several lessons. Therefore it may not be completed in one class period. It may take several class periods to complete a Unit. If Unit Plans are given in Teacher's Guides, they might be very useful for the science teachers specially the new teachers.

A new teacher feels difficulty in treating a topic in his class not because he does not know the subject matter, but because he does not know exactly how much subject matter in a certain topic suits the varying age-levels of the students. Again he faces the difficulty in selecting the teaching material. He also finds it difficult to decide what activities should be undertaken to cast a lasting impression on the minds of the students. Very often, the teachers specially the new ones do not have enough practice of how to evaluate how far the students have followed what they have been taught.

But for the many experienced science teachers it may be quite easy. Thus, a beginning teacher may take advantage of their experiences, but they are not always available to him. But if NCERT and SCERTs invite such experienced science teachers to develop Unit Plans on some selected science topics, it would be of great help not only to freshers, but to others too. Such a Unit Plan may also be termed as Teaching Unit.'

Steps of a Unit Plan. A Unit Plan may be written in the following steps:

1. Subject: (Physics, Chemistry, Biology or Science)
2. Topic: (Heading of the Unit)
3. Class: (To whom the Unit is to be taught)
4. Time: (No. of class periods)
5. Aids: (To be used during the entire unit)
6. Content: (Syllabus to be covered)
7. Sub-units: (No. and Name)

8. Objectives: (To be achieved after completing the Unit)

For ***Each Sub-Unit***

9. Sub-unit No. and Name (Heading)

10. Time: (No. of class periods)

11. Teacher's Activities

12. Student's Activities

13. Joint Activities (Teacher's and student's)

14. Assignment

15. Follow-up Activities

16. Evaluation

17. References

Under these steps A Sample Unit Plan "Lifting of Heavy Bodies by Smaller Forces" for IX Physics is developed and is given here for guidance. Similar Unit Plans may also be developed in other science subjects — Chemistry or Biology and for any class level.

A Sample Unit Plan

Subject: Physics

Topic: Lifting of Heavy Bodies by Smaller Forces

*Class:*IX

Time: 11 periods, each of 30-40 minutes duration

Aids: Tool chest. Planks of wood, 16 mm film projector/VCR/ VCP.

Introduction. Here a teacher is not to teach all that is given in the chapter on 'simple machines' found in any secondary physics textbook. What is important in the class level we are going to teach, *i.e;* the intellectual level of me learners.

1. Intricate mathematical calculations should be avoided.
2. Subject-matter not in keeping with the cognitive level of learners should be eliminated.
3. A teacher, however, may add something new that he deems necessary, even if it is not given in the textbook.

This Unit may be divided into the following sub-units:

1. Classification of different devices
2. Levers
3. Wheel and axle, and pulley
4. Inclined plane, and jack.

Objectives

1. To find out from children what devices they have used or seen being used for lifting heavy bodies.
2. To classify these devices into different categories.
3. To help the children understand how these devices are used in everyday living.
4. To help the children construct such devices or their models.
5. To enable the children to distinguish between the utility of the various devices in various situations.

Sub-Unit 1: Classification of Different Devices

Time: 2 Class periods (60-80 minutes) *The Teacher's Activity:* To pose the following problems:

1. How can a child defeat a team of wrestlers in a tug of war?
2. How can a man have his truck lifted in order to remove a flat tyre?
3. How could a new born baby lift his father?
4. How can a man lift his scooter on a platform, which is about one metre above the road?

The Student's Activity: With the help of past experiences the students will:

1. try to solve these problems, and
2. suggest why certain devices are used and not others. (These devices will be listed on the blackboard).

Part Played by the Teacher: The teacher will give finishing touches to the list of the devices suggested by the students. He may ask the students to bring, either the actual devices or the models to the next class meeting. The teacher's own enthusiasm and initiative in this direction will be of supreme importance.

Joint-Activity (Teacher's and Student's): The following day, the devices brought by the students the actual ones or in the form of models should, after demonstration and explanation, be classified into:

1. Lever
2. Wheel and axle
3. Pulley
4. Inclined plane
5. Jack

Sub-Unit 2: Levers

Time: 2 Periods (60-80 minutes) *Main Activity:* Projection of 16 mm film on 'Levers' showing its video:

1. What is a lever and how is it used?
2. Experiments with levers.
3. How often levers are used in everyday life?

Teacher's Activity

1. The teacher should see the film beforehand. If the commentary is in English and the language is too difficult for the students, the teacher should prepare his own commentary (in Hindi or any other regional language) and give his commentary stopping the sound of the projector.
2. Pre-projection activities should include the introduction of the topic to be viewed by the students, so that they should know what they are going to leam from the film. Follow-up activities should include clarifying concepts not followed by the students.

Assignment: Classroom activities may be co-ordinated with science club activities. Students may engage themselves in making models and drawings of levers. A time-limit for the completion of the work should be set up by the teacher,

Sub-Unit 3: Wheel and Axle and Pulley

Time: 2 periods (60-80 minutes)

Main Activity: Projection of 16 mm film on "Wheel, and Axle, and Pulley" or showing its video:

1. The construction of the wheel and axle device.
2. How this device increases force and speed?
3. In what situations pulleys are used?
4. Types of pulleys.
5. How a small child can defeat a strong man in a tug of war by using pulleys?
6. How all these devices help us in everyday life?

Teacher's Activity: Same as in Sub-unit 2.

Assignment: Similar to Sub-unit 2, to suit what is taught in Sub-unit 3.

Sub-Unit 4: Inclined Plane and Jack

Time: 2 periods (60-80 minutes)

Main Activity: Projection of 16 mm film "Inclined Plane, Wedge and Screw" or showing its video:

1. What is an inclined plane and how is it used to increase force.
2. What is a wedge, and how is it used in everyday life?
3. What is a screw, and why is it considered a machine?

Teacher's Activity: Same as in Sub-unit 2.

Assignment: Similar to Sub-unit 2 to suit what is taught in Sub-unit 4.

Follow-up Activities

Time: 2 periods (60-80 minutes)

1. A display in the laboratory of the charts and models made by students.
2. Those who have made the models and charts could be asked to explain their work to other students.

Note : This activity will need the supervision of the teacher.

Evaluation

Time: 1 period (30-40 minutes)

The construction of an objective type test on the matter covered, and to see if the objectives of the Unit have been achieved.

References

1.16 mm films

(a) Levers — English, 11 minutes

(b) Wheel and Axle, and Pulley — English, 11 minutes

(c) Inclined Plane, Wedge and Screw — English, 11 minutes.

Note : These films or videos can be borrowed from The Central Institute of Educational Technology (CIET), NCERT, New Delhi.
2. UNESCO Source Book of Science Teaching.

EXERCISE

1. What is the need of lesson planning?
2. "Objectives, Content, Methods and Evaluation" are the four important features of what a lesson plan should contain? Discuss.
3. Why do we ask questions during teaching-learning process?
4. What is the role of motivation when teaching science? How can you motivate your students in your science classes?
5. What are the various steps of a lesson plan? Give a brief description of each step.
6. What are the various steps of preparation in lesson planning? Discuss.
7. What are the various steps of introduction of a lesson plan? Discuss.
8. What is the utility of stating the aim and specific objectives in the lesson plan? Discuss.
9. Your method of teaching should make the students think, do, see, say and hear. Discuss.

15

Curriculum (India)

Science Curriculum Programmes at national level began after the establishment of National Council of Educational Research and Training (NCERT) on 1st September 1961 with its headquarters at New Delhi. Besides many functions, NCERT develops curriculum, instructional materials, techniques of evaluation, teaching aids, kits and equipment etc.

In the last four decades, NCERT has developed several National Science Curriculum Programmes at all the school levels —primary, middle, secondary and senior secondary. In this chapter some of the several National Science Curriculum Programmes are discussed.

Programme of UNICEF

With a view to studying the existing science education programme in India a planning mission from UNESCO visited several States and Union Territories in 1964 and made some recommendations for improvement in teaching of science in Indian schools. In order to expedite the implementation of the scheme, it was decided by the Government of India, Ministry of Education and Social Welfare to launch a pilot project from the beginning of the next academic year. The pilot project covered Primary classes (I-V) and Middle classes (VI-VIII), and was funded by UNICEF. This project was called UNICEF-Assisted Science Education Programme (SEP).

Practical Aspects

Under this project NCERT developed a national primary

science programme, "SCIENCE IS DOING" in 1970. Its adapted, adopted and translated (in regional languages) versions were used in most of the primary schools in the country. This programme was a package of:

(a) Class III-V Text Books;

(b) Class III-V Teacher's Guides;

(c) Primary Science Kit and Kit Guide;

(d) Class I-II Syllabus;

(e) Two 16 mm films for Teacher Training;

(i) Science is Doing; and (ii) Primary Science Kit.

In spite of such a good primary science programme when we went into the classrooms, we found that science was not doing; science was either reading, telling or in very few cases 'science was demonstrating.

Cognitive Development Studies

In Delhi Directorate of Education, Siddiqis conducted research studies on cognitive development of primary school children, during 1975-77 on 1206 Delhi Primary school children. It was found that majority of primary school children (95.6 per cent) is either pre-operational or concrete operational, and a very small percentage (4.4 per cent) is at formal operational stage. Similar results could also be obtained in other parts of the country. This shows that working with concrete objects or doing experiments is a very important part of primary science education.

The following recommendations are based on these studies for the purpose of providing guidelines to teachers who teach science to primary school children and to science educators who develop instructional material — textbooks, teachers' guides, audio-visual aids etc., and design teaching techniques:

1. Discourage traditional teaching techniques like book reading and teacher telling.
2. Involve children in activities with concrete objects and doing experiments with their own hands.
3. Encourage children to find out facts of science by doing experiments and not to memories

4. Delete the science concepts and skills from the existing science texts which are not compatible with the cognitive level of children.
5. Delete the activities from the existing science texts which are not compatible with the cognitive level of children.
6. Introduce only those concepts which are compatible with the cognitive level of children of a particular class and in which use of concrete objects in their immediate environment may be possible.
7. Use local resources and environment which is full of real and concrete objects when teaching science to primary school children.

Similar studies could also be conducted on children at other school levels and the results could possibly have a positive effect on science teaching at all levels. These studies reveal that if our primary school teachers used environment and local resources and teach science through environmental approach, the learning will be more meaningful.

Studies in Environment

The National Policy on Education (Kothari Education Commission Report 1964-66) adopted by the Government of India recommends that science should form an integral part of general education for the first ten years of schooling. Therefore, NCERT examined the question of what type of science courses should be introduced at various levels of school system of 10+2 pattern. One of the major recommendations of the NCERT is that the child should learn the method of inquiry in science and should begin to appreciate science and technology in the life and the world around him. The NCERT recommends further that in classes I and II science should be taught as Environmental Studies (EVS), which includes both the natural and the social environment. Later on in classes III, IV and V, two subjects, *viz.*, EVS (social science) and EVS (general science) should be taught. There are certain areas where there will be variation depending upon the environment of the child. Hence, it is proposed that the equipment and materials locally available should be used for the teaching of science. Cycle, bullock cart, motor pump etc., available in the village set-up can be used in explaining many important concepts in science. Nature Should be used as a laboratory for science teaching.

EVS Objectives

On the basis of this (the Kothari Commission Report) NCERT had laid down certain objectives for teaching science through environment. They are stated as follows:

1. The main objective is to enable children to observe their environment and to enrich their experience, thereby developing skills in the processes of science, such as observing, communicating, measuring, hypothesising, and experimenting to test the hypotheses.
2. Besides developing skills in some processes of science, the children, through EVS (General Science) if given knowledge of scientific facts and principles, have a better understanding of the phenomena taking place in the environment around them.
3. The understanding of the environment through application of scientific method (the processes of science) will help children to develop a scientific attitude in life, which may comprise such components as rational outlook, open-mindedness, a positive inclination for democratic, secular, and socialistic outlook to situation in life, opposition to the prejudices based on sex, caste, religion, language or region.
4. Children will be helped to develop their creative faculties — their imagination and independent thinking for locating problems, suggesting solutions and trying out their ideas.

Primary Curriculum Revised

'Science is Doing' syllabus for classes I-V was revised. Environment which is full of concrete objects was taken into consideration when the revised science syllabus was framed, and the instructional materials were developed based on the revised Environment Studies (EVS) syllabus. The new curriculum, 'EVS Programme' developed by NCERT has the following materials:

(i) EVS class I-II (science and social studies) Teacher's Guide;

(ii) EVS (science) textbooks for class III, IV and V.

This programme is to be adopted or adapted by the States and Union Territories depending upon their own environment and local resources.

Activities Handbook

UNICEF also funded the interested States and Union Territories for developing 'Handbook of Activities Using Environment and Local Resources' for the use of primary school teachers teaching science, so that they could use NCERT developed EVS textbooks more effectively when teaching science with environmental approach.

Science Branch, Directorate of Education, Delhi also took this project. According to the findings of the Siddiqis' Research studies on the "Cognitive Development of Primary School Children (1975-77)" majority of primary school children (95.6 per cent) are either pre-operational or concrete operational and they need concrete objects to learn science concepts and skills. Our environment is full of real and concrete objects, which the children can use to learn science. Based on the findings of these research studies and their implications a "Handbook of Activities Using Environment and Local Resources" was developed by Science Branch, Directorate of Education, Delhi for the use of primary school teachers teaching science and social studies to classes I and II and science to classes III, IV and V. This UNICEF assisted programme consists of an Environmental kit and a package of seveit booklets:

(i) Class I Activities;

(ii) Class II Activities;

(iii) Class III Activities;

(iv) Class IV Activities;

(v) Class V Activities;

(vi) Envircnmental Kit Guide;

(vii) Class I-II (science and social studies) and classes III-V (science) syllabus.

This is the bank of activities for use of teachers. For one minc idea several activities have been developed to be fit in differei environments. This programme was tried out and revise according to the feedback received from experimental schools. Its English version is also available which might be useful for those who are interested or engaged in developing such materials in other States and Union Territories of the country as well as in other countries.

Programmes at Middle Level

Upto early sixties science at middle level was a general science course. It had a little content and in it no importance was given to science processes. Learning science was a book reading process with no emphasis on experimentation and demonstration. Only once a while some very innovative teachers used to do some demonstrations when teaching science. This process continued till 1964 when UNESCO came into picture, and a new disciplined science course came into existence for middle classes.

Programme under Discipline

This was a package of physics, chemistry and biology courses at the middle stage. These courses were introductory in nature and helped the students to familiarise with the basic concepts and processes compatible with the cognitive levels of students at this stage.

The main objectives of the science course were:

(i) to develop scientific knowledge;

(ii) to develop processes of science such as observation, experimentation, problem-solving and investigatory approach;

(iii) to develop scientific attitude;

(iv) to develop mechanical, experimental and mental skills;

(v) to develop the interest of science in children; and

(vi) to appreciate the role of science in everyday life.

Based on these objectives NCERT developed disciplined science courses in physics, chemistry and biology in mid-sixties. These courses were oriented in such a way that teaching of science was based on first hand experiences, practical experiments, which might be in the form of demonstrations by the teacher and individual laboratory exercises and up-to-date facts of science with suitable examples and illustrations from everyday life.

Physics Course. The physics course was a 3-year programme (VI, VII and VIII). The main objectives of physics teaching were:

To enable the child to:

(i) obtain the knowledge and understanding of the basic concepts and laws of physics;

(ii) acquaint themselves with the application of laws in everyday life;

(iii) obtain the understanding of the physical phenomena and basic laws governing them;

(iv) develop skills in solving problems, handling equipment and performing experiments;

(v) develop scientific attitudes and the spirit of scientific enquiry;

(vi) appreciate the laws of physical science in everyday life.

Based on these objectives, the physics programmes developed by NCERT was a package of:

(a) Class VI-VIII Physics textbooks;

(b) Class VI-VIII Physics teachers' guides;

(c) Class VI-VIII Physics test items;

(d) Class VI-VIII Physics kits (3 — one for each class) and kit guides;

(e) teacher training films (Physics kit — Parts I, II and III).

Chemistry Course. The Chemistry course was a 2-year programme (VII and VIII). The main objectives of Chemistry Teaching were:

To provide the children with:

(i) knowledge of the nature of substances, their properties and their atom-molecular composition;

(ii) knowledge and understanding of the nature of chemical changes, their types and basic laws governing them;

(iii) development of power of observation and ability to explain the chemical phenomena involved in the processes studied;

(iv) acquaintance with language of chemistry;

(v) development of skills in solving problems, handling substances and equipments to do experiments;

(vi) development of computational skills;

(vii) development of scientific attitude and spirit of scientific enquiry;

(viii) application of the role of chemistry in everyday life.

Based on the objectives, the chemistry programme developed by NCERT was a package of:

(a) Class VII-VIII Chemistry textbooks;

(b) Class VII-VIII Chemistry teachers' guides;

(c) Class VII-VIII Chemistry test items;

(d) Class VII-VIII Chemistry kit and kit guide;

(e) Teacher training films (Chemistry Demonstration Kit).

Biology Course. The Biology course was a 3-year programme (VI, VII and VIII). The main objectives of Biology Teaching were:

(i) To acquaint the students with the world of living things which surround them;

(ii) To discover the main laws and regularities governing the life processes;

(iii) To give an understanding of the nature of biographical science;

(iv) To create interest in pupils in life sciences enabling them in the solution of problems of everyday life;

(v) To give knowledge of:

(a) plants and their functions (Botany);
(b) animals and their functions (Zoology);
(c) the structure and functions of the human body (Human Physiology);
(d) man and his environment.

Based on these objectives, the biology programme developed by NCERT was a package of:

(a) Class VI-VIII Biology textbooks;

(b) Class VI-VIII Biology teachers' guides;

(c) Class VI-VIII Biology test items;

(d) Class VI-VIII Biology kit and kit guide;

(e) Teacher training film (Biology kit — Parts I, II and III). The Disciplined Science textbooks were written in such a way that science teachers in schools would have physics, chemistry and biology kits, but they could not be supplied to all the schools. Thus again, science teaching became a book reading or teacher telling process. Disciplined science curricula developed during sixties were assessed as inappropriate for the eighties. Isolated disciplines served to cut science off from our common humanity. For this it was decided to seek a curriculum with more attention to integrative system and operations that can interweave diverse disciplines.

Integrated Projects

During seventies a number of integrated science teaching projects and programmes were developed in various countries. These programmes embody a wide range of different approaches to integrate science teaching, including processes, concept, units, environment, applied science, thematic projects and patterns. As a part of 10+2 curriculum the NCERT also developed an integrated science programme for middle classes (VI-VIII).

If we review the overall aims and objectives of integrated science programmes, we find these three aspects are reflected, *i.e.*,

(a) the nature of science; (b) the nature of learners, and (c) the nature of society.

The Nature of Science

(i) The simple cognitive skills, such as the ability to recall knowledge, comprehend the basic concepts and themes of science such as the nature of matter, energy and its transformations, the nature and properties of living things, etc., and their application in novel situations.

(ii) The process skilis such as the ability to observe, measure, classify and predict. It is these skills that will largely influence the way in which the subject matter is taught.

(iii) The development of attitudes such as honesty and open-mindedness, and the realisation of the tentative nature of science theories. These are unlikely to arise from the courses unless the approach to practical investigation rejects true query.

(iv) The skills appropriate to science: these would include not only the ability to manipulate apparatus, but also to construct and interpret tables, charts and graphs, as well as to be able to find relevant information from sources of reference.

The Nature of Learners. It seems that many integrated science teaching programmes, most of which cover a period of several years of schooling, attempt to reflect the findings of research in the development of science and mathematics concepts in children. It looks, there appears to be considerable awareness in the designers of integrated science schemes that curriculum development should be geared to the thought of the child and not just to be logical structure of the subject.

The Nature of Society

(i) In the selection of aims for the course as a whole greater attention is paid to the overall needs of society. One reason for the widespread popularity of integrated science courses is an awareness that they can better reflect the aspirations of society than courses in single science discipline.

(ii) In the selection of subject matter, the social significance of science has been given prominence and technology has also crept into integrated science courses. Thus, the Integrated Science Project places heavy emphasis on integration of science, technology and society.

Based on these objectives a full curriculum package containing syllabus, textbooks, teachers' guides, kit and kit guide was developed during 1975-80. The process of development includes participation and interaction of more than a hundred people belonging to the category of scientists, subject teachers, method masters, science educators and classroom teachers. All worked to fulfil certain predetermined objectives drawn on the basis of the curriculum frame work prepared by NCERT in 1975.

This integrated science curriculum was finally implemented. Some states have already introduced it and many are contemplating its introduction. In the States and organisations where this curriculum has been introduced, it has been observed that the textbooks are being used as if these are mere amalgamation of physics, chemistry and biology. The curriculum is not being implemented in the intended spirit.

Integrated science teaching covers all those approaches to teaching science:

(a) in which concepts and principles of science (physics, chemistry, biology, etc.) are presented in such a way as to express to fundamental unity of scientific thought,

(b) which emphasis the processes and methodology of the scientific outlook, and

(c) which embody a scientific study of the environment and technological recruitments for everyday life. The NCERT integrated science curriculum can be analysed keeping an eye over the above given definition of integrated science.

Programmes at Different Levels

The Education Commission headed by Professor D.S. Kothari, was appointed by the Government of India in July 1964. It submitted its report in July 1966, recommending guiding principles and working policies for the development of Indian Education at all stages and in all respects. Based on its recommendations 10+2+3 Education Scheme started in Delhi Schools, Central Schools and other schools under Central Board of Secondary Education (CBSE) throughout the country in July 1975, in which science was compulsory (as a part of general education) like other subjects upto class X. The first Secondary School Examination was conducted by CBSE in 1977. The same year the new Science Course was introduced at +2 stage in class XI in Senior Secondary Schools, and in 1979 the first batch of class XII students appeared in Senior Secondary Examination conducted by CBSE. NCERT developed secondary and senior secondary science curricula were used in the schools under CBSE.

Disciplined Course at Secondary Level

This programme developed by NCERT in 1975 was a package of three textbooks — physics, chemistry and life science. These textbooks after being written were placed before a group of selected science teachers for review. Only after minor changes these textbooks were in the market for the use of students.

A and B Courses at Secondary Level

This secondary science course lived A.r four years and in 1979 it split up into two courses — Science A-Course and Science B-Course, according to the recommendations of Ishwarbhai Patel Review Committee.

A. *A-Course.* The syllabus of the programme was framed by CBSE, and the books were written by private publishers. This was a package of the following nine books:

(i) Physics Theory Part I for Class IX

(ii) Physics Theory Part II for Class X

(iii) Physics Practical for Classes IX and X

(iv) Chemistry Theory Part I for Class IX

(v) Chemistry Theory Part II for Class X

(vi) Chemistry Practical for Classes IX and X

(vii) Life Science Theory Part I for Class IX

(viii) Life Science Theory Part II for Class X

(ix) Life Science Practical tor Classes IX and X.

B. *B-Course.* This course was developed by NCERT in 1979. This was a package of two textbooks:

(i) Science Part I for Class IX

(ii) Science Part II for Class X

For science practical, private publishers published science practical books (Physics, Chemistry and Life Science all in one) based on CBSE prescribed syllabus.

These NCERT developed science textbooks were written on integrated approach, and not as separate textbook of physics, chemistry and life science, as it is clear from the sequence of chapters in the two textbooks.

Science Part I (for Class IX)

Chapter

1. Our Universe
2. Living World: An Introduction

3. Motion
4. Moments and Couples
5. Work and Energy
6. Atomic and Molecular Masses, Mole Concept and Chemical Equation
7. Behaviour of Gases
8. Flotation
9. Elasticity of Solids
10. The Structure of the Atom
11. Chemical Bonding
12. Oxidation and Reduction
13. Periodic Classification of Elements
14. The Halogens
15. Oxygen and Sulphur
16. Nitrogen and Phosphorus
17. Organisation of Life
18. Man and His Environment

Science Part II (for Class X)

Chapter

19. Wave Motion
20. Reflection and Refraction of Light
21. Carbon
22. Compounds of Carbon — Organic Chemistry
23. Life Processes
24. Genetics and Evolution
25. Electricity
26. Magnetism
27. Solutions and Electrolytic Dissociation

28. The Rates of Reactions and Chemical Equilibrium
29. Combustion and Fuels
30. Human Biology, Health and Nutrition
31. Metals and Metallurgical Processes
32. Some Applications of Science.

A-Course versus B-Course

If we look at these two science courses, we find that Science A-Course consists of a vast syllabus as compared to Science B-Course. Science A-Course includes nine books (three in each Physics, Chemistry and Life Science), while in Science B-Course all the three subjects (Physics, Chemistry and Life Science) are amalgamated in one book (in two parts), plus book for science practical.

According to the Ishwarbhai Patel Review Committee on the curriculum for the ten year school, published by the Ministry of Education and Social Welfare (1978) the aim of framing Science A-Course was "to develop special interest in students for the science subjects," while Science B-Course aimed at imparting in students a broad based knowledge of science along with other subjects.

This means that the study of Science A-Course demanded an intensive teaching and teachers are expected to put in some more work, and show extra interest in the teaching of this course. But the number of periods allotted per week (usually 9, each of duration 30-40 minutes) to the teaching of Science A-Course remained the same as are allotted to the teaching of Science B-Course. There were only 3 periods per week allotted to each subject physics, chemistry and life science (theory and practical).

Under these conditions it was proposed that in order to make Science A-Course more useful and popular among the students the following recommendations (the first two of the Review Committee, 1978) may be considered by the curriculum developers and educational administrators:

1. The main concepts should be studied and unnecessary details which overload the syllabus should be avoided.
2. The content of the course should be capable of being taught or studied within the time allotted.

3. The Science A-Course should cover the pre-requisites of the senior secondary (XI-XII) science.

Science for All

One of the recommendations of the Education Commission under the chairmanship of Dr. D.S. Kothari was that the science should be made a compulsory subject in school education.

The recommendation was accepted and science was made compulsory up to class X in several States and Union Territories, creating a lot of problems. In the old 3 years Higher Secondary Scheme (IX-XI), a selected number of students (about 33 per cent) who were really interested in science used to take science in class IX. But now like other subjects science is also a required course upto class X. Therefore all students including a big majority of those who perhaps do not have any interest and aptitude for science have to take science. Now the question arises, must every student be forced to learn the same science for which he has no aptitude and interest or may a special curriculum in science be developed for such students so that science may be interesting even for them.

Fresh Courses

The Science A and B Course started in 1979 finished in 1984 after living for five years. The Central Board of Secondary Education, New Delhi started one science course from 1984. It is 3 in 1 — Physics, Chemistry and Biology.

Senior Secondary Course

This programme was developed by NCERT in *1977-78,* starting with textbooks in Physics, Chemistry and Biology for Senior Secondary (XI-XII) students. Afterwards teachers' guides and test-items were also written on these texts. This programme was introduced at +2 stage in class XI in Senior Secondary Schools in July *1977,* and in 1979 the first batch of class XII students appeared in Senior Secondary Examination conducted by CBSE.

After visiting hundreds of schools, observing science classes, interviewing science teachers, students, principals and parents some key problems regarding science education at +2 stage have been identified. They are as follows:

1. There seems to be a big gap between senior secondary science (Physics, Chemistry and Biology) and secondary science courses.
2. It looks that there is no co-ordination between theory and practicals in science Specially in physics at +2 stage.
3. The science laboratories at +2 stage are not equipped enough with all the needed facilities for all the experiments, investigatory projects as well as demonstration experiments.
4. Students, teachers, administrators and parents seem to be not satisfied with the science courses at +2 stage.
5. Science courses at +2 stage do not fulfil the basic admission test requirements of some professional courses like engineering and medicine, as students seeking admission to these courses need extra content coaching.
6. At +2 stage in class XII besides experiments in Physics, Chemistry and Biology students are also to work on one investigatory science project (in each Physics, Chemistry and Biology). It looks that many science teachers are not clear as to what the difference between a science project and investigatory science project is, and they need orientation in guiding their students on some investigatory science projects.

Senior Secondary Science courses were revised afterwards but solutions to such problems (mentioned above) were not taken into consideration satisfactorily when revising these courses.

Conclusions

The responsibility of drawing up science curricula, writing of textbooks and designing of teaching aids for the introduction of science in schools has been given to NCERT. The curricula has been drawn up and textbooks written by those who perhaps have never taught in schools (Indian Express, May 5, 1981). They have tried to compress in the textbooks, a variety of topics some of which have little utility or relevance. What students upto the secondary stage (in general education) should learn, is the application of science to everyday life and not theoretical science. Better science perhaps was taught before as Raman, Saha, and

Bhabha were products of pre-independence science. In spite of the Ishwarbhai Patel Committee Report on Curricula Reform for the ten years school submitted in 1978, the curricula have not been updated. Even the Minister of Education presiding over the annual general meeting of the NCERT on March 11, 1981 regretted that attempts at improving the quality of education in terms of upgrading curricula were not heartening.

Morarji Desai, the then Prime Minister, while addressing the members of the Ishwarbhai Patel Review Committee on the curriculum for the ten year school at New Delhi stated, "the books that I did carry in college are being carried by school students today. The students are burdened by how many books, I do not know."

Knowledge of science doubles every decade. We are to keep pace with the new development. The problem is how much knowledge in science should be given to a child at a particular level, so that he is not burdened.

Is the capacity of a child to absorb knowledge limited? Professor V.N. Wanchoo, President, All India Science Teachers Association, in his Presidential Address in the 22nd All India Science Teachers' Conference at Trivandrum in December 1978, has tried to answer this question:

"Research on theory of learning and the development of brain during the last two decades indicate that a child is capable of learning any amount of knowledge at his level. What is really lacking in this country, are the management and transmission technique of information and the process and the channels through which such information should be imparted at different school levels. The exploration of knowledge is affecting all the countries uniformly. Others deviate their attention to the problems of management of information, and we appoint committees which end up by making some marginal changes in the syllabus. Deleting an information in one class and adding an item of information in another class, will not serve any purpose; and this is what exactly Ishwarbhai Patel Committee has done in recommending changes in the Ten-Year School Curriculum proposed by NCERT".

EXERCISE

1. (a) Describe 'Science is Doing' programme?

   (b) How is EVS programme different from 'Science is Doing'?

2. 'Handbook of Activities Using Environment and Local Resources' is based on the findings of the Research Studies on the Cognitive Development of Primary School Children. Discuss.

3. What is the difference between:

   (a) Disciplined Science Programme, and

   (b) Integrated Science Programme? Discuss.

4. What is the difference between:

   (a) Science A-Course and

   (b) Science B-Course. Which course do you think will be a better course as a prerequisite of senior secondary science? Discuss.

5. What are some key problems regarding science education at +2 stage? What do you think will be the possible solutions? Discuss.

6. In the past two decades several national science programme came up, but people seem to be dissatisfied. Discuss.

16

Curriculum (World)

A level of public education has reached in developing as well as in developed countries where a considerable portion of the population has become interested in a question that until recently was the concern only of specialists:

"What shall we teach and to what end? The new spirit perhaps reflects the profound scientific revolution of our times as well. One of the places in which this renewal of concern has expressed itself is in curriculum planning for the elementary and secondary schools. There has been an unprecedented participation in curriculum development by university scholars and scientists, men distinguished for their work at the frontiers of their respective disciplines. They have been preparing courses of study for elementary and secondary schools not only reflecting recent advances in science and scholarship but also embodying bold ideas about the nature of schools experiences.

In the last four decades (mostly in early sixties) several innovative science education programmes like PSSC, Project Physics, CHEM-Study, Chemical Bond Approach (CBA), BSCS, Nuffield Science Courses, ISCS, AAAS, ESS, SCIS etc., came up in the developed world mostly in United States and United Kingdom. Some of them are discussed here, to give you an idea, so that you will be able to compare with the ones we have in our country.

PSSC Physics

(a) The Physical Science Study Committee is a group of American University and secondary school physics teachers who developed an improved beginning physics course called PSSC physics. The project started in 1956 with the grant from the National Science Foundation, which gave the main financial support. The Ford Foundation and the Alfred P. Sloan Foundation also contributed to the support of the programme. The PSSC physics course is the work of several hundred people, mainly school and college physics teachers, over a period of four years.

The PSSC physics course is much more than a textbook. It is a co-ordinated set of resources for the teaching of high school physics (XI-XII). It includes:

1. PSSC Physics Textbook
2. PSSC Physics Laboratory Guide
3. PSSC Physics Laboratory Apparatus
4. PSSC Physics Closely Related Films
5. PSSC Physics Tests
6. PSSC Physics Supplementary Reading Material
7. PSSC Physics Teachers' Resource Book and Guide (in four parts) In the following pages PSSC Physics content, laboratory experiments and films are listed, to give you some idea of PSSC materials.

PSSC Physics Contents (2nd Edition)

Part I — The Universe

Chapter

1. An Introduction to Physics
2. Time and Measurement (E-1"; F-1", 2,3)
3. Space and Its Measures (E-2,3; F-4,5)
4. Functions and Scaling (E-4; F-6)
5. Motion Along a Straight Line Path (E-5; F-7)
6. Motion in Space (F-8,9)
7. Mass and the Elements
8. Atoms and Molecules (E-6; F-10,11,12,13)

9. The Nature of a Gas (E-7; F-14,15)
10. Measurement (F-16)

Part II — Optics and Waves

11. How Light Behaves
12. Reflection and Images (E-8,9)
13. Reflection (E-10,11)
14. The Particle Model of Light (E-12; F-17,18)
15. Introduction to Waves (E-13; F-19)
16. Waves and Light (E-14,15,16,17)
17. Interference (E-18,19; F-20)
18. Light Waves (E-20,21,22,23)

Part III — Mechanics

19. Newton's Law of Motion (E-24,25,26; F-21,22,23)
20. Motion at the Earth Surface (E-27,28; F-24,25)
21. Universal Gravitation and the Solar System (E-29; F-26,27)
22. Momentum (E-30,31,32)
23. Work and Kinetic Energy (E-33; F-28,29,30)
24. Potential Energy (E-34,35)
25. Heat, Molecular Motion, and Conservation of Energy (E-36; F-31,32)

Part IV — Electricity and Atomic Structure

26. Some Qualitative Facts About Electricity (E-37,38)
27. Coulomb's Law and the Elementary Electric Charge (E-.39, 40, 41, 42; F-33, 34,35,36,37)
28. Energy of Motion of Charges in Electric Fields (E-43; F-38,39,40)
29. Electric Circuits (E-44,45; F-41)
30. The Magnetic Field (E-46,47,48,49; F-42,43,44)
31. Electromagnetic Induction and Electromagnetic Waves (F 45)

32. Exploring the Atom (P-46)

33. Photons and Matter Waves (E-50; F-46,47,48,49,50)

34. Quantum Systems and the Structure of Atoms (E-51; F-51) the PSSC course consists of four parts:

    I. The Universe.
    II. Optics and Waves.
    III. Mechanics, and
    IV. Electricity and Atomic Structure.

Part I is a general introduction to the fundamental physical notations of time, space and matter. It gives the almost boundless range of dimensions from the immensely large to the infinitesimally small, from billions of years to microseconds. Student learns that instruments serve as an extension of his senses. Laboratory experience shows how we first measure by direct counting, and then extend our range of measurements by calibrating and using simple instruments such as stroboscopes and range finders.

From these experiments of measuring time and space, the student moves to an understanding of velocity and acceleration, vector and relative motion. He then goes on to the study of matter, which we see moving through space in the course of time. In the first examination of matter, the concepts of mass and its conservation are developed. Then the evidence of physicists and chemists are used to find that matter is made of relatively few kinds of atoms. Direct experience is provided in the laboratory. There, for example, students compute the size of a molecule from measurements of thin films of oil. Films extend this direct laboratory experience by showing experiments which are beyond the reach of students.

Throughout, the student is led to realise that physics is a single subject of study, and time, space and matter cannot be separated.

Part II is started with light. The student moves into the study of sharp and diffuse shadows, reflection in mirrors, and refraction of light at optical boundaries. The development of the subject leads to develop a particle theory (or model) of light, which proves inadequate and the students find that another model (a wave model) is needed. Here the laboratory experiments provide an excellent source of experience, and the student becomes familiar with the properties of waves. He observes the behaviour of waves on springs and on the surface of water. He learns properties of waves like reflection, refraction, interference and diffraction directly from ripple tank, and relates his knowledge to conclude that the smears of light around street lights, the colours of slicks, and the formation of images by lenses are all aspects of the wave nature of light.

Part III deals with motion from a dynamical point of view. With simple laboratory experiments, the students discover Newton's laws of motion. They learns to predict motions when forces are known and to determine forces when motions are known. From here they follow the Newton's law of gravitational attraction.

The laws of conversation of momentum and energy are introduced through a combination of theory and laboratory explanation. These laws form a substantial portion of Part III, and their use is stressed in situations where detailed observations of the motion are not possible, as in Chadwick's discovery of the neutron and in the kinetic theory of gases.

Part IV introduces the student to electricity and through it to the physics of the atom. Here the student uses the knowledge of dynamics gained in Part III. This part begins with qualitative observations, then proceeds to a quantitative study of the forces between charges. Students learns how to measure very small electric forces and discover that electric charge comes in natural units. Then the motion of charged particles in electric fields is studied and students learns how to determine the masses of electrons and protons.

Next comes a discussion of magnetic fields produced by magnets and currents, and a discussion of the forces they exert on moving charges. As a final part of electricity, the induction laws are discussed, which give the student a qualitative feeling for electromagnetic nature of light. Many of the fundamental ideas are explored in the laboratory, as for example. Coulomb's law, the magnetic field around a current, the force exerted by a magnetic field on a current carrying wire etc.

Now the knowledge gained is used on a large scale to probe the structure of atoms. Following the work of Rutherford, a nuclear model of the atom is established. But some questions remain unanswered like 'why is such an atom stable?' 'why does it not collapse by emitting light?' In searching for the answers to such questions students discover that light is both grainy and wavy. Furthermore, it is found that although matter behaves like particles in some respect, it also behaves like waves. By combining both properties 'the hydrogen atom and the structure of its energy levels' can be understood. In this part of the course, because direct experimentation becomes harder and more expensive, films bring the student such experiments as the Millikan experiment and the interference of photons. At the end of the course students arrive at a modern model of atoms.

Laboratory Experiments

Part I

Experiments

1. Short Time Intervals (Chapter 2)
2. Large Distances (Chapter 3)
3. Small Distances (Chapter 3)
4. Analysis of an Experiment (Chapter 4)
5. Motion: Velocity and Acceleration (Chapter 5)
6. Molecular Layers (Chapter 8)
7. Temperature Scale (Chapter 9)

Part II

8. Reflection from a Plane Mirror (Chapter 12)
9. Images Formed by a Concave Mirror (Chapter 12)
10. Refraction (Chapter 13)
11. Images Formed by a Converging Lens (Chapter 13)
12. The "Refraction" of Particles (Chapter 14)
13. Waves on a Coil Spring (Chapter 15)
14. Pulses in a Ripple Tank (Chapter 16)
15. Periodic Waves (Chapter 16)
16. Refraction of Waves (Chapter 16)
17. Waves and Obstacles (Chapter 16)

18. Waves from Two Point Sources (Chapter 17)
19. Interference and Phase (Chapter 17)
20. Young's Experiment (Chapter 18)
21. Diffraction of Light by a Single Slit (Chapter 18)
22. Resolution (Chapter 18)
23. Measurement of Short Distances by Inference (Chapter 18)

Part III

24. Changes in Velocity with a Constant Force (Chapter 19)
25. The Dependence of Acceleration on Force and Mass (Chapter 19)
26. Inertia and Gravitational Mass (Chapter 19)
27. Forces on a Ball in Flight (Chapter 20)
28. Centripetal Force (Chapter 20)
29. Law of Equal Areas (Chapter 21)
30. Momentum Changes in an Explosion (Chapter 22)
31. The Cart and the Brick (Chapter 22)
32. A Collision in Two Dimensions (Chapter 22)
33. Simulated Nuclear Collision (Chapter 23)
34. Changes in Potential Energy (Chapter 24)
35. The Energy of a Simple Pendulum (Chapter 24)
36. A Head-on Collision (Chapter 25)

Part IV

37. Electrified Objects (Chapter 26)
38. Electrostatic Induction (Chapter 26)
39. The Force Between Two Charged Spheres (Chapter 27)
40. The Addition of Electric Forces (Chapter 27)
41. Driving Force and Terminal Velocity (Chapter 27)
42. The Millikan Experiment (Chapter 27)

43. The Charge Carried by Ions in Solution (Chapter 28)
44. The Charge on a Capacitor (Chapter 29)
45. Energy Transferred by an Electric Motor (Chapter 29)
46. The Magnetic Field Due to Current (Chapter 30)
47. The Measurement of a Magnetic Field in Fundamental Units (Chapter 30)
48. The Mass of the Electron (Chapter 30)
49. The Magnetic Field Near a Long Straight Wire (Chapter 30)
50. Randomness in Radioactive Decay (Chapter 33)
51. The Spectrum of Hydrogen and Blanck's Constant (Chapter 34) All the above experiments are given in the PSSC Physics Laboratory Guide. This guide is designed to help students with their laboratory work. It provides a general introduction to the problems at hand, gives students technical hints, but leaves the thinking to them. Students are on their own a great deal.

Throughout the guide students find many questions. Finding the answer to these questions may sometimes require a little thought about what they have done before, or it may require a short calculation. Sometimes more experimentation is called for. It is upto the students to decide what to do in each case.

Most of the experiments in this guide are so presented as to have the way for reading the text. Students are guided to investigate physical phenomena rather than just verifying known conclusions. When a student performs experiments, the results of which are not known to him in advance, he gains a feeling of personal participation in the discoveries of science; both science and the role of the scientist become more meaningful to him. For this reason, detailed instructions have been limited to purely technical aspects of the experiments; and the necessary guidance on the physical ideas is supplied in short introductions and by asking leading questions.

Students need not end an experiment at any definite point. Usually there is a first basic part of the experiment which all students can complete. Other students proceeding at their own pace, go to the more advanced questions which are raised at the end of the description of each experiment. The procedure allows both the teacher and the student a considerable amount of choice, although there is enough direction so that important ideas are sure to be emphasised. Furthermore, this procedure stimulates an appreciable number of students to go into interesting, related investigations on their own.

During the course of laboratory work students learn that experiments are generated as a result of ideas, that experiments are designed so that their results can be interpreted, and that they are incomplete unless they are analysed.

The laboratory is a vital component of the PSSC course. It makes unique and key contributions to the success of the course. In certain parts of the course the laboratory carries the main burden of developing the subject.

PSSC Films

Part I

1. Short Time Intervals.
2. Time and Clocks.
3. Long Time Intervals.
4. Measuring Large Distances (30 minutes).
5. Measuring Small Distances (20 minutes).
6. Change of Scale (23 minutes).
7. Straight Line Kinematics (33 minutes).
8. Vectors (28 minutes).
9. Vector Kinematics (16 minutes).
10. Measuring Small Distance.
11. Elements, Compounds and Mixtures (Colour, 33 minutes).
12. Definite and Multiple Proportions (30 minutes).
13. Crystals (25 minutes).
14. Behaviour of Gases (15 minutes).
15. Random Events (31 minutes).

16. Measurements (22 minutes).

Part II

17. The Pressure of Light (21 minutes).
18. The Speed of Light (23 minutes).
19. Simple Waves (27 minutes).
20. Sound and Waves in Air (35 minutes).

Part III

21. Forces (22 minutes).
22. Inertia (27 minutes).
23. Inertial Mass (20 minutes).
24. Falling Bodies (30 minutes).
25. Deflecting Forces (26 minutes).
26. Universal Gravitation.
27. Elliptic Orbits (18 minutes).
28. Elastic Collisions and Stored Energy.
29. Momentum, Energy and Centre of Mass (25 minutes).
30. Energy and Work (28 minutes).
31. Mechanical and Thermal Energy (22 minutes).
32. Conservation of Energy (27 minutes).

Part IV

33. Coulomb's Law (28 minutes).
34. Electric Fields (24 minutes).
35. The Millikan Experiment (30 minutes).
36. Coulomb's Force Constant (34 minutes).
37. Electric Lines of Force (7 minutes).
38. Counting Electrical Charges in Motion (23 minutes).
39. Elementary Charges and Transfer of Kinetic Energy (33 minutes).

40. EMF (20 minutes).
41. Electric Potential Energy and Potential Difference Parts I and II (54 minutes).
42. A Magnet Laboratory (20 minutes).
43. Electrons in Uniform Magnetic Field (10 minutes).
44. Mass of Electron (18 minutes).
45. Electromagnetic Waves (33 minutes).
46. Rutherford Atom (40 minutes).
47. Photons (18 minutes).
48. Interference of Photons (13 minutes).
49. Photoelectric Effect (28 minutes).
50. Matter Waves (28 minutes).
51. The Franck-Hertz Experiment (30 minutes).

The PSSC films are part of a complex which includes the text and the laboratory. They bear little resemblance to other physics films used in the secondary schools. Each PSSC film presumes to some degree a knowledge of what has been presented earlier in the course, and is intended in part to open these specified areas which the student will later traverse. Most PSSC films include an experiment which cannot be done in the school laboratory or demonstrated in the classroom. In others, an attempt is made to present an experiment carried out with relatively simple materials, and within the capacity of an earnest student to duplicate. Some films summarised and integrate a topic by presenting several experiments or phenomena which could not be assembled by the teacher. Finally, certain difficult-portions of the course are presented on film in the belief that the student will be best served if all the learning tools — the text, the laboratory, classroom discussion and film — are used for the coverage of the topic. Most of the films are of use in any physics course, but their best and most efficient use is within the context of the PSSC course.

Stephan White, who had a major part in producing the PSSC films reports that these films serve the classroom by directing attention to those aspects of the subjects which will best stimulate classroom discussion. For example, the PSSC film "Energy and

Work" deliberately calls attention to the temperature rise in a nail on which work is being done, and thus opens a discussion of thermal energy when the class will meet next. And the film, wherever possible, serves the individual directly the suggesting work he himself can carry on outside the school; it is for this reason that many PSSC films contain sophisticated experiments performed by simple apparatus.

Each film shows a real scientist in action, presenting him not as a disembodied intellect but as a normal, active, occasionally fallible human being dealing rigorously and respectfully with real problems and deriving not only satisfaction but at times excitement from the intellectual pursuit in which he is engaged. Experiments which are shown in the films were carefully performed and accurately reported.

Some Tests

Two complete sets, each containing ten achievement tests, have been prepared with the co-operation of the Education Testing Service. These are objective (multiple choice) tests. Because of their emphasis on the application of knowledge, rather than recall of facts, the tests are valuable as teaching devices as well as for testing purposes.

Reading Material for Reference

PSSC supplementary Reading Material is a package of the science study series which offers to students and to the general public the writing of distinguished authors on the most string.and fundamental topics of physics, from the smallest known particles to the whole universe. Some of the books tell of the role of physics in the world of man, his technology and civilisation. Others are biographical in nature, telling the fascinating stories of the great discoverers and their discoveries.

The main objective of PSSC Physics course was to present subject matter effectively, not only for coverage but also for structure. The PSSC course does not attempt to study the entire spectrum of physics, but it selects certain basic principles and factual knowledge which contribute to an understanding of two fundamental concepts of modern physics — the wave-particle duality in nature and the modern concept of an atom. What might be called a "traditional" general physics course seeks to familiarise the student with virtually all aspects of physics, emphasising "classical" physics. While it (the traditional physics) is more broad in coverage than the PSSC course, it is also more superficial in depth. According to Bruner PSSC Physics is an example of excellent instances of a well conceived sequence designed to lead the student to an understanding of basic ideas and structure.

CHEM-Study

(a) CHEM-Study (Chemical Education Material Study) is a national chemistry programme for American High Schools (class X-XII). It is usually taught in Class XI. The CHEM-Study materials include a text, a laboratory manual, a teachers' guide, ten films, programmed instruction in Chemical Arithmetic, and objective multiple choice unit and evaluation tests.

In the summer of 1960 a group of eminent chemists and enthusiastic chemistry teachers met at Harvey Mudd College, in Clavemont to write a textbook and a laboratory manual. This material was tried out in 24 high schools during 1960-61. About 1300 students were involved in this try out. The feed back of this try out was used by second writing team in the summer of 1961 at the University of California in Berkeley. This group produced second experimental editions of the textbook and the laboratory manual, and developed a complete teachers' guide. During 1961-62 this revised material and teachers guide were tried out in 130 high schools scattered across the United States. This time about 13,000 students were involved in the tryout. Some additional experimental schools were again added to the tryout programme during 1962-63.

CHEM-Study is an experiment-based chemistry course. The course stresses productive learning and thinking rather than rote learning. Each succeeding step has 'discovery' based on laboratory work. The student really struggles with the problem and is motivated enough to do some problem solving. Let's see how students are trained in keen observation through simple experiments in CHEM-Study. There is an experiment on lit candle where the student is asked to write down as many observations as he can make. He then compares his list (usually 10 to 12 observations) with the list of a professional chemist, which has 53 observations. The big difference in the number and the quality of observations comes as a surprise and eye opener to most of the CHEM-Study students.

About three-fourths of the experiments are quantitative in nature, but mathematics involved in doing calculation is not difficult. A good VII or VIII Class Mathematics background, will enable the students to perform practically all the operations.

CHEM-Study experiments allow students to make their own discoveries of the principles which unify chemistry and make it easier to understand. It emphasises careful observations and quantitative measurements under controlled experimental conditions. It stresses the preparation of tables for recording data. It involves challenging discussions and questions, helping in the application of principles, observed in the experiments to new situations.

Material for Instruction

The textbook consists of 25 chapters and lab manual has the guidelines for 41 experiments. The development of each chapter is based on the observations and results of some experiments, which the students perform and discuss before going into the textbook. The teachers' guide provides guidelines to teachers for their role when their students use textbook and lab manual. How experiments are integrated with theory in CHEM-Study is given below.

Theory and Experiment Integrated

Chapter 1. Chemistry: An Experimental Science

Experiments

1. Scientific observation and description.
2. Behaviour of solids on warming.
3. The melting temperature of a pure substance.
4. Combustion of a candle: a class experiment.

   (a) Further investigations of a burning candle.
5. Heat effects.

Chapter 2. A Scientific Model: The Atomic Theory

Experiments

6. The weights of equal volumes of gases.

7. The behaviour of solid copper immersed in a water solution of the compound silver nitrate.

Chapter 3. Chemical Reactions

Experiments

8. Mass relationships accompanying chemical changes I.

    (a) Mass relationships accompanying chemical changes II.

    (b) The formula of a hydrate.

Chapter 4. The Gas Phase: Kinetic Theory

Experiments

9. A quantitative investigation of the reaction of a metal with hydrochloric acid.

Chapter 5. Liquids and Solids: Condensed Phases of Matter

Experiments

10. An investigation of the reacting volumes of two solutions of known concentration.

11. Reactions between ions in solution.

Chapter 6. Structure of the Atom and the Periodic Table

Experiments

Nil

Chapter 7. Energy Effects in Chemical Fractions

Experiments

12. A study of reactions.

13. The heat of reactions.

Chapter 8. The Rates of Chemical Reactions

Experiments

14. A study of reaction rates I.

    (a) A study of reaction rates II.

Chapter 9. Equilibrium in Chemical Reactions

Experiments

15. Chemical equilibrium.

Chapter 10. Solubility Equilibria

Experiments

16. Determination of the solubility product of silver acetate.

Chapter 11. Aqueous Acids and Bases

Experiments

17. The heat of acid-base reactions.
18. The determination of the hydrogen ion concentration for solutions using indicators.
19. Applying Le Chatelier's Principle to some reversible reactions.

Chapter 12. Oxidation-Reduction Reactions

Experiments

20. An introduction to oxidation reduction.
21. Electrochemical cells.

Chapter 13. Chemical Calculations

Experiments

22. Ionic Reactions
23. A quantitative titration.

Chapter 14. Why We Believe in Atoms

Experiments

24. Construction of a logical model.
25. The relation between moles of copper, moles of silver and moles of electrons involved during electrolysis.

Chapter 15. Electrons and the Periodic Table .

Experiments

Nil

Chapter 16. Molecules in the Gas Phase

Experiments

26. The investigation of some of the properties of a pair of Cis-Trans Isomers.

Chapter 17. The Bonding of Solids and Liquids

Experiments

27. The packing of atoms or ions in crystals.

Chapter 18. The Chemistry of Carbon Compounds

Experiments

28. Some reactions of hydrocarbons and of alcohols.
29. Some derivatives of organic acids.

    (a) The preparation of some polymers.

Chapter 19. The Halogens

Experiments

30. The electrolysis of aqueous potassium iodide.
31. Some chemistry of iodine.

Chapter 20. The Third Row of the Periodic Table

Experiments

32. Some chemistry of the elements of row 3.
33. Development of a scheme of qualitative analysis using reagents labelled A, B and C.

Chapter 21. The Second Column of the Periodic Table: The Alkaline Earths

Experiments

34. The relative solubilities of some compounds of the metals of Column 2 — Qualitative analysis.
35. Qualitative Analysis of Ag, Hg, Pb'2.
36. Development of a scheme for the analysis of an unknown containing various ions.

Chapter 22. The First Row Transition Elements

Experiments

37. The separation of some transition metal ions with an ion-exchange resin.
38. Some investigation into the corrosion of iron.
39. Preparation of a complex salt and a double salt.

40. Preparation of potassium dichromate.

41. Preparation of chrome alum.

Chapter 23. Some Sixth and Seventh Row Elements

Experiments

Nil

Chapter 24. Some Aspects of Biochemistry: An Application of Chemistry

Experiments

Nil

Chapter 25. Geochemistry: The Earth as a Source of Material

Experiments

Nil

Appendices (in the Laboratory Manual)

A-L A Description of a Burning Candle.

A-2. Laboratory Techniques.

A-3. Measurement — The Metric System.

A-4. Experimental Errors.

A-5. Some Mathematics Useful in Chemistry-Exponents, Graphing Relationships.

A-6. Optional Experiments: 4(a), 8(a), 8(b), 14(a) and 29(b).

A-7. Names, Formulas, and Charges of Some Common Ions.

A-8. Oxidation-Reduction Half-Reactions in Aqueous Solutions.

A-9. Relative Strengths of Acids and Bases in Aqueous Solutions.

A-10. Solubility of Some Inorganic Compounds in Water.

After seeing the integration of experiments with theory, one can think how students in CHEM-Study build up their knowledge in chemistry. In this programme the student usually does the experiment before he reads the material from the textbook or before the material is discussed in the class. The student discovers many fundamental ideas and relations himself and discusses them with his classmates, instead or reading them from the textbook or hearing them by the teacher.

Curriculum for Biological Science

(a) In 1959, the American Institute of Bic!ogical Science, with the financial support of the National Science Foundation (NSP), established the Biological Sciences Curriculum Study (BSCS) to conduct an intensive investigation of biological education in the secondary schools of the United States. The function of the BSCS, as stated in the original proposal was "to evaluate the content of present, biology courses, to determine what biological knowledge can and should be learned at each level and to recommend how this latter goal can be achieved."

It was found that many better and imaginative teachers were dissatisfied with the kind of books and other material with which they had to work. Until late fifties biology all over the world was being taught in a very traditional way, mainly emphasising on the type of study of various living organisms in the form of isolated facts and simple generalisations. This kind of biology emphasised on rote memorisation of lists of names, facts and dates. The innovative teachers wanted to teach modern biology in an imaginative, investigation and inquiry oriented manner. Biological Sciences Curriculum Study has played an important role in the improvement of biological education. They have recognised the need of collaboration among the different people the research biologists educators high school biology teachers. They have recommended that a different approach to the teachmg of biology was needed, one that was more suited to modern concepts of biology.

The writing team started working in summer of 1960 under the directorship of William V Mayer of University of Colorado, Boulder Colorado. The aim was not to get the material from the most recent journals into the textbooks, but to select the material most appropriate for the youth, to develop and present the materials so as to contribute to the development of attitudes and skills as well as the relevant knowledge. They have also recognised the fact that for many students high school is terminal.

The initial goal of the BSCS was the production of classroom material for the average students in a first course of biology at the Secondary School level. They were convened to produce three versions of textbook with co-ordinated student laboratory manuals and teachers' guides.

The materials were structured around a series of 9 major themes (1) science as investigations and enquiry, (2) the history of biological concepts, (3) complimentary of structure and function, (4) diversity of type and unity of pattern (5) Change of organisms through time as evolution, (6) genetic continuity, (7) the complimentarily of the organism and its environment, (8) regulation and homeostasis, and (9) the biological basis of behaviour. These themes were presented through the use of a variety of organisms best illustrating the concept in consideration. The various themes were interweaved with organisms and levels of organisation that has given biology a structure as a science. The BSCS programme has presented a balanced approach to the science of biology without presenting excessive details. Content has been carefully selected by the learned biologists and educators.

Materials Developed by BSCS

The BSCS recognised that there was no single best way to organise a course in high school biology. They have selected three patterns, each different in approach from the others but all within the general framework of BSCS objectives including the unifying biological themes. For easy identification they are referred as Blue Green and Yellow versions.

17

Textbook and Material Projects

1. ***The Blue Version: Biological Science Molecule to Man*** **(Molecular Approach).** This book approaches the study of biology from a molecular level with emphasis upon recent advances in physiology and biochemical evolution. The book contained 29 chapters grouped into 8 units. There are 66 laboratory investigations integrated into text chapters and an additional 20 supplementary investigations at the end of the book. Ten appendices covering 25 pages providing enrichment material for a more detailed coverage of such topics as genetic code, fermentation photosynthesis kreb cycle, respiratory chain and more extensive classification living things.

2. ***The Green Version: High School Biology*** **(Ecological Approach).** The approach of this book is through the study of ecological and behavioural aspect of biology. A major emphasis is placed upon the biological community and world biome.

The whole course is woven together in 20 chapters grouped into 6 sections. The 6 sections are:

1. The world of life: The Biosphere;
2. Diversity among living things;
3. Patterns in the Biosphere;
4. Within the individual organisms;
5. Continuity of the Biosphere; and
6. Man and the Biosphere.

Here also the laboratory investigations are integrated with the text chapters. They are placed at a point in the course where firsthand experience is most pertinent, most feasible and most efficient.

This course was planned for the middle 60 per cent in interest and achievement *i.e.* average tenth grade students. However by wise use of the "problems" and "suggested readings" appended to each chapter and of the suggestions. "For further Investigation" the teacher may carry above average students beyond the classroom and into other BSCS material.

3. ***The Yellow Version: Biological Science — An Inquiry into Life*** **(Cellular Approach).** This is organised around the 4 major concepts of biological unity diversity, continuity and interaction, stressing the cellular level of organisation.

Part 1 of "Unity" includes 8 chapters, 20 chapters are included in Part 2 of "Diversity" where variety of living organisms are discussed as micro organisms, plants and animals. Part 3 of "Continuity" has two main diversions: the short aspect or evolution. 6 chapters are included in Part 3. Part 4 "Interaction" includes 5 chapters.

Altogether there are 39 chapters. There is a separate "Student Laboratory Guide" containing 90 laboratory exercises interwoven with each chapter.

Mostly students take biology in class X, they could use any one of the versions. These three versions were written for average and above average students. Some students had problems using these materials, they were unable to achieve satisfactory academic success. As a result of this a new textbook "Patterns and Processes" was developed for below average students.

4. ***Biological Science: Patterns and Processes*** **(published in 1966).** This book was written for low achievers. Five major areas of biological sciences are included in "Pattern and Processes." These are "ecological relationships," "cell energy processes," "reproduction and development," "genetic continuity," and "organic evolution."

Teachers Editions of the Textbooks

The team of authors has also developed the teachers editions of the textbooks where additional notes, suggested patterns of discussions, and hints for teaching are given.

The Teachers Guides for Various Textbooks and Laboratory Manuals

In addition to the teachers' editions of textbooks the teachers' guides were also published. In these books the entire sequence of the course is presented topic by topic. The teacher is given the possible student responses to the discussion questions given at the end of each chapter. It also provides suggestions for helping the students with reading, evaluation etc. The teachers' guide also outlines the quantities of material needed for laboratory activities and gives directions for preparing special solutions and media. In short, the teachers' guides are designed to help the teachers to be successful in teaching the students.

Laboratory Guides

BSCS writers wished laboratory work to lead to an understanding of scientific inquiry and investigation. In Blue and Green Versions and also Pattern and Processes laboratory exercises are written in the text but in Yellow Version there is a separate student laboratory Guide. The writers felt that a major purpose of studying science is to understand and to appreciate the spirit in which scientists work. The laboratory activities are written in guided discovery approach.

Supplementary Materials

(i) ***Laboratory Blocks.*** A set of 13 books in the form of laboratory books each to be completed in a six-week "block" of time were developed called laboratory blocks on variety of topics such as "Animal growth and development," "Plant growth and development". "The complementarity of structure and function". "Animal behaviour" etc. The Blocks were designed originally for the use with tenth grade classes along with any version, but they have been used for eleventh and twelfth grade classes. It was recommended to use only one block in a regular nine month course. Sequences of blocks have been used in advance biology course for students who already finished one year biology course. The objective of using the blocks is to give opportunity to carry out a series of investigations on the given topic to develop an understanding of the nature of research in biological science as well as scientific enterprises as a whole.

(ii) ***Equipment and Techniques Resource Book.*** This book discusses techniques and equipment in some fields like laboratory animals, their housing, culture of microorganisms, equipment and techniques for plant growth etc.

(iii) ***BSCS Biology Second Course:*** The Interaction of Experiments and Ideas were developed for secondary students who already had a course in biology. The 24 sections of the book are divided into three major parts:

1. The Nature of Biological Sciences
2. Experiments and Ideas in Biological Investigations
3. Problems and Prospects — social implications of biological understanding. The commercial edition was available in September 1965.

(iv) ***Evaluation Aids.*** For each of three versions quarterly achievement tests have been developed; BSCS Comprehensive Final Examination and the test on processes of science are common to all versions. These tests were only available to classroom teachers teaching BSCS materials.

(v) ***Teacher's Handbook.*** A biology teacher's handbook, suitable for use with the three BSCS versions has been published. It helps the teacher not only in current biology but also in the manner in which BSCS biology is taught.

(vi) ***BSCS Pamphlet Series.*** It was primarily intended for interested teachers and students at high school level. Each pamphlet covers a specific area in biology.

(vii) ***BSCS Films Programme***

(a) ***BSCS technique films*** — Nine BSCS Biological technique films have been prepared to assist teachers in mastering certain laboratory techniques needed in performing various laboratory investigations. The films vary in length from one to fourteen minutes.

(b) ***Single topic films*** — The single topic films are silent and about four minutes in length. They are designed to show an experiment or result of an experiment. They provide the kind of experience which cannot readily be demonstrated in the class or laboratory. The films are available in 8 mm and 16 mm, they are mostly coloured. The 8 mm films are available in film loop cartridges designed for use in automatic projection device.

(c) ***The BSCS Inquiry Slide sets*** — Each set contains several 35 mm slides presenting a sequence of visual data for observation. Along with visuals some questions are also projected that involve students in loosely structured patterns of enquiry and discussion. Slides are accompanied by teacher's guide also.

(viii) ***BSCS Research Problems in Biology.*** A series of four volumes of Research problems in Biology was initiated by the BSCS special student committee. Each volume consists of 40 separate investigations. They were developed to help the student carry forward individual research.

In addition to these publications, BSCS has contributed to the development of other materials also like BSCS Newsletter for current informations, bulletin series consisting of monographs on topics related to biological education, special publications for specific guidelines to assist teacher training facilities for preparation of teachers to teach BSCS course.

In-service Teachers Training Programme for BSCS

Although biology teachers may have general knowledge of BSCS biology but they need an orientation in the objectives and philosophy as well as special orientation to teach BSCS biology effectively. For this purpose various types of in-service programmes were organised. Often these programmes were arranged by colleges and university departments as in-service institutes, summer institutes, or academic year institutes. These in-service programmes were funded by National Science Foundation (NSF). Every year summer institutes were organised at various places in United States. BSCS summer institutes were also organised in some developing countries including India. The first BSCS summer institute was organised in India in Madras in the summer of 1963. Since then many summer institutes were organised mainly for BSCS Yellow Version. The Yellow Version Text and laboratory manual are familiar to many biology teachers here.

An Indian adaptation of BSCS Yellow Version, laboratory and teachers' manual were prepared at a special summer institute held in 1967 (May-June) under the auspices of Madurai University and sponsored by the UGC, NCERT, USAID and NSF in India. Though these books were extensively used as reference books by many teachers but were never used as textbooks. But BSCS has left an impact on our science teachers as well as on curricula which came afterwards.

In United States since eighties BSCS is not being taught as such in most of the schools but the material is still being utilised by many teachers. It has its importance being the first course very different from traditional biology towards investigation. BSCS is still committed to producing quality educational materials that make a difference. In December 1982 the main BSCS moved from Boulder, Colorado to Colorado College Colorado Springs and the New Director was Jack L. Carter, who came to India and participated in All India Science Teachers' Association Silver Jubilee Conference, December 1981 at New Delhi, organising several Biology Seminars and addressing our science teachers.

Nuffield Teaching Project

(a) In late fifties and early sixties in most of the developed countries there arose a dissatisfaction amongst the science educators and innovative science teachers. They were not satisfied with the kind of courses and material they had to work with, where stress was on rote learning and unimaginative teaching.

In England the first move towards change in curriculum was made by some innovative teachers themselves. The Nuffield Foundation Science Teaching Project arose from a general interest in curriculum development in science. This interest was originally fostered by bodies such as *Association for Science Education* (ASE).

They looked critically at syllabi for Physics, Chemistry and Biology to make recommendations for future. Association for Science Education extended its work and Nuffield Foundation assisted by giving funds and work began early in 1962 on Nuffield Science Teaching Project. Nuffield Foundation is a British charitable educational foundation. The trustees of the Nuffield Foundation considered it important and allocated large resources to it.

Aims and Objectives of Nuffield Science Teaching Project

Their objectives were:

1. To make science intelligible and accessible to pupils of all kinds in schools of all kinds.
2. To make science a more useful tool, both intellectually and practically.
3. To develop material that will help teachers to present science in lively and exciting manner.
4. To develop and encourage an attitude of curiosity and enquiry.
5. To develop programme which is relevant to the world outside the classroom.
6. To show science is a carefully woven fabric of the three subjects — Physics, Chemistry and Biology.
7. To develop a critical approach to the subject with an emphasis on experimentation and enquiry rather than on the mere assimilation of facts.
8. The aim is not only to produce a new syllabus, but a new approach to teaching.

The first assignment of Nuffield Foundation was the development of material for teaching science from age level 11-16 with special reference to O-level (Ordinary level equivalent to our class Xth) Physics, Chemistry and Biology at Secondary level. The programme was then extended to the teaching of science in sixth form, in primary schools and in secondary classes which were not studying for O-level examination.

Brain Young was the Director of the Nuffield Foundation. The work was started and the teams of teachers were seconded to the project to develop new teaching materials — books, films and apparatus.

Nuffield Physics Project

The Physics team was the first to establish and Mr. Donald McGill, of Scottish Education Department was appointed organiser in May 1962 and in spite of his untimely death in March 1963 the inspiration which he brought to the work is evident in the final material.

(i) ***Approach.*** Students see physics as a consistent and logical whole as a fabric of knowledge in which something learnt in one place proves useful somewhere else, and a later discovery throws light back on earlier work. Students think things out for themselves when learning physics. Much gain in understanding does not come from the formal learning of definitions or the working of examples by substituting numerical values in formulae. It is more important to know the meaning of formula and where it comes from, than to learn that formula by heart.

(ii) ***The Course.*** The course developed for O-level is constructed on the following pattern:

First Year

1. Materials and Molecules.
2. Making a Microbalance.
3. Rough Measurement.
4. Looking for a Law of. Levers.
5. Investigation of Springs.
6. Air Pressure and Molecules.
7. Measurement of a Molecule.
8. Energy.

Second Year

1. Forces.
2. Electric Circuits.
3. Electric Currents.
4. More Forces.
5. Energy.
6. Heat.
7. Heat Transfer.

Third Year

1. Waves.
2. Optics.
3. Motion and Force.
4. Molecules in Motion.
5. Electromagnetism.
6. Cells and Voltage.
7. Electrostatics.
8. A Fruitful Theory

Fourth Year

1. Physical Bases of Newtonian Mechanics.
2. Kinetic Theory of Gases.
3. Universal Conservation of Energy.
4. Power.
5. Electricity.

6. Electrons.

Fifth Year

1. Motion in an Orbit. 2. Electrons in Orbits.

3. The Grand Theory planetary, astronomy and the development of theory.

4. Oscillations and Waves. 5. Interference of Light Waves.

6. Radioactivity. 7. Waves and Particles.

Nuffield Chemistry Project

The Nuffield Chemistry Project's proposal is a contribution to the reappraisal of the place of science in education. The chemistry project was intended for children of average and above average ability in the 11-16 years of age group.

Most of their students would not continue to study science after the age of 16 years. For them the course must be pertinent, satisfying and enlightening part of their school experiences and must be a completed part. There are also those whose interests will take them into engineering industry or further academic studies. For this important minority, the course must also act as an adequate basis and stimulation for further work whatever its nature may be. In developing the proposal, the varying need of both groups have been kept in mind.

Nuffield Biology Project

The essence of the Nuffield course in biology is 'science for all.' In devising it, the intention of the writers has been to provide a balanced and up-to-date view of the subject suitable for pupils who will leave school at the age of 16 and do no more further biology. For some, it will also provide a jumping off point for further study at A-Level.

The course has been built around a number of fundamental themes. Such issues as the relationship of structure and function, adaptation and the interaction of organism and environment recur again and again in different contexts throughout the five-year period. The course is designed to foster a critical approach to the subject with an emphasis on experimentation and enquiry rather than on the mere assimilation of facts. In terms of a conventional syllabus this means that less factual matter is included.

The course falls into two parts: the first two years are introductory, and the remaining three constitute the intermediate phase. The first phase has a broad general approach, the next phase becomes more quantitative with greater emphasis on experimentation and reasoning.

Instructional Material Developed by Nuffield Science Teaching Project

Title	Age Range%	Ability Range%	Publishers
1	2	3	4
Nuffield Junior Science	5-11 (mainly 7-11)	All	Coffins
Nuffield Combined Science	11-13	1970	Longman Penguin
Nuffield O-level Chemistry, Physics and Biology	11-16	1966-67	Longman Penguin
Nuffield Secondary Science	13-16	1971	Longman
Nuffield A-level Physics, Biological Sciences, Chemistry, Physical Science	16-18	1970 to 1973 University Courses	Penguin

(i) *Textbooks.* Textbooks were developed by the writing teams of Nuffield Science teaching project. The texts were so designed that variety of teaching approaches can be adopted. Texts are intended to provide a clear indication of overall structure of the course, how subject matter can be approached in investigatory manner, how laboratory experiments can be related to the books and the films. However no separate laboratory manuals have been provided, the texts include the details of laboratory work also.

(ii) *Teachers' Guides.* They are available for various textbooks which also help in teaching methodology. If they also give experimental details, the guides help the inexperienced teachers to achieve at least a certain minimum standard.

(iii) *Films and Other Visual-Aids.* Elaborate experiments that cannot be shown in class can be shown with the help of films, Nuffield Biology course textbooks are supplemented with films.

The film loops are also available, they are silent but detailed teaching notes are provided with them. Suggestions are also made for class discussions in them.

All the new trend science programmes including Nuffield emphasise an enquiry and process approach rather than facts. All these stress on qualitative insight rather than quantitative approach.

Nuffield books are not very interestingly being followed in several schools in England today, as the essence of these books is guided discovery whereas trend over the years has changed to investigatory approach.

EXERCISE

1. (a) Discuss PSSC Physics Course in terms of its various components.

   (b) Compare the PSSC Physics Programme with the Senior Secondary Physics Course being taught in our schools.

2. (a) Discuss CHEM-Study in terms of integration of theory with practicals. (b) Compare the CHEM-Study Programme with the Senior Secondary Chemistry Course being taught in our schools.

3. (a) How is BSCS different in its philosophy and structure from the traditional biology courses? Discuss.

   (b) Compare the three versions of BSCS.

   (c) How is the "patterns and Processes different from the three BSCS' versions?

   (d) Name the various BSCS instructional materials.

   (e) Compare BSCS Programme with the Senior Secondary Biology Course being taught in our schools.

4. (a) What are the objectives of Nuffield Science Project?

   (b) Discuss Nuffield Projects in Physics, Chemistry and Biology.

   (c) What materials were developed by Nuffield ? Discuss.

18

Social Service

For the porpose of harmonious development of the child personality, it is inevitable not only to expose him to scholastic areas for intellectual development but also to put him in situations where he may get opportunities to work with his hands and develop proper attitudes towards manual labour. In addition, there is an urgent need to bridge the gap between the world of school and the world of work. This gap will widen further, if not controlled, due to the modern technological developments and the increasingly technology-based society of the future. Processes and skills of work are changing. An cearly initiation of children into these is possible only through work experience or socially useful productive work (SUPW). That is why the Education Commission (1964-66) made a strong case for introducing work experience as an essential component of general education at all stages of school education. As a matter of fact, the work experience or SUPW approach should permeate the entire curriculum.

SUPW provides the basis for the development of knowledge, skills and attitudes useful for latter participation in productive work. SUPW should cover production, maintenance and the technological process as well as human relations, organisation and management and marketing. The areas of work chosen should have local significance and should be such as to develop the competence of the students. It is not just learning to work, it is work education.

SUPW programmes can serve the following objectives. Their main purpose should be to develop proper attitudes towards work, to inculcate dignity of labour, banish status and class distinctions, and to stress the principle of productivity. Whenever possible SUPW should help to appreciate the need for and utility of labour-saving devices, gadgets, tools that are so much a part of modern life, and the techniques involved in their use and the underlying scientific principles. Various activities of SUPW must necessarily be related to the community needs and its services. A carefully directed SUPW programme would also help to discover the aptitude of a student for gainful vocations which demand certain types of skills, physical ability, attitudes towards others with whom they have to work and responsibility in performing their Jobs and discharging their duties.

At the primary stage, SUPW should begin with simple, creative, self-expressional activities performed with locally available material and simple tools. It is desirable to avoid any activity with an element of monotony in it. At middle and secondary levels, the use of the tools should be introduced in a scientific manner.

As a science teacher you are likely to teach also some SUPW subject along with science subjects — Physics, Chemistry and Biology. It is a general practice in schools that physics teachers teach electronics and electrical gadgets, chemistry teachers teach photography, and biology teachers teach gardening. It is not necessary that science teachers should only teach some science based SUPW subject. They may also develop and teach SUPW Course selecting some activities according to .their interest from the list given in the suggested SUPW syllabus given in this chapter or adding some other activities from their own experiences. Some activities like cleanliness suggested in the syllabus may be useful and interesting in any subject as well as in science.

If you learn, therefore, to teach some SUPW subjects in your B.Ed. programme you may be an asset to the school where you will teach science as a regular teacher, otherwise you will need an immediate in-service teacher training to teach SUPW course, as soon as you join a school as a regular teacher.

The Perspective

The concept of manual work as a tool of education is not very new in our country. It was recognised long before the advent of formal education. In ancient India the students used to live in their schools *(ashrams)* with their teacher *(guru)*. They had to do every kind of manual work for living and learning. Education was related to the life of students and the dichotomy between education and work was not existing.

When formal education was introduced in the country, education became bookish and it started preparing students for white collared jobs. There was no provision of manual work in formal education. This limitation was pointed out in the Woods Education Despatch (1854) which contemplated the introduction of prevocational education at the secondary stage. But practically, no action was taken in this direction. Wood and Abbott (1937) also stressed the need of manual work in education for the sake of harmonious development of child's personality.

Deploring the ineffectiveness of bookish education, Rabindranath Tagore also stressed the role of manual work in education for all-round development of the child. Mahatma Gandhi insisted for the first time that education should centre around manual and productive work. This proposal of Mahatma Gandhi was accepted at the Wardha National Education Conference in October 1937. This proposal when accepted was given a practical shape by the Zakir Hussain Committee and Basic Education was accepted as the national pattern of education at the primary level in 1938.

Kothari Commission (1966) suggested that Work Experience should form an integral part of general education (Class I to X). The Commission also clarified that the concept of work-experience was essentially similar to the Mahatma Gandhi's philosophy of Basic Education and it might be described as a redefinition of his thinking in terms of the changes in society due to the development of industrialisation. Consequently, great emphasis was given to work experience in the new 10+2 pattern of education.

In June 1977, Ishwarbhai Patel Committee pointed out that "work-experience which was intended to be an integral feature of the curriculum, at all stages, did not find a proper place in teaching-learning process that followed the introduction of the new pattern." This Committee recommended a scheme having three components — humanities, science, and work (Socially Useful Productive Wor' and Community Services), together with aesthetic appreciation to illuminate the curriculum.

Adiseshiah Committee also accepted the concept and objectives of Socially Useful Productive Work (SUPW) as defined by Ishwarbhai Patel Committee, for plus two stage with minor modifications.

The National Education Conference (December 18 to 20,1977) held in New Delhi, under the chairmanship of Shri Sriman Narain, recommended that 50 per cent of the total school time ought to be devoted to productive, creative and recreational activities, at least half of which should be focused on SUPW of various kinds. It also urged, as did Patel Committee, that the existing burden on student of textbooks, due to a large number of compulsory subjects, should be tided proportionately.

Aims and Objectives

The objectives of SUPW may be stated as follows:

(i) To prepare students to practise and perform manual work individually and collectively;

(ii) To acquaint students with the world of work and services to the community and develop in them a sense of respect for manual work;

(iii) To develop a desire to be useful members of society and contribute their best to the common good;

(iv) To indicate positive attitudes of team work and socially desirable values like self-reliance, dignity of labour, tolerance, co-operation, sympathy and helpfulness;

(v) To help in understanding the principles involved in the various forms of work;

(vi) To lead children to participate increasingly in productive work as they go from one stage of education to another and, thereby, enable them to earn while they learn;

(vii) To provide opportunities of creative self-expression anc for the development of problem solving abilities;

(viii) To provide for the development of vocational preparedness,

(ix) To develop in the students an awareness of social problems and inculcate in them positive attitudes towards community service.

Ideas and Suggestions

The SUPW syllabus should be flexible. It is not desirable to prescribe a uniform SUPW syllabus for all the schools, as is the practice with other subjects. The SUPW syllabus should depend upon the local needs and facilities available. It is suggested that SUPW syllabus should have three components:

(i) Study of the world of work through observation and enquiry;

(ii) Experimentation with material, tools and techniques; and

(iii) Work practice.

The first two components are concerned with preparation for actual participation in productive work and services. This makes the common core programme of SUPW. The third component, "work practice" may lead to remuneration or earning. Thus the SUPW syllabus will have two components:

(a) A common core programme, comprising components (i) and (ii) above, and

(b) Work practice, the third component of the syllabus.

The purpose of the common core programme will be to bring about attitudinal changes and to develop readiness for work practice. The purpose of work practice is to give a vocational bias to the programme. It will, therefore, be repetitive in nature and, it is hoped that it will be remunerative either in kind or cash.

When framing SUPW syllabus, the content identified may be put in the following six areas:

(i) Health and Hygiene;

(ii) Food;

(iii) Shelter;

(iv) Clothing;

(v) Culture and Recreation; and

(vi) Community Work and Social Service.

Some suggestive activities for various levels pertaining to the above six areas are as follows.

Middle Stage

Common Core Programme

(i) ***Health and Hygiene*** — Dusting of furniture, cleaning of classrooms and science laboratories, school buildings, the school compound and its vicinity.

(ii) ***Food*** — Vegetable gardening or pot culture, cooking of meals.

(iii) ***Shelter*** — Construction with plastic, pliable and rigid material, maintenance of articles of use.

(iv) ***Clothing*** — Spinning and simple hand weaving or knitting, washing of clothes, stitching, mending.

(v) ***Culture and Recreation*** — Recreating the classroom, preparation for important national days, festivals and school function.

(vi) ***Community Work and Social Service*** — Cleaning the neighbourhood, planting and care of shade trees, running of co-operative stores, the school panchayat, helping adults in productive work.

Work Practice. This should be in the form of projects. A suggestive list is as follows: Few projects according to the need and interest of students and availability of time may be selected in each class from the following list.

(i) ***Health and Hygiene*** — Making of tooth powder, soap, disinfectants, detergent powder, hair oil, brooms, waste paper baskets, dust bins, first-aid boxes, health posters, scrap books on health and hygiene, keeping health records, keeping the neighbourhood clean, working at health centres.

(ii) ***Food*** — Growing of selected vegetables and flower plants in plots or pots — where possible, also for sale; seed collecting, soil testing, experimentation with different kinds of soils, different types of seeds, different kinds of manures; vegetative propagating, by grafting of propagation by breeding, vegetative propagation by grafting, vegetative reproductivity, layering, soil conservation;

making of jam, jelly, ketchup, sauce, pickles, fruit juices, confectionery or bakery items; working in canteen, or stalls for a specified period; packing of food material.

(iii) ***Shelter*** — Making stationery items, white washing, polishing doors, windows and furniture; caning chairs, repairs of furniture, casual labour work in the school.

(iv) ***Clothing***—Spinning, making school bags, school uniforms, handkerchiefs, table cloths, pillow cases, knitting, making mats.

(v) ***Culture and Recreation*** — Toy making, artificial flowers making, pottery painting, making games material, greeting cards, fancy covers for book and book binding, fancy candle making.

(vi) ***Community Work and Social Service***— Helping adults in their work as. projects, such as keeping a specified area clean, helping in the case of the sick, first-aid, helping at functions and during festivals, traffic control, helping in the literacy campaign.

Secondary Stage

At this level more emphasis should be given to work practice. A suggestive list of activities (crafts/services) is given below, some activities according to the need and interest of students and availability of time may be selected in each class from the following list.

(i) ***Health and Hygiene*** — Growing medicinal plants, eradication of communicable diseases, paramedical service; cleanliness of the neighbourhood, well and pond, and die disposal of garbage; construction of toilet facilities and composite pits; making tooth picks, tooth powder, soap, detergents, disinfectants, first-aid boxes; construction of waste-paper baskets, dust bins, garbage cans, brooms, brushes, dusters, mops etc.; detection of adulteration.

(ii) ***Food*** — Agro-industries; kitchen gardening; pot culture; crop and seed production; repair of farm implements; soil conservation and desert control; horticulture, animal husbandry, and dairying, beekeeping, poultry farming, fish culture, distribution of fertilisers and insecticides, processing and preservation of food, hydroponics, mushroom culture; khandsari, gur and candy making; canning; making jam, jelly, squashes, pickles; packing food, marketing, bakery; confectionary, cooking.

(iii) ***Shelter*** — Pottery, masonry work, workshop practice — mechanical, electrical, electronics; cane and bamboo work; black-smithy, wood work, carpet weaving; home, village and town planning; minor repairs in buildings, fittings, furniture and household articles, decorating the home, gardening, interior decorations, construction of decorative pieces, chalk and candle making.

(iv) ***Clothing*** — Production of cotton, wool, silk and other fibres, weaving, dress making, knitting, hosiery work, embroidery work, dress designing, leather work, spinning of different fibres; dyeing, printing and repair of garments, laundry work.

(v) ***Culture and Recreation*** — Making toys and puppets, making and repairing musical instruments; making games material, printing, book binding, photography, stage craft, making costumes, holding exhibitions.

(vi) ***Community Work and Social Service*** — Identification of problems relating to health and hygiene, supply of drinking water and adult literacy; rendering help in solving these problems; helping teachers in tackling school drop-out problem by visiting houses of children and finding out their difficulties; motivating the people in slum and unhygienic areas to maintain cleanliness of their surroundings by joining hands with them in cleanliness campaigns; helping the illiterate people in the community by way of writing letters, filling in application forms and reading telegrams for them; helping in road construction and digging of well etc. in the community and their maintenance; during natural calamities involving students in the relief work and help the people in the affected areas; serving the sick people in the community; tree plantation; checking the soil erosion; canal repair and maintenance.

Senior Secondary Stage

(a) ***Common Core Programme*** — The work done in the previous classes should be further extended at this level.

(b) ***Work Practice*** — This should include mass production of work done previously as well as community and social work.

(c) ***Subject Related Suggested SUPW Activities***

(i) ***Physics.*** Gaining the basic knowledge about how to prevent electric shock accidents; giving the knowledge about how the lightning and the thunder occur and what are the use of lightning and thunder; giving an idea about how we receive the sound from the radio which is relayed from the radio station: preparing hot water with the help of solar heat energy; giving the knowledge about how to produce artificial rain; giving an idea of how to get electricity from the water and the steam; giving the basic knowledge about how to operate the machines like washing machine, grinding machine, electric cookers etc.; giving the knowledge about how the sound is produced from various sound instruments; giving them the basic knowledge and practice about electronics and electrical gadgets.

(ii) ***Chemistry.*** Preparation of soap and washing soda; explaining the uses of dettol and phenyl for cleanliness: preparation of tincture-iodine and .simple ointments for wounds; preparation of dyes; explaining the preparation of bleaching powder; explaining the equipping technique and uses of gobar gas plant in the houses making use of animal waste; explaining the uses and preparation of ammonium nitrate; explaining the fixation of nitrogen; explaining the uses of insecticides; demonstrating the method of purifying water; giving them the basic knowledge and practice about various processes involved in photography.

(iii) ***Biology.*** Helping the farmers to get rid of the insect pest; learning methods of vegetative propagation; introducing modern techniques of incubation in poultry; practising the way of getting uniform fruiting and blossoming through simple techniques using chemicals (hormones); leathering of economically important animals; making them aware of economic zoology; providing them the knowledge of crop rotation; helping them to know about the various sources of nitrogen manure in the form of nitrogen yielding plants (legumes) and easily available cultures to increase the yield; making them aware of contamination; giving them the basic knowledge and practice about various processes and techniques involved in gardening.

The Evaluation

The evaluation work in SUPW should be carried out at three levels:

(i) By the teacher;

(ii) By the children; and

(iii) By the parents and community members.

The teacher should note the behaviour of children and the skills learnt by them during SUPW activities. The students should maintain diary of the daily work and experiences gained along with their reactions. The parents and the community members involved in organising SUPW activities should be consulted while assessing students behaviour and participation.

Tools of Evaluation

(i) ***Attendance.*** A record of attendance should be maintained in SUPW classes (indoor or outdoor) as is usually done in other subject classes.

(ii) ***Observation.*** What needs to be evaluated is not only the product (goods or services), but also the process and the quality of learning, for which observation is a reliable technique. 'Anecdotal Records' and 'Check lists' may be used when this techniques of evaluation is used.

(iii) ***Self-Evaluation.*** Self-evaluation of their work by the students may prove to be a good measure. It may lead to some exaggerations in the beginning but, if persisted in, will turn out to be a very reliable tool of evaluation.

(iv) ***Written Tests.*** Written examination in SUPW does not seem to be necessary. It may cause even some disadvantages. Assessment, therefore, should take the form of *demonstration, viva voce, or examination of the product or service.*

(v) ***Feedback from Parents.*** Parents and guardians may be able to give valuable feedback of their children's work (SUPW) at home, which will help the teacher in evaluation.

(vi) ***Feedback from Community Members.*** In case of community service projects, the assessment by the beneficiaries may also be a good source of evaluation.

Students' Grading

According to the Central Board of Education (CBSE), New Delhi, the assessment should be done on the following 7 points scale:

Grade A (Excellent)	75 percent and above
Grade B (Very Good)	60-74 percent

Grade C (Good)	53-59 percent
Grade D (Quite Satisfactory)	45-52 percent
Grade E (Just Satisfactory)	33-44 percent
Grade F (Poor)	15-32 percent
Grade G (Very Poor) Below	15 percent

In order to ensure that the objectives of SUPW programme are achieved, it is necessary to follow the problem solving approach. Students should be made aware of the problems related to their needs; they should be led to arrive at solutions by discussing the material, tools and techniques necessary for performing such work and services. A built-in system of evaluation should be developed to enable the students to improve their performance and to enable teachers to give a fair assessment of their work.

EXERCISE

1. What is the place of SUPW in school curriculum? Discuss.
2. Give a historical perspective of SUPW?
3. What should be the objectives of SUPW?
4. Suppose you are asked to teach SUPW at middle, secondary or senior secondary level. Seeing your background identify the SUPW syllabus, you will like to use.
5. How will you evaluate your students involved in SUPW activities? Discuss.
6. What methods of teaching will you like to use in SUPW classes?
7. Components of SUPW should be infused in science subjects. Discuss.
8. As a science teacher, with the background you have in your field, what SUPW subject will you like to teach? Discuss.

Additional Reading

Bhaskara Rao, Digumarti (1994). *Scientific Aptitude,* New Delhi: Ashish Publishing House. ISBN 81-7024-658-X.

Bhaskara Rao, Digumarti (1995). *Animal Kingdom.* New Delhi: Discovery Publishing House. ISBN 81-7141-274-2.

Bhaskara Rao, Digumarti (1995). *Batracology.* New Delhi: Discovery Publishing House. ISBN 81-7141-279-3.

Bhaskara Rao, Digumarti (1997), *Scientific Attitude.* New Delhi: Discovery Publishing House. ISBN 81-7141-308-0.

Bhaskara Rao, Digumarti (1996). *Scientific Attitude vis-à-vis Scientific Aptitude.* New Delhi: Discovery Publishing House. ISBN 81-7141-308-0.

Bhaskara Rao, Digumarti, Editor (1996). *Encyclopaedia of Education for All,* 5 Volumes. New Delhi: APH Publishing Corporation. ISBN 81-7024-759-4 (set).

Vol. I *Education for All: The World Conference.* ISBN 81-7024-760-8.

Vol. II *Education for All: The EPA-9 Summit.* ISBN 81-7024-761-6.

Vol. III *Education for All: Quality Education for All.* ISBN 81-7024-762-6.

Vol. IV *Education for All: Planning and Monitoring.* ISBN 81-7024-763-4.

Vol. V *Education for All: The Indian Scenario.* ISBN 81-7024-764-0.

Bhaskara Rao, Digumarti, Editor (1996). *Global Perceptions on Peace Education,* 3 Volumes. New Delhi: Discovery Publishing House. ISBN 81-7141-319-6.

Bhaskara Rao, Digumarti, Editor (1996). *National Policy on Education*. 2 Volumes. New Delhi: Anmol Publications Pvt. Ltd. ISBN 81-7488-323-1.

Bhaskara Rao, Digumarti, Editor (1997). *Care the Child*, 2 Volumes. New Delhi: Discovery Publishing House. ISBN 81-7141-394-3.

Bhaskara Rao, Digumarti, Editor (1997). *Education for the 21st Century*. New Delhi: Discovery Publishing House. ISBN 81-7141-389-7.

Bhaskara Rao, Digumarti, Editor (1997). *Reflections on Scientific Attitude*. New Delhi: Discovery Publishing House, ISBN 81-7141-319-6.

Bhaskara Rao, Digumarti, Editor (1997). *Success Story of a Primary Education Project*. New Delhi: APH Publishing Corporation. ISBN 81-7024-850-7.

Bhaskara Rao, Digumarti, Editor (1997). *World Food Summit*. New Delhi: Discovery Publishing House. ISBN 81-7141-386-2.

Bhaskara Rao, Digumarti, Editor (1998). *Adolescence Education*. New Delhi: Discovery Publishing House. ISBN 81-7141-432-X.

Bhaskara Rao, Digumarti, Editor (1998). *Community and School Nutrition Education*. New Delhi: Discovery Publishing House. ISBN 81-7141-435-4.

Bhaskara Rao, Digumarti, Editor (1998). *District Primary Education Programme*. New Delhi: Discovery Publishing House. ISBN 81-7141-396-X.

Bhaskara Rao, Digumarti, Editor (1998). *Earth Summit*, 2 Volumes. New Delhi: Discovery Publishing House. ISBN 81-7141-435-4.

Bhaskara Rao, Digumarti, Editor (1998). *National Policy on Education: Towards an Enlightened and Humane Society*, New Delhi: Discovery Publishing House. ISBN 81-7141-426-5.

Bhaskara Rao, Digumarti, Editor (1998). *Reforming School Education*. New Delhi: Discovery Publishing House. ISBN 81-7141-403-6.

Bhaskara Rao, Digumarti, Editor (1998). *Teacher Education in India*. New Delhi: Discovery Publishing House. ISBN 81-7141-406-0.

Bhaskara Rao, Digumarti, Editor (1998). *World Summit for Social Development*. New Delhi: Discovery Publishing House. ISBN 81-7141-420-6.

Bhaskara Rao, Digumarti, Editor (2000). *Education for All: Achieving the Goal*, 3 Volumes, New Delhi: APH Publishing Corporation. ISBN 81-7648-152-1.

Vol. I *The Global Consensus*. ISBN 81-7648-155-6.

Vol. II *Mid-Decade Review Reports of Regional Seminars*. ISBN 81-7648-154-8.

Vol. III *Issues and Trends*. ISBN 81-7648-155-6.

Bhaskara Rao, Digumarti, Editor (2000), *International Encyclopaedia of AIDS*, 11 Volumes in 13 Parts. New Delhi: Discovery Publishing House. ISBN 81-7141-6 (Set).

Vol. 1 *Introduction to HIV/AIDS*. ISBN 81-7141-523-7.

Vol. 2 *HIV/AIDS—Issues and Challenges*, 2 Parts. ISBN 81-7141-524-5.

Vol. 3 *HIV/AIDS Socio Economic Realities*. ISBN 81 7141 524-3.

Vol. 4 *HIV/AIDS—Law Ethics and Human Rights*, 2 Parts. ISBN 81-7141-526-1.

Vol. 5 *AIDS and NGOs*. ISBN 81-7141-527-X.

Vol. 6 *AIDS and Home Care*. ISBN 81-7141-528-8.

Vol. 7 *STD Case Management*. ISBN 81-7141-529-6.

Vol. 8 *HIV/AIDS Prevention and Care—Teaching Modules for Nurses and Midwives*. ISBN 81-7141-530-X.

Vol. 9 *HIV Prevention Education for Education for Educational Institutions*. ISBN 81-7141-531-8.

Vol. 10 *Instructional Modules for AIDS Education*. ISBN 81-7141-532-6.

Vol. 11 *School Health Education to Prevent AIDS and STD—A Package for Curriculum Planners*. ISBN 81-7141-5338-4.

Bhaskara Rao, Digumarti, Editor (2000). *International Encyclopaedia of Science and Technology Education*, 11 Volumes. New Delhi: Discovery Publishing House. ISBN 81-7141-548-2 (Set).

Vol. 1 *Science and Technology Education*. ISBN 81-7141-568-7.

Vol. 2 *Science Education in Developing Countries*. ISBN 81-7141-570-9.

Vol. 3 *Organisational Structure of Science*. ISBN 81-7141-570-9.

Vol. 4 *Science Education in Asia and the Pacific*. ISBN 81-7141-571-7.

Vol. 5 *Science and Technology Education for All*. ISBN 81-7141-572-5.

Vol. 6 *Values, Ethics, Talent and Girls in Science and Technology Education*. ISBN 81-7141-573-3.

Vol. 7 *Popularization of Science and Technology Education*. ISBN 81-7141-574-1.

Vol. 8 *Science, Power and Society*. ISBN 81-7141-575-X.

Vol. 9 *Information Technology*. ISBN 81-7141-576-8.

Vol. 10 *Teacher Training in Science and Technology Education*. ISBN 81-7141-577-6.

Vol. 11 *Teacher Training in Science and Technology: A Curriculum Framework*. ISBN 81-7141-578-4.

Bhaskara Rao, Digumarti, Editor (2001). *Distance Education in Different Countries*. New Delhi: APH Publishing Corporation. ISBN 81-7648-229-3.

Bhaskara Rao, Digumarti, Editor (2001). *Decentralised Management of Education (Management of Education in Panchayati Raj and Municipal Bodies)*. New Delhi: Discovery Publishing House. ISBN 81-7141-617-9.

Bhaskara Rao, Digumarti, Editor (2001). *Electrochemistry for Environmental Protection*. New Delhi: Discovery Publishing House. ISBN 81-7141-619-5.

Bhaskara Rao, Digumarti, Editor (2001). *Global Educational Studies*. New Delhi: Discovery Publishing House. ISBN 81-7141-616-0.

Bhaskara Rao, Digumarti, Editor (2001). *Global Synthesis of Educational Assessment*. New Delhi: Discovery Publishing House. ISBN 81-7141-613-6.

Bhaskara Rao, Digumarti, Editor (2000). *International Encyclopaedia of Human Rights*. 7 Volumes in 13 Parts. New Delhi: Discovery Publishing House. (Royal Size). ISBN 81-7141-567-9 (Set).

Vol. 1 *International Instruments of Human Rights*, 2 Parts. ISBN 81-7141-595-4.

Vol. 2 *Regional Instruments of Human Rights*. ISBN 81-7141-604-7.

Vol. 3 *Human Rights and the United Nations*, 2 Parts. ISBN 81-7141-605-5.

Vol. 4 *Fact Files of Human Rights*, 3 Parts. ISBN 81-7141-605-3.

Vol. 5 *Study Stories of Human Rights*, 3 Parts. ISBN 81-7141-607-3.

Vol. 6 *International Meetings on Human Rights*, 2 Parts. ISBN 81-7141-608-X.

Vol. 7 *Professional Training in Human Rights*. ISBN 81-7141-609-8.

Bhaskara Rao, Digumarti, Editor (2001). *Jomtein Decade of Education*. New Delhi: Discovery Publishing House. ISBN 81-7141-618-7.

Bhaskara Rao, Digumarti, Editor (2001). *Nuclear Materials: Issues and Concerns*, 2 Volumes. New Delhi: Discovery Publishing House. ISBN 81-7141-611-X.

Bhaskara Rao, Digumarti, Editor (2001). *World Conference on Education for All*. New Delhi: APH Publishing Corporation. ISBN 81-7141-274-9.

Bhaskara Rao, Digumarti, Editor (2001). *World Conference on Higher Education*, New Delhi: Discovery Publishing House. ISBN 81-7141-610-1.

Bhaskara Rao, Digumarti, Editor (2001). *World Conference on Science*. New Delhi: Discovery Publishing House. ISBN 81-7141-612-8.

Bhaskara Rao, Digumarti, Editor (2003). *Inspiring Experience in Teacher Education*. New Delhi: Discovery Publishing House. ISBN 81-7141-656-X.

Bhaskara Rao, Digumarti, Editor (2003). *International Studies in Education*, 3 Volumes, New Delhi: Discovery Publishing House. ISBN 81-7141-647-0.

Bhaskara Rao, Digumarti, Editor (2003). *Military Conversion: Impact on Science and Technology*, New Delhi: Discovery Publishing House. ISBN 81-7141-578-4.

Bhaskara Rao, Digumarti, Editor (2003). *United Nations Millennium Summit*. New Delhi: Discovery Publishing House. ISBN 81-7141-632-2.

Bhaskara Rao, Digumarti, Editor (2003). *World Assembly on Aging*. New Delhi: Discovery Publishing House. ISBN 81-7141-637-3.

Bhaskara Rao, Digumarti, Editor (2004). *World Conference on Human Rights*. New Delhi: Discovery Publishing House. ISBN 81-7141-661-6.

Bhaskara Rao, Digumarti, Editor (2003). *World Education Forum*. New Delhi: Discovery Publishing House. ISBN 81-7141-639-X.

Bhaskara Rao, Digumarti, Editor (2004). *Education Employment and Human Resource Development*. New Delhi: Discovery Publishing House. ISBN 81-7141-681-0.

Bhaskara Rao, Digumarti, Editor (2004). *Successfully Schooling*. New Delhi: Discovery Publishing House. ISBN 81-7141-677-2.

Bhaskara Rao, Digumarti, Editor (2004). *European Education and Teachers*. New Delhi: Discovery Publishing House. ISBN 81-7141-702-7.

Bhaskara Rao, Digumarti, Editor (2004). *Teachers in a Changing World*. New Delhi: Discovery Publishing House. ISBN 81-7141-694-2.

Bhaskara Rao, Digumarti, Editor (2004). *Learning to Live Together*, 4 Volumes. New Delhi: Discovery Publishing House.

Vol. 1 *International Conference on Learning to Live Together.*

Vol. 2 *Globalisation and Living Together.*

Vol. 3 *Curriculum for Learning to Live Together.*

Vol. 4 *Science Education for the Contemporary Society.*

Bhaskara Rao, Digumarti (2004). *International Guidelines on Open and Distance Education*, New Delhi: Discovery Publishing House.

Bhaskara Rao, Digumarti, Editor (2004). *Adult Learning in the 21st Century*. New Delhi: Discovery Publishing House.

Bhaskara Rao, Digumarti, Editor (2004). *Educational Practices: Research and Recommendations*. New Delhi: Discovery Publishing House.

Bhaskara Rao, Digumarti, Editor (2004). *Chernobyl: Never Again*. New Delhi: APH Publishing Corporation.

Bhaskara Rao, Digumarti, Editor (2004). *Virology and Immunology*. New Delhi: APH Publishing Corporation.

Bhaskara Rao, Digumarti, C.A.P. Swami and B.S.V. Dutt (1997). *Self-Evaluation in Student Teaching*. New Delhi: Discovery Publishing House. ISBN 81-7141-374-9.

Bhaskara Rao, Digumarti and B.S.V. Dutt, Editors (2003). *Education: Programmes and Policies*. New Delhi: APH Publishing Corporation. ISBN 81-7648-470-9.

Bhaskara Rao, Digumarti and D. Naresh Kumar (2004). *School Teacher Effectiveness*. New Delhi: Discovery Publishing House.

Bhaskara Rao, Digumarti and D. Sridhar (2002). *Job Satisfaction of School Teachers*. New Delhi: Discovery Publishing House. ISBN 81-7141-652-7.

Bhaskara Rao, Digumarti and Digumarti Pushpa Latha (1994). *Achievement in Biology*. New Delhi: Discovery Publishing House. ISBN 81-7141-264-5.

Bhaskara Rao, Digumarti, C. Sridevi and K. Vijaya (1995). *Achievement in Social Studies*. New Delhi: Discovery Publishing House. ISBN 81-7141-281-5.

Bhaskara Rao, Digumarti and Digumarti Pushpa Latha (1995). *Achievement in English*. New Delhi: Discovery Publishing House. ISBN 81-7141-283-1.

Bhaskara Rao, Digumarti and Digumarti Pushpa Latha (1994). *Achievement in Science*. New Delhi: Discovery Publishing House. ISBN 81-7141-280-70.

Bhaskara Rao, Digumarti and Digumarti Pushpa Latha (1995). *Achievement in Mathematics*. New Delhi: Discovery Publishing House. ISBN 81-7141-278-5.

Bhaskara Rao, Digumarti and Digumarti Pushpa Latha, Editors (1998). *International Encyclopaedia of Women*. 5 Volumes. New Delhi: Discovery Publishing House. ISBN 81-7141-410-9.

Vol. 1 *Status of World's Women*. ISBN 81-7141-494-X.

Vol. 2 *Women, Education and Empowerment*. ISBN 81-7141-498-1.

Vol. 3 *Women Challenges and Advancement*. ISBN 81-7141-497-4.

Vol. 4 *Women and Family Health*. ISBN 81-7141-497-4.

Vol. 5 *Women and International Action*. ISBN 81-7141-498-2.

Bhaskara Rao, Digumarti, Digumarti Pushpa Latha and Digumarti Harshitha, Editors (2001). *Biological Warfare*. New Delhi: Discovery Publishing House. ISBN 81-7141-597-0.

Bhaskara Rao, Digumarti, Digumarti Pushpa Latha and Digumarti Harshitha, Editors (2001). *Women as Educators*. New Delhi: Discovery Publishing House. ISBN 81-7141-602-0.

Bhaskara Rao, Digumarti and Digumarti Harshitha, Editors (2001). *Education in India*. New Delhi: APH Publishing Corporation. ISBN 81-7141-207-2.

Bhaskara Rao, Digumarti, Digumarti Pushpa Latha and Digumarti Harshitha, Editors (2001). *Assessing Learning Achievement*. New Delhi: Discovery Publishing House. ISBN 81-7141-601-2.

Bhaskara Rao, Digumarti, Digumarti Pushpa Latha and Digumarti Harshitha, Editors (2001). *Energy Security*. New Delhi: Discovery Publishing House. ISBN 81-7141-598-9.

Bhaskara Rao, Digumarti, Digumarti Harshitha and K.R.S.S. Rao, Editors (1999). *Advanced Biotechnology*. New Delhi: Discovery Publishing House. ISBN 81-7141-516-4.

Bhaskara Rao, Digumarti and K.R.S. Sambhasiva Rao, Editors (1996). *Current Trends in Indian Education*. New Delhi: Discovery Publishing House. ISBN 81-7141-311-0.

Bhaskara Rao, Digumarti and K. Vijaya (1995). *A Text Book of Evaluation*. Ambala Cantt: The Associated Publishers.

Bhaskara Rao, Digumarti and N.V.M. Mohana Rao (2002). *Problems of Mentally Handicapped Children*. New Delhi: Discovery Publishing House. ISBN 81-7141-645-4.

Bhaskara Rao, Digumarti and S. Chandra Mohan (2002). *Sports Management*. New Delhi: APH Publishing Corporation. ISBN 81-7648-467-9.

Bhaskara Rao, Digumarti and Sk. Johni Basha (2004). *Teachers' Population Education Awareness*. New Delhi: APH Publishing Corporation.

Bhaskara Rao, Digumarti, V.V. Rao, V.V. Lakshmi and V.V. Krishna, Editors (1999). *Status and Advancement of Women*. New Delhi: APH Publishing Corporation. ISBN 81-7648-169-6.

Babu, P.C., Author and Digumarti Bhaskara Rao, Editor (2004). *Flowers of Wisdom*. New Delhi: Discovery Publishing House. ISBN 81-7141-695-0.

Bhagya Lakshmi, Lingineni, Author and Digumarti Bhaskara Rao, Editor (2000). *Reading and Comprehension*. New Delhi: Discovery Publishing House. ISBN 81-7141-543-1.

Bhuvaneswara Lakshmi, Gadde, Author and Digumarti Bhaskara Rao, Editor (2000). *Attitude Towards Science*. New Delhi: Discovery Publishing House. ISBN 81-7141-541-6.

Devraj, T.A.S., Author and Digumarti Bhaskara Rao, Editor (1997). *Trace Analysis of Uranium and Thorium*. New Delhi: Discovery Publishing House. ISBN 81-7141-375-7.

Durga Rani, K., Author and Digumarti Bhaskara Rao, Editor (2000). *Educational Aspirations and Scientific Attitudes*. New Delhi: Discovery Publishing House. ISBN 81-7141-555-55.

Dutt, B.S.V. and Digumarti Bhaskara Rao (2001). *Empowering Primary Teachers*. New Delhi: Discovery Publishing House. ISBN 81-7141-615.2.

Ediger, Marlow and Digumarti Bhaskara Rao (1996). *Science Curriculum*. New Delhi: Discovery Publishing House. ISBN 81-7141-321-8.

Ediger, Marlow and Digumarti Bhaskara Rao (2000). *Teaching Mathematics Successfully*. New Delhi: Discovery Publishing House. ISBN 81-7141-552-0.

Ediger, Marlow and Digumarti Bhaskara Rao (2001). *Teaching Science Successfully*. New Delhi: Discovery Publishing House. ISBN 81-7141-600-4.

Ediger, Marlow and Digumarti Bhaskara Rao (2001). *Teaching Social Studies Successfully*. New Delhi: Discovery Publishing House. ISBN 81-7141-596-2.

Ediger, Marlow and Digumarti Bhaskara Rao (2002). *Philosophy and Curriculum*. New Delhi: Discovery Publishing House. ISBN 81-7141-631-4.

Ediger, Marlow and Digumarti Bhaskara Rao (2002). *Improving School Administration*. New Delhi: Discovery Publishing House. ISBN 81-7141-633-0.

Ediger, Marlow and Digumarti Bhaskara Rao (2002). *Elementary Curriculum*. New Delhi: Discovery Publishing House. ISBN 81-7141-658-6.

Ediger, Marlow and Digumarti Bhaskara Rao (2003). *Language Arts Curriculum*. New Delhi: Discovery Publishing House. ISBN 81-7141-657-8.

Ediger, Marlow and Digumarti Bhaskara Rao (2004). *Teaching Language Arts Successfully*. New Delhi: Discovery Publishing House. ISBN 81-7141-678-0.

Ediger, Marlow and Digumarti Bhaskara Rao (2004). *Teaching Mathematics in Elementary Schools*. New Delhi: Discovery Publishing House. ISBN 81-7141-687-X.

Ediger, Marlow and Digumarti Bhaskara Rao (2004). *Teaching Science in Elementary Schools*. New Delhi: Discovery Publishing House. ISBN 81-7141-709-4.

Ediger, Marlow and Digumarti Bhaskara Rao (2004). *School Curriculum and Administration*. New Delhi: Discovery Publishing House. ISBN 81-7141-709-4.

Ediger, Marlow and Digumarti Bhaskara Rao (2004). *Modern Elementary School*. New Delhi: Discovery Publishing House.

Ediger, Marlow and Digumarti Bhaskara Rao (2004): *Relevancy in Elementary Curriculum*. New Delhi: Discovery Publishing House. ISBN 81-7141-751-5.

Ediger, Marlow and Digumarti Bhaskara Rao, (2004). *Teaching Social Studies in Elementary Schools*. New Delhi: Discovery Publishing House.

Ediger Marlow, B.S.V. Dutt and Digumarti Bhaskara Rao (2004). *Teaching English Successfully*. New Delhi: Discovery Publishing House. ISBN 81-7141-707-8.

Harshitha, Digumarti and Digumarti Bhaskara Rao, Editors (2004). *Educational Innovations*. New Delhi: Discovery Publishing House.

Indira Devi, Author and J. Prasanth Kumar and Digumarti Bhaskara Rao, Editors (2004). *Values in Language Text Books*. New Delhi: Discovery Publishing House.

Jayasree, Kandi, Author and Digumarti Bhaskara Rao, Editor (1999). *Correlates of Socialisation*. New Delhi: Discovery Publishing House. ISBN 81-7141-517-2.

John Babu, Chikati, Author and T.J.R. Prasad, G.M. Madhukar and Digumarti Bhaskara Rao, Editors (1996). *Problem Solving in Mathematics*. New Delhi: APH Publishing Corporation. ISBN 81-7648-273-0.

Lalitha, T., Author and K.S. Prabhakaram, D.S.N. Sastry and Digumarti Bhaskara Rao, Editors (2004). *Educational Philosophic Beliefs*. New Delhi: Discovery Publishing House. ISBN 81-7141-765-5.

Madhu Bala, Jampala, Author and Digumarti Bhaskara Rao, Editor (2004). *Adjustment Problems of Hearing Impaired*. New Delhi: Discovery Publishing House.

Marja, Talvi and Digumarti Bhaskara Rao, Editors (1996). *Educational Leadership and Social Changes*. New Delhi: Discovery Publishing House. ISBN 81-7141-320-X.

Nirmala Jyothi, M., Author and Digumarti Bhaskara Rao, Editor (2003). *Non-detention Systems in School Education*. New Delhi: Discovery Publishing House. ISBN 81-7141-654-3.

Prabhakaram, K.S., Author and Digumarti Bhaskara Rao, Editor (1998). *Concept Attainment Model in Mathematics Teaching*. New Delhi: Discovery Publishing House. ISBN 81-7141-424-9.

Prasanth Kumar, J., Author and Digumarti Bhaskara Rao, Editor (1998). *Effectiveness of Distance Education System*. New Delhi: Discovery Publishing House. ISBN 81-7141-437-0.

Prasanth Kumar, J., Author and G. Sundara Rao and Digumarti Bhaskara Rao, Editors (2000). *Open University Student Support Services*. New Delhi: Discovery Publishing House. ISBN 81-7141-550-4.

Ramatulasamma, K., Author and Digumarti Bhaskara Rao, Editor (2002). *Job Satisfaction of Teacher Educators*, New Delhi: Discovery Publishing House. ISBN 81-7141-655-1.

Rama Krishnaiah, D., Author and Digumarti Bhaskara Rao, Editor (1998). *Job Satisfaction of College Teachers*, New Delhi: Discovery Publishing House. ISBN 81-7141-438-9.

Rama Kumar Ratnam, M., Author and Digumarti Bhaskara Rao, Editor (1998). *Dukka: Suffering in Early Buddhism*. New Delhi: Discovery Publishing House. ISBN 81-7141-653-5.

Rathaiah, Lavu and Digumarti Bhaskara Rao, Editors (1996). *International Innovations in Education*. New Delhi: Discovery Publishing House. ISBN 81-7141-359-5.

Ramesh, Ganta and Digumarti Bhaskara Rao, Editors (1998). *Environmental Education: Problems and Prospects*. New Delhi: Discovery Publishing House. ISBN 81-7141-423-0.

Rathaiah, Lavu and Digumarti Bhaskara Rao (1997). *Achievement Correlates*. New Delhi: Discovery Publishing House. ISBN 81-7141-385-4.

Reddy, Sudhakar Y., Author, and Digumarti Bhaskara Rao, Editor (2003). *Creativity in Adolescents*. New Delhi: Discovery Publishing House. ISBN 81-7141-659-4.

Reddy, M.S., Author and Digumarti Bhaskara Rao, Editor (2004). *Creativity in College Students*. New Delhi: Discovery Publishing House. ISBN 81-7141-697-7.

Radramamba, B., Author and Digumarti Bhaskara Rao, Editor (2003). *Problems of Teaching*. New Delhi: APH Publishing Corporation. ISBN 81-7648-462-8.

Sanjeeva Rao, P.C., Author and Digumarti Bhaskara Rao, Editor (1996). *A Text Book of Geology*. New Delhi: Discovery Publishing House. ISBN 81-7141-313-7.

Satya Narayana V., Author and Digumarti Bhaskara Rao, Editor (2001). *Physical Education, Social Attitudes and Leadership Qualities*. New Delhi: Discovery Publishing House. ISBN 81-7141-593-8.

Srinivasulu Reddy, M., and K.R.S. Sambasiva Rao, Authors and Digumarti Bhaskara Rao, Editor (1999). *A Text Book of Aquaculture*. New Delhi: Discovery Publishing House. ISBN 81-7141-482-6.

Srinivasa Rao, Mandalapu, Author and Digumarti Bhaskara Rao, Editor (2004). *Achievement Motivation and Achievement in Mathematics*. New Delhi: Discovery Publishing House. ISBN 81-7141-674-8.

Vanaja, M. Author and Digumarti Bhaskara Rao, Editor (1999). *Inquiry Training Model*. New Delhi: Discovery Publishing House. ISBN 81-7141-515-6.

Vanaja. M. and N. Sneha Latha, Authors and Digumarti Bhaskara Rao, Editor (2004). *Student Shyness*. New Delhi: APH Publishing Corporation.

Valeri V. Koustiouk, Author and Digumarti Bhaskara Rao, Editor (2002). *A Text Book of Cryogenics*. New Delhi: Discovery Publishing House. ISBN 81-7141-642-X.

Valeri V. Koustiouk, Author and Digumarti Bhaskara Rao, Editor (2004). *Refrigeration and Environment*. New Delhi: APH Publishing Corporation.

Veena Kumari, Balusu and Digumarti Bhaskara Rao (1996). *Operation Black Board*. New Delhi: Ashish Publishing Corporation. ISBN 81-7024-711-X.

Veena Kumari, Balusu, Author and Digumarti Bhaskara Rao, Editor (2000). *Psycho-Social Correlates of Achievement*, New Delhi: Discovery Publishing House. ISBN 81-7141-547-4.

Vanaja, M., Author and Digumarti Bhaskara Rao, Editor (1999). *Inquiry Training Model*. New Delhi: Discovery Publishing House. ISBN 81-7141-515-6.

Venkata Rao, P. and Digumarti Bhaskara Rao (1989). *A Text Book of Zoology—Junior Intermediate*. Guntur: Vignan Publishers.

Venkata Rao, P. and Digumarti Bhaskara Rao (1989). *A Text Book of Zoology—Senior Intermediate*. Guntur: Vignan Publishers.

Venugopala Rao, K., Author and Digumarti Bhaskara Rao, Editor (2000). *Teacher Morale in Secondary Schools*. New Delhi: Discovery Publishing House. ISBN 81-7141-551-2.

Vidya, C., Author and Digumarti Bhaskara Rao. Editor (1996). *A Text Book of Nutrition*. New Delhi: Discovery Publishing House. ISBN 81-7141-309-9.

Vidya Bharathi, D., Author and Digumarti Bhaskara Rao, Editor (2000). *Educational Philosophies of Swami Vivekananda and John Dewey*. New Delhi: APH Publishing Corporation. ISBN 81-7648-309-9.

Books in Telugu Language

Bhaskara Rao, Digumarti (1986). *Dhrushya Sravana Bodhanapakaranalu* (Audio Visual Teaching Aids). Guntur: Nagarjuna Publishers.

Bhaskara Rao, Digumarti (1993). *Jeevasashtra Bodhana* (Teaching of Biology). Guntur: Nagarjuna Publishers.

Bhaskara Rao, Digumarti (1995). *Vignanasasthra Bodhana* (Teaching of Science) Guntur: Nagarjuna Publishers.

Bhaskara Rao, Digumarti (1997). *Vidya Manovignana Seshtram* (Educational Psychology). Guntur: Creative Press.

Bhaskara Rao, Digumarti (1998). *DSC Study Material*. Guntur: Nagarjuna Publishers.

Bhaskara Rao, Digumarti (1998). *Upadhyayudu Vidya*. (Teacher and Education). Guntur: Nagarjuna Publishers.

Bhaskara Rao, Digumarti (1998). *Vidya Drukpadalu* (Prespectives of Education). Guntur: Nagarjuna Publishers.

Bhaskara Rao, Digumarti (1999). *EdCET Teaching Aptitude*. Guntur: Nagarjuna Publishers.

Bhaskara Rao, Digumarti (2001). *Bharata Samajamulo Upadyayudu Vidya* (Teacher and Education in Emerging Indian Society). Guntur: Nagarjuna Publishers.

Bhaskara Rao, Digumarti (2001). *Bhoutika Sastra Bodhana Paddathulu* (Methods of Teaching Physical Science). Guntur: Nagarjuna Publishers.

Bhaskara Rao, Digumarti (2001). *Jeeva Sastra Bodhana Padhathulu* (Methods of Teaching Biology). Guntur: Nagarjuna Publishers.

Bhaskara Rao, Digumarti (2001). *Vidya Manovignana Sastram* (Educational Psychology). Guntur: Nagarjuna Publishers.

Bhaskara Rao, Digumarti (2003). *Patsala Yajamanyam/Paripalana* (School Management and Administration). Guntur: Nagarjuna Publishers.

Bhaskara Rao, Digumarti (2004). *Vidya Sanketika Sastram mariyu Computer Vidya* (Educational Technology and Computer Education). Guntur: Nagarjuna Publishers.